W9-AHZ-672

Compliments of
Abbott Laboratories
and K·Tab®

POTASSIUM CHLORIDE
EXTENDED-RELEASE
TABLETS, USP

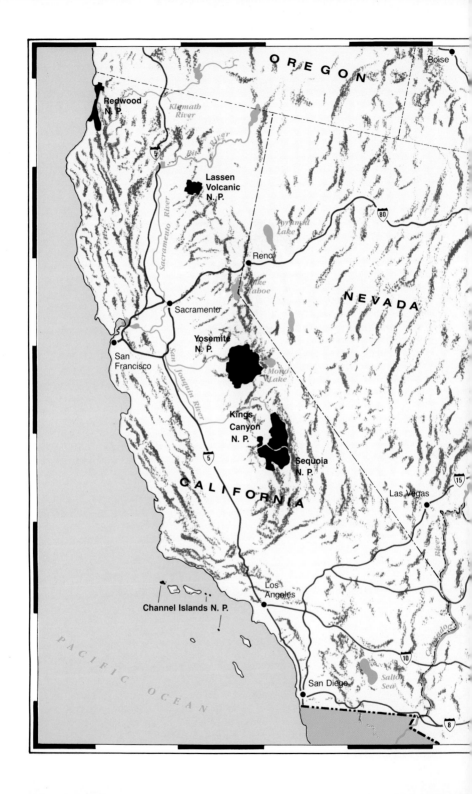

0   50   100   200

NATIONAL PARKS
OF THE
PACIFIC
SOUTHWEST
AND HAWAII

Interstate _____
State boundary _._.—._.—
International boundary .—.—.—

See appropriate chapters for detailed park maps.

IDAHO

Great
Salt Lake

Salt
Lake
City

UTAH

Cheyenne

80

COLORADO

70

Denver

25

KAUAI

NIIHAU

OAHU

Honolulu   H1

MOLOKAI

MAUI

Haleakala N. P.

HAWAII

HAWAII

Hawaii
Volcanoes
N. P.

PACIFIC OCEAN

0   50   100   200
INSERT MAP SCALE

Phoenix

ARIZONA

NEW

MEXICO

THE SIERRA CLUB GUIDES
TO THE
NATIONAL PARKS
OF THE
PACIFIC
SOUTHWEST
AND HAWAII

Published by
Stewart, Tabori & Chang

Front cover: El Capitan, Yosemite National Park
(© Jeff Gnass)

Frontispiece: Coast view, Redwood National Park
(© Ed Cooper)

Back cover: Redwood forest, Redwood National Park
(© David Muench)

Text by:

Joseph E. Brown—Channel Islands and Redwood
Barbara B. Decker and Robert W. Decker—Haleakala, Hawaii Volcanoes, Lassen Volcanic
David Lavender—Kings Canyon and Sequoia

Consulting Editor: James V. Murfin

Project Editor: Irene Pavitt

Designer: J. C. Suarès

Photo Editor: Christine A. Pullo

Illustrations and maps © Bill Russell

Library of Congress Cataloging in Publication Data
Main entry under title:

Sierra Club guide to the national parks of the Pacific Southwest.

Includes index.
1. National parks and reserves—California—
Guide-books. 2. National parks and reserves—
Hawaii—Guide-books. 3. California—Description
and travel—1981—Guide-books. 4. Hawaii—
Description and travel—1981- —Guide-books.
I. Brown, Joseph E., 1929- . II. Sierra Club.
F859.3.S56 1984   917.94'0453   83-17848
ISBN 0-394-72490-9 (Random House)

Created and published by Stewart, Tabori & Chang, Inc.
Text pp. 13–27, 31–55, 59–89, 93–115, 119–139, 143–163, 167–195,
199–233 copyright © 1984 Stewart, Tabori & Chang, Inc.
740 Broadway, New York, N.Y. 10003.

Photographs, drawings, and maps copyright © 1984 Stewart,
Tabori & Chang, Inc. and as indicated on this page and in
the photo credits on pp. 251 and 252.

Printed and bound in Japan.

THIS COUNTRY'S FORTY-EIGHT NATIONAL PARKS CON-
tain natural wonders more varied and extraordinary than
those found in any other nation on earth. Embodied and
preserved in them is the beauty of a vast land, which only
a few centuries ago was wilderness. Every year, 50 million
people visit these parks, testifying to a deep appreciation of the treasures they offer.

Recognizing the need for park guide books that are practical as well
as beautiful, Stewart, Tabori & Chang is proud to present *The Sierra
Club Guides to the National Parks*. These books have been created
with the cooperation of the Sierra Club, which has been committed to
conservation since 1892, and with the participation of the National
Park Service and Random House. The five regional guides planned for
the series—the Desert Southwest, the Pacific Southwest and Hawaii,
the Rocky Mountains and the Great Plains, the Pacific Northwest and
Alaska, and the East and Middle West—take you through each of the
national parks of the United States.

Leading nature writers and photographers, experts in their fields,
have provided text and photographs that work together as a tour of
the parks. One chapter is devoted to each park, beginning with its
discovery and use by man, moving on to its natural and geological
history, its animal and plant life, and finally exploring its sites, trails,
and trips. Each chapter also includes an up-to-date facilities chart, trail
guides, and park and trail maps created especially for the book. An
extensive full-color appendix of the most commonly seen animals and
plants is included at the end of each book.

M A P S

MAP OF THE NATIONAL PARKS OF THE PACIFIC SOUTHWEST AND
HAWAII 2–3

Channel Islands
PARK MAP 14–15

Haleakala
PARK MAP 32–33

Hawaii Volcanoes
PARK MAP 60–61
KILAUEA CALDERA TRAIL MAP 81

Kings Canyon
PARK MAP 94–95
GRANT GROVE TRAIL MAP 109

Lassen Volcanic
PARK MAP 120–121

Redwood
REDWOOD NORTH AREA MAP 144–145
SOUTH AREA TRAIL MAP 161

Sequoia
PARK MAP 94–95
GIANT FOREST TRAIL MAP 189

Yosemite
PARK MAP 200–201
YOSEMITE VALLEY TRAIL MAP 224–225

C O N T E N T S

PREFACE

7

Channel Islands

10

Haleakala

28

Hawaii Volcanoes

56

Kings Canyon

90

Lassen Volcanic

116

Redwood

140

Sequoia

164

Yosemite

196

APPENDIX OF
ANIMALS & PLANTS

235

PHOTO CREDITS

251

INDEX

253

CHANNEL ISLANDS
NATIONAL PARK

California sea lions are one of six species of seals and sea lions on San Miguel Island.

CHANNEL ISLANDS NATIONAL PARK
1901 SPINNAKER DRIVE, VENTURA, CALIFORNIA 93001
TEL.: (805) 644-8157

Highlights: Anacapa Island □ Santa Barbara Island □ San Miguel Island □ Arch Rock □ Signal Peak □ Landing Cove

Access: To park headquarters, drive from Ventura (no public transit available). To islands, take private or charter vessels from Ventura, Oxnard, or Santa Barbara.

Hours: Visitor Center, daily, 8 A.M.–5 P.M.; longer hours between Memorial Day and Labor Day. Closed Christmas. Access to islands is subject to weather and permit restrictions.

Fees: None.

Parking: At park headquarters.

Gas, food, lodging: In Ventura, Oxnard, and Santa Barbara.

Visitor Center: At Ventura harbor. Offers exhibits and films; postcards, books, and posters for sale.

Museum: Exhibits in Visitor Center.

Pets: Not permitted in park headquarters or ashore on Anacapa Island, San Miguel Island, and Santa Barbara Island.

Picnicking: On Anacapa Island, Santa Barbara Island, and at park headquarters.

Hiking: Permitted on Santa Barbara Island and East Anacapa Island without permit; on San Miguel Island with permit.

Backpacking: Permitted on Anacapa Island and Santa Barbara Island with permit. Carry water.

Campgrounds: Tent camping with permit on Anacapa Island and Santa Barbara Island. Primitive only: no gas, food, electricity, or water.

Tours: Guided tours on islands by arrangement; contact park headquarters for further information. In English.

Other activities: Scuba diving, swimming (generally requires a full wet suit), fishing (license required).

Facilities for disabled: At park headquarters: parking, restrooms, theater, exhibits, and observation tower.

For additional information, see also Sites, Trails, and Trips on pages 24–25 and the map on pages 14–15.

ONE OF THE MOST RECENT ADDITIONS TO THE NAtional park system, Channel Islands National Park is a striking and awe-inspiring contrast to the teeming southern California megalopolis that appears to be but a stone's throw away. Reached only by boat, the five islands are a primitive anachronism in the Space Age, a refuge where seals and whales and sea birds enjoy freedom from human influences, and where the ever-changing drama of the relentless ocean constantly unfolds before the visitor.

Four of the five islands are related geologically; all are related historically. Yet each exhibits its own features and its own specialized habitats for wildlife. Covering only a little more than 127,000 acres of land area, the islands are constantly exposed to the sea's influence. Surf pounds rocky shoreline; winds funneled through the Santa Barbara Channel can be a mariner's nightmare in winter or a weekend sailor's delight in summer. In season, great stands of yellow coreopsis—one of the islands' most noted plants—form a vivid backdrop for birdwatching and nature studies. Trails lead to high points with incredible vistas of the other islands, the mainland to the east, and the Pacific to the west. The island shoreline reveals ragged, surf-carved caves that echo to the din of colonies of barking seals and sea lions.

Arch Rock rises from the surf off East Anacapa Island, which is 11 miles from the California mainland.

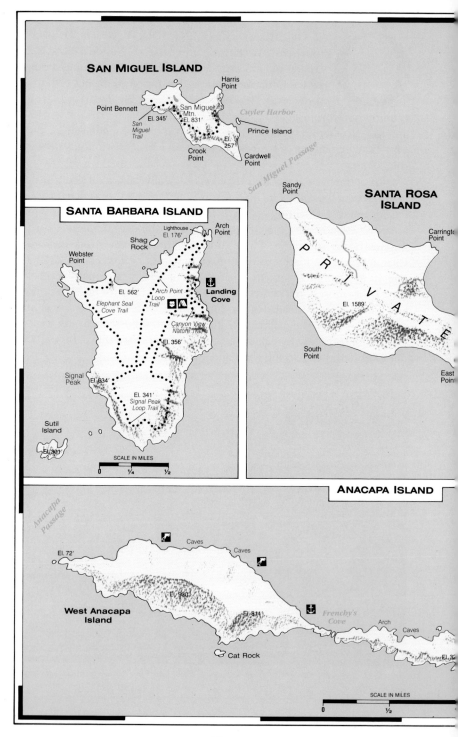

SAN MIGUEL ISLAND

Point Bennett
El. 345'
San Miguel Trail
San Miguel Mtn. El. 831'
Harris Point
Cuyler Harbor
Prince Island
El. 257
Crook Point
Cardwell Point

San Miguel Passage

SANTA BARBARA ISLAND

Lighthouse El. 176'
Arch Point
Shag Rock
Webster Point
El. 562'
Elephant Seal Cove Trail
Arch Point Loop Trail
Landing Cove
Canyon View Nature Trail
El. 356'
Signal Peak
El. 634'
El. 341'
Signal Peak Loop Trail
Sutil Island
El. 301'

SCALE IN MILES
0   ¼   ½

Sandy Point

SANTA ROSA ISLAND

P R I V A T E

Carringto Point
El. 1589'
South Point
East Poin

ANACAPA ISLAND

Anacapa Passage
Caves
Caves
El. 72'
El. 930'
El. 814'
Frenchy's Cove
Arch
Caves
West Anacapa Island
Cat Rock
El. 3

SCALE IN MILES
0   ½

14

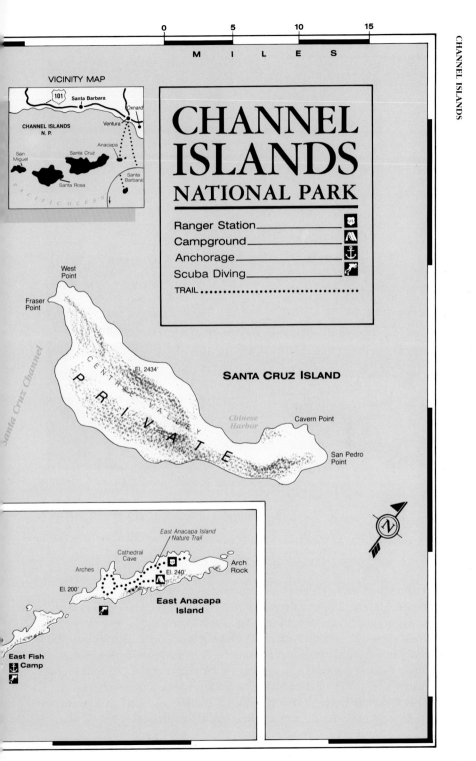

0   5   10   15

M   I   L   E   S

VICINITY MAP

101 Santa Barbara

Oxnard

Ventura

CHANNEL ISLANDS
N. P.

Anacapa

San
Miguel

Santa Cruz

Santa
Barbara

Santa Rosa

PACIFIC OCEAN

CHANNEL ISLANDS

NATIONAL PARK

Ranger Station

Campground

Anchorage

Scuba Diving

TRAIL ••••••••••••••••••••••••••••••••••

West
Point

Fraser
Point

Santa Cruz Channel

CENTRAL VALLEY

El. 2434'

P R I V A T E

SANTA CRUZ ISLAND

*Chinese
Harbor*

Cavern Point

San Pedro
Point

East Anacapa Island
Nature Trail

Cathedral
Cave

Arches

El. 240'

Arch
Rock

El. 200'

**East Anacapa
Island**

East Fish
Camp

A memorial to Portuguese explorer Joao Rodrigues Cabrilho, who is believed to have been buried on San Miguel Island.

H I S T O R Y

The Chumash

Among the Channel Islands' first inhabitants were coastal Indians known as the Chumash. When they first arrived remains questionable, but it was sometime between 11,000 and 30,000 years ago. The Chumash crisscrossed the Santa Barbara Channel between the islands and the mainland in sturdy boats called tomols. They subsisted on shellfish and other marine organisms as well as on berries, nuts, roots, bulbs, and plants, which they obtained through trading with mainland populations. The Chumash were a well-developed society and had an extensive trade network when the first white explorers arrived.

Exploration

The first European explorer to see the Channel Islands was Joao Rodrigues Cabrilho, a Portuguese navigator who sailed under the flag of Spain. Cabrilho sighted the Channel Islands in 1542, and is believed to be buried on San Miguel, where he died from injuries early in that year. A succession of other explorers and visitors followed, including sealers and whalers whose trail of exploitation is evident even today. Fur seals were their particular victims, and by the late 1800s the sea otter was hunted to near extinction. A few ranchers and farmers settled on the islands in the late nineteenth century.

Establishment of the Park

In 1938, President Franklin D. Roosevelt proclaimed two of the islands —Anacapa and Santa Barbara—a national monument. Their status was elevated in 1980 to that of a national park, and the islands of San Miguel, Santa Cruz, and Santa Rosa were added. (Santa Catalina, San Clemente, and San Nicolas are not part of Channel Islands National Park.)

But ownership is complex. The navy owns San Miguel, but it is administered by the National Park Service. Landing permits are required. The largest islands, Santa Cruz and Santa Rosa, are privately owned. Permits to land must be obtained from the owners. Most of Santa Cruz is owned by a company that is turning over its property to the nonprofit Nature Conservancy; at some future date, the National Park Service may own the remaining part of the island. The federal government is also committed to eventual purchase of all of Santa Rosa. No permit is needed to visit Anacapa Island and Santa Barbara Island.

In addition, a 1-mile area around all of the National Park Service-administered islands is designated, as are all features—natural, archeological, and historic—within the 250,000-acre park. A national marine sanctuary extends 6 nautical miles around each of the islands that compose Channel Islands National Park.

G   E   O   L   O   G   Y

The four northern Channel Islands are the seaward extension of the Santa Monica Mountains. Fossil remains found on Santa Rosa, Santa Cruz, and San Miguel indicate that these islands probably were joined to one another and to the mainland until about 600,000 years ago. At that time, intense earthquakes, accompanied by faulting and folding, caused this seaward expanse to separate from the mainland.

Overleaf: Channel Islands' tidepools, such as this one at Point Bennett on San Miguel Island, are part of a national marine sanctuary. Collecting specimens is forbidden.

Climate and Precipitation

During the summer, days are usually sunny, although sometimes the islands are veiled in fog. Swimming is possible in 68° F ocean water, and air temperatures seldom exceed 80° F. Winter is the season of rainfall (about 12 inches), the highest winds, and the fiercest seas.

Wildlife

Channel Islands' wildlife mixes species of the ocean, land, and air. The largest mammal is the California gray whale, which swims past the islands in winter toward calving grounds in Mexico. In spring, large numbers of pinnipeds haul out of the ocean to form breeding colonies, and playful porpoises frolic just past the surf. Elsewhere in the coastal waters is a teeming variety of life, ranging from the microscopic to the largest creature on earth, the whale: plankton, sharks, succulent abalone, lobsters, many game fish, and the infinite variety of animals such as

The island fox is found only on the Channel Islands.

starfish and the flowerlike anemone that are found in tidepools alternately exposed and covered by changing tides.

Of the islands' birds, the western gull is perhaps the most familiar resident, along with many of its sea-bird cousins such as the Brandt's cormorant, brown pelican (an endangered visitor), and sandpiper. Wildlife ashore consists of smaller animals and birds, mostly rodents, songbirds, and the distinctive island fox, which is endemic to the Channel Islands.

Flora

Channel Islands' plants are generally hardy species, since they must be tolerant of salt water and wind. Morning glory, buckwheat, exquisite lotuses, mallows, and locoweeds are examples. The "tree sunflower" (giant coreopsis) is found on all five islands, and the Santa Barbara ice plant is an example of an exotic species. Tree species are few in number, but three—the ironwood tree, the Torrey pine, and the Santa Cruz Island pine —are found only on the Channel Islands and in a few isolated sections on the mainland.

Checkermallow.   *Brown pelican.*

Top: Strawberry anemone.
Center: Spawning starfish.
Bottom: Kelp fish.
Right: California gray whale.

There are small Visitor Centers on the islands, but it is wise to check well in advance with the National Park Service Visitor Center in mainland Oxnard, California, for specifics. Camping is permitted, but even on a day trip, the visitor always should come "self-contained."

Anacapa Island

Closest of the five islands to the California mainland (11 miles), 700-acre Anacapa is actually three small islets, the highest of which rises to an elevation of 930 feet. East and Middle Anacapa are made up of rolling plateaus sandwiched between steeply rising cliffs. Vegetation is scrubby and brownish most of the year, but ablaze in wildflower color a few days after spring rains. Birds are seen in profusion: gulls, scoter ducks, black oyster catchers, and brown pelicans. Whales swim by offshore in winter. California sea lions and harbor seals haul ashore during the breeding season and prefer rocky ledges.

Santa Barbara Island

Santa Barbara Island, only 640 acres in area, is almost entirely surrounded by high cliffs that rise to two hilltops, the higher of which is 635-foot Signal Peak. The only safe landing is at Landing Cove, which is protected from prevailing westerly winds. An easy, .25-mile self-guiding nature trail introduces visitors to the island's resources. There are also 5 miles of trails for visitors to explore on their own and a primitive campground near the ranger station. Because of past farming and grazing practices, plant growth is sparse, consisting mainly of introduced grasses and ice plant. Both animals and plants are making a comeback, however, notably the once-threatened, 6,000-pound elephant seal, which forms breeding colonies in winter. Sharp eyes will spot land birds such as the American kestrel, burrowing owl, horned lark, and meadow lark, as well as land animals such as the deer mouse.

San Miguel Island

Westernmost of the islands, 10,000-acre San Miguel has a history of shipwrecks, battered as it constantly is by ocean swells that fetch thousands of miles across the Pacific. Its isolated location, however, seems ideal for five of the major colonizing sea-bird species of southern California: auklets, cormorants, gulls, guillemots, and snowy plovers. American kestrels, red-tailed hawks, and barn owls hunt smaller prey over fields of buckwheat, live-forever, and rose mallow. No visitor should miss the island's barren forests of wind-carved caliche, the fossilized remains of ancient vegetation strewn across a lunarlike landscape amid drifting sands. At Point Bennett, six species of seals and sea lions may be seen; five of these species breed here.

Santa Rosa Island

Santa Rosa Island, privately owned and inaccessible to the public, has been called an "archaeological and zoological treasure." Buried remains of a 6-foot dwarf mammoth, carbon-dated at 30,000 to 40,000 years, have been found associated with possible man-made tools. This find has touched off a scientific debate over when humans actually arrived in North America. Deeply eroded gullies, sea caves, and a few beaches are noted features of this 53,000-acre island.

Santa Cruz Island

Like Santa Rosa, Santa Cruz Island is privately owned and inaccessible to the public, and at 65,000 acres is the largest of all eight Channel Islands. It has several rugged peaks and a pastoral central valley. Gently flowing fresh-water creeks and streams feed an abundant biotic community.

Trails of Channel Islands National Park

Anacapa Island
East Anacapa Island Nature Trail: Starts and ends at the information station; 1.5 miles; figure-eight loop with fourteen observation points winds through unique wildflowers and plant life; excellent opportunities to see wildlife.

Santa Barbara Island
Canyon View Nature Trail: Starts and ends at information center near Landing Cove; .25 mile; .33 hour; introduces the island's resources; leads by one of the more interesting of the island's canyons; picturesque views of the ocean; superb birdwatching.

There are 5 miles of other trails available for explorers: Arch Point Loop Trail, Elephant Seal Cove Trail, and Signal Peak Loop Trail; all trails lead by sea gull rookeries and unique plant communities; outstanding opportunities to observe seals and sea lions.

San Miguel Island
San Miguel Trail: Starts at the ranger station overlooking Cuyler Harbor; ends at Point Bennett; 14 miles round trip; tour meets at beach area and is under the guidance of a park ranger (there are no self-guided tours); permits required; passes remains of old ranch complex and a unique caliche forest. **See map on pages 14–15.**

Overleaf: Yellow coreopsis, or "tree sunflowers," flourish on all of the islands.

HALEAKALA
NATIONAL PARK

HALEAKALA NATIONAL PARK
P.O. BOX 369, MAKAWAO, HAWAII 96768
TEL.: (808) 572-9306 OR (808) 572-7749
(Park Weather Tape)

Highlights: Silversword □ Hosmer Grove □ Leleiwi Overlook □ Kalahaku Overlook □ Puu Ulaula □ Pele's Paint Pot □ Kipahulu □ Oheo □ Waimoku Falls □ Hawaiian Planting Area □ Makahiku Falls

Access: To park entrance (near Crater District): 19 miles from Pukalani: 27 miles from Kahului. To Kipahulu District: 9 miles from Hana; 61 miles from Kahului and airport.

Hours: Daily 24 hours, year-round. Portions of the park closed during disasters, ice on road, and so on.

Fees: None.

Parking: At Oheo, Red Hill, Haleakala Visitor Center, Kalahaku, Leleiwi, Halemauu, park headquarters, and Hosmer Grove. For campers at Oheo and Hosmer Grove.

Food, lodging: Not available in park. Crater District: available 12 miles below park entrance. Kipahulu District: in Hana.

Gas: Not available in park. Crater District: in Pukalani. Kipahulu District: in Hana.

Visitor Center: In Crater District, on rim. Offers hourly interpretive talks until noon.

Pets: Permitted on leash, except on trails and in back country.

Picnicking: At Hosmer Grove, park headquarters in Crater District, Oheo Gulch in Kipahulu District.

Hiking: On designated trails. Carry water.

Backpacking: Permit required, see campgrounds entry. Check with park headquarters before going into crater.

Campgrounds: Crater District: Hosmer Grove, no permit required, up to 25 campers/night, fires in grills only; Paliku and Holua, permits required, up to 25 campers/night, no open fires. Kipahulu District: up to 50 campers/night, fires in grills only, no drinkable water available.

Tours: Crater District: at crater rim, crater trails, and Hosmer Grove. Kipahulu District: at trail side. All tours depend on availability of staff. In English.

Facilities for disabled: Water fountains, restrooms, parking stalls with ramps, and paved walkways.

Other activities: Swimming and horseback riding.

Please be aware that the high elevation of the Crater District may pose problems for people with certain medical conditions. Remember that all visitors to the Crater District should bring a jacket or sweater.

For additional information, see also Sites, Trails, and Trips on pages 48–54 and the map on pages 32–33.

HAWAII'S MASSIVE HALEAKALA VOLCANO RISES 10,023 feet into the tropical sky from a sea-level base 33 miles in diameter. Haleakala National Park encompasses the huge crater at the top of the mountain—an immense bowl that is 7.5 miles long, 2.5 miles wide, and .5 mile deep—with an unearthly but strangely beautiful panorama of stark cliffs, multihued cinder cones, and jumbled lava flows on a scale almost impossible to comprehend. This stark, barren place is the home of the Haleakala silversword, a unique plant that had been vandalized and grazed almost into extinction, and the rare Hawaiian goose, the nene.

In spite of the impression of long-dead volcanic fires, Haleakala is still considered to be active; it is the only Hawaiian volcano that is still alive except for those on the much younger Big Island of Hawaii. Its last eruption was around 1790.

Haleakala National Park extends from the summit down Kipahulu Valley on the southeastern flank of the mountain to the coast near Hana. This verdant, mist-shrouded valley with sheer cliffs and shimmering waterfalls descends in just 7.6 miles from a subalpine zone with frequent frosts to a subtropical rain forest and a section of the lovely Maui coast.

Lava formations circa 1860.

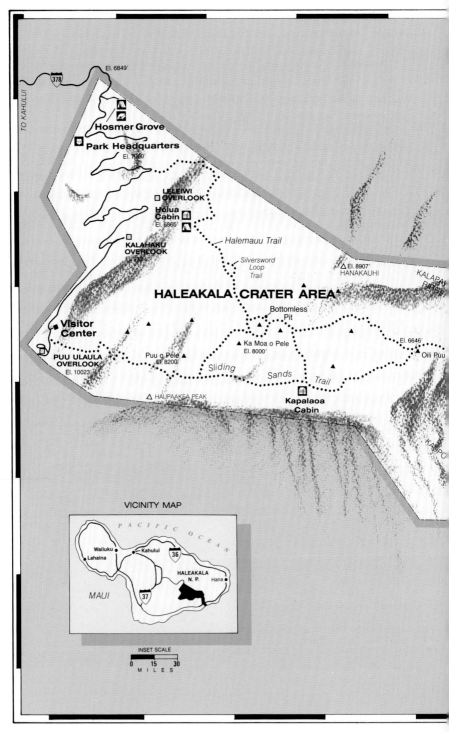

El. 6849'

378

TO KAHULUI

Hosmer Grove

Park Headquarters
El. 7000'

LELEIWI
OVERLOOK

Holua
Cabin
El. 6865'

KALAHAKU
OVERLOOK
El. 9324'

Halemauu Trail

Silversword
Loop
Trail

El. 8907'
HANAKAUHI

KALAPAWI
RIDGE

HALEAKALA CRATER AREA

Bottomless
Pit

Visitor
Center

Ka Moa o Pele
El. 8000'

El. 6646'

Oili Puu

Puu o Pele
El. 8200'

PUU ULAULA
OVERLOOK
El. 10023'

Sliding

Sands

Trail

△ HAUPAAKEA PEAK

Kapalaoa
Cabin

KAUPO

VICINITY MAP

PACIFIC OCEAN

Wailuku

Kahului

36

Lahaina

HALEAKALA
N. P.

Hana

MAUI

37

INSET SCALE

0   15   30
M I L E S

32

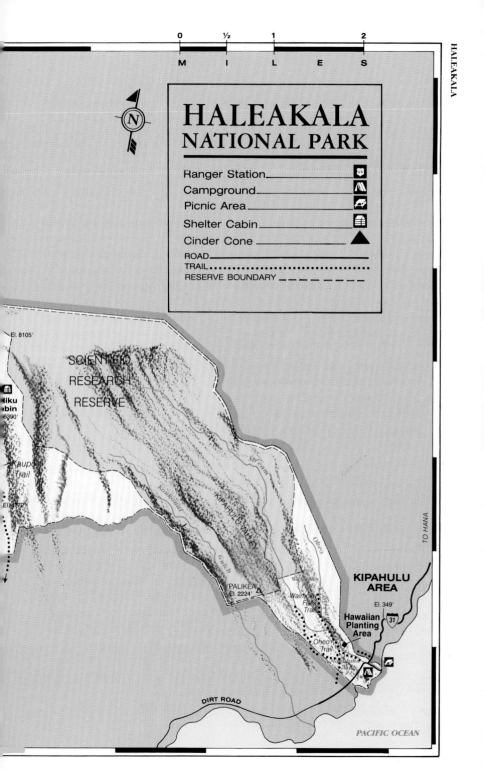

HALEAKALA
NATIONAL PARK

Ranger Station —
Campground —
Picnic Area —
Shelter Cabin —
Cinder Cone —
ROAD —
TRAIL ••••••••••••••••••••••
RESERVE BOUNDARY — — — — —

El. 8105'

SCIENTIFIC
RESEARCH
RESERVE

liku
bin
6390'

Kaupo
Trail

El. 4772'

KIPAHULU VALLEY

Koukouai Gulch

Stream

Oheo

TO HANA

PALIKEA
El. 2224'

Waimoku
Falls
Trail

KIPAHULU
AREA

El. 349'

Hawaiian
Planting
Area

31

Oheo
Trail

DIRT ROAD

PACIFIC OCEAN

Although clouds often shroud the lower slopes of Haleakala and some-times fill the crater, the summit is usually in sunshine. The impression everywhere is of dazzling light, which is partly what made this a sacred place for early Hawaiians; the Hawaiian words *Hale•a•ka•lā* mean "House of the Sun."

Hawaiian Legend

Stories tell of an early time when days were only three or four hours long because the sun was so lazy and full of sleep that he would hurry through the sky to get back to bed. The whimsical demigod Maui lived in Hana with his mother, a maker of fine tapa cloth. The shortness of the days made it difficult for her to sun-dry her tapa, so the mischie-vous Maui thought of a plan to lengthen the day. He noticed that the sun rose over the rim of Haleakala by thrusting first one long sunbeam and then another over the rim, much as a spider climbs over a rock. One night Maui took sixteen rope snares and hid in a cave near the summit; when the first of the sun's legs snaked over the edge, Maui threw a rope around it and made it fast. This he did with each leg in turn, and then he tied the ropes to a wiliwili tree. The sun was in no position to bargain, and had to agree to Maui's demand that he walk slowly and steadily across the sky, as he has done to this day.

Early Hawaiians

The first Polynesian settlers arrived in Hawaii about A.D. 750, and over the next several hundred years a flourishing, if sometimes warlike, soci-ety evolved. Most Hawaiian villages were in coastal areas where there were fertile lands, abundant water, and an ocean full of fish. There is no evidence that Hawaiians ever made their homes in the hostile envi-ronment of Haleakala Crater, but it was central to their unique land-division system. The ancient land sections, or *ahupuaa*, radiated like spokes of a wheel from a point on the northeastern rim of Haleakala Crater; thus each district had a pie-shaped piece of land, giving all people access to the ocean, the coast, and the uplands for sustenance. A particularly dense type of lava rock from the crater was quarried for adzes. There can still be seen in a few places the remains of a cross-island trail, which was used by ancient travelers in preference to routes through dense rain forests and deep valleys.

Most archeological evidence, though, shows that early Hawaiians visited Haleakala Crater only occasionally, and viewed it as a sacred

An old-time pack outfit meanders across Haleakala Crater.

place. Archeological remains have been found inside the park.

Early Explorers

One characteristic of Westerners seems to be their inability to resist climbing to the highest point in sight. Missionaries from New England had hardly arrived in Hawaii when three of them went on record in August 1828 as the first non-Hawaiians to reach the summit of Haleakala. They brought back and published a vivid description of the terrors and beauties of "Pele's dreadful reign."

The next recorded exploration of Haleakala Crater was by naval Lieutenant Charles Wilkes and his United States Exploring Expedition of 1841. They did a detailed study of the crater and published a map of the area. To their credit, they recorded the mountain's name as Haleakala —the name that was used locally—even though the custom of the time was to name important landmarks after dignitaries and patrons.

Marauding Animals

By the turn of the century, the "visitors" that were having the biggest impact on Haleakala Crater were animals. Cattle ranchers on Maui were in need of upland pasture, and for a while large herds of cattle were driven up to spend the summer in Haleakala Crater—an enormous natural corral. Wild goats, too, were becoming a problem. Brought to the islands originally by Captains James Cook and George Vancouver to use for food for future voyages, goats multiplied so rapidly because they had no predators that they presented a severe threat to native vegetation, especially in such a fragile environment as the crater.

Establishment of the Park

In 1916, thanks partly to the eruption of Lassen Peak in California two years earlier, which awakened the public's interest in volcanoes, President Woodrow Wilson signed into law a bill to create Hawaii National Park. The park included the active volcanoes Kilauea and Mauna Loa on the island of Hawaii, and the summit crater of Haleakala Volcano.

Park status came none too soon; the rare and beautiful silversword plants that grow only on the high slopes and crater of Haleakala were being destroyed by the thousands through the carelessness of hikers and sightseers. Introduced animals—pigs, goats, and cattle—were also taking a heavy toll on native plants and thus destroying the habitat of native birds. Rats had arrived on Maui accidentally from ships, and mongooses had been brought in to combat the rats; as it turned out, both animals preyed on ground-nesting birds and drove several species almost into extinction.

The new national park status not only gave protection to the unique and fragile ecosystems of Haleakala Crater, but also made it possible to preserve and interpret the extraordinary volcanic features of the area.

The park was increased in size in 1951, when 9,000 acres of the upper Kipahulu Valley were added. In 1969, the Nature Conservancy and the state of Hawaii donated 880 acres in the Kipahulu coastal area to the National Park Service; in 1976, the boundary was extended to include an additional 837 acres of coastal lands and water. Since 1961, Haleakala has had full status as a national park, separate from the volcanoes on the island of Hawaii.

G   E   O   L   O   G   Y

Early Volcanism

Maui, the second-youngest island of the Hawaiian chain, is made up of Haleakala and the smaller, older West Maui Volcano. These mountains are part of a huge undersea volcanic massif that consists of the islands of Molokai, Lanai, and Kahoolawe as well.

Thousands of years ago during the great ice ages, much of the world's water was locked up in continental ice sheets; sea levels were as much as 300 feet lower than they are now. The now-separate islands were joined above water into one large island that geologists call Maui Nui, which was made up of seven volcanoes and was about one-half the present size of the Big Island of Hawaii. As glaciers melted and sea levels rose, the islands became isolated again; in fact, when seas were higher than they are now, the isthmus between East and West Maui was covered, separating those mountains into two islands.

A cinder and rock pattern on the crater's rim, which is 21 miles around and 2.5 miles wide.

Hawaiian volcanos are born on the deep ocean floor, below as much as 3 miles of water. Quiet outpouring of lava goes on intermittently, and undetected, for thousands of years before the mound reaches the surface. When the growing volcano is a few hundred feet below sea level, gas in lava is able to expand; explosive eruptions start, accompanied by steam blasts and huge ash falls. For a time, it is a contest between the continuing eruptions and the erosive action of the sea, with the sea often the winner. But if the volcano is vigorous and persistent, it can grow; once above water, the growing mountain is armored against wave action by quieter lava flows.

In this way, Haleakala emerged from the sea about 1 million years ago to take its place as the youngest—and last—volcano of the Maui Nui group. It is the only one of the group that is still considered active.

The building stage lasted for tens of thousands of years, with voluminous lava flows piling up an imposing mountain. Haleakala grew strongly and steadily, probably to an elevation of over 13,000 feet. Then for some reason that is not fully understood by geologists, the rate of volcanism slowed. At the same time, world climate became exceptionally wet, and Haleakala was again in a deadly battle with erosion, caused by torrential rains and flooding streams. It was during this period that the spectacular Haleakala Crater was formed.

Lava from the 1790 eruption has been eroded by water into smooth dark pebbles.

Haleakala Crater

This tremendous natural bowl is fondly known locally as "the world's largest extinct volcanic crater," a phrase that makes geologists flinch. In the first place, the volcano is almost surely not extinct, but only dormant. Moreover, the term "volcanic crater," strictly speaking, implies creation by volcanic action—explosion or collapse. Haleakala's crater seems to be largely the result of massive erosion that took place about 100,000 years ago, when rainfall was much greater than it is now and when volcanic activity had lessened. Geologists think that as much as 3,000 feet of the summit was worn away, and that the heads of Kaupo and Keanae valleys were so deeply eroded that they met in the summit area and created the huge craterlike depression. When volcanic activity resumed, this area was filled with the unearthly cinder cones and lava flows that are seen today. Finally, other volcanic craters are larger than Haleakala.

A view from the air shows a line of large cinder cones that runs from Hana at the eastern tip of Maui, westward to the summit, across the summit crater, and down the southwestern flank to the ocean at La Perouse Bay. These late cinder cones—symptoms of old age in a volcano—form the clearly defined rift zones along which several eruptions have taken place in the last 1,000 years.

Late Volcanism

There is no precise historical record of Haleakala's most recent eruption, but a piece of detective work places it at about 1790. When the explorer Jean François Galoup de La Perouse mapped Maui's shoreline in 1786, he showed a broad, shallow bay between two points on the southwest coast. A few years later, Vancouver charted the same area; his map of 1793 shows a prominent peninsula between those points. Since the peninsula lava flow looks very young, and also local legend tells of eruptions at approximately that time, 1790 seems like a reasonable date. The area south of the flow is now known as La Perouse Bay.

Just offshore nearby is Molokini, a tiny, crescent-shaped islet that was formed by an undersea eruption where the rift zone extends into the ocean. Hot lava exploded violently from contact with the sea and built a typical tuff cone, which has been partially destroyed by wave action. If sea levels were to fall, Molokini would be connected to Maui.

The history of Haleakala suggests that since the last eruption occurred about 200 years ago, another could happen within the next 100 years, but there is no way to predict its precise time or place.

Overleaf: A cinder cone, with the peaks of Mauna Loa and Mauna Kea on the island Hawaii in the distance.

Climate

The Hawaiian Islands in general can claim uniformly mild, subtropical weather, but there are also microclimates with startling extremes of rainfall and temperature. Haleakala National Park could be considered a showcase of those extremes; it extends from the warm, sunny coastal area, through the upland rain forest (where the clouds that ring the mountain almost every day drop copious amounts of rain), to the desert-dry alpine conditions of the crater itself.

Weather near the summit is extremely variable; it can be cold, wet, and windy at any time of the year. In general, though, summit temperatures range from 35° F to 77° F in summer, and from 26° F to 75° F in winter. Severe weather sometimes occurs in winter, when the northeast trade winds weaken and allow subtropical storms to sweep in from the south. Frost is not uncommon at the summit, and some winters see an occasional snowfall.

Hawaii's Island Ecology

The Hawaiian chain is isolated in the North Pacific, 2,500 miles from the nearest continent. All the flora and fauna that colonized the islands before the arrival of humans came by air, on ocean currents, or attached to migratory birds. The odds against any form of life making this journey successfully were immense, but time is always on the side of evolution. Over tens of thousands of years, isolated seeds, spores, insects, and birds found their way to these volcanic islands. Although only a tiny percentage of those that arrived were able to survive the transition, those that did flourished, rapidly evolving and diversifying; climate and topography were ideal for survival, and competitors were scarce.

Hawaii has only two native mammals, a small bat and the Hawaiian monk seal; significantly, one arrived by flying and the other by swimming. Plants and birds, however, had a remarkably successful evolutionary history in Hawaii until humans and their introduced animals reversed the trend and brought many species to the verge of extinction. Haleakala National Park is the last refuge for several endangered species.

Native Plants

Probably the most famous natural feature in the park is a plant, the Haleakala silversword. A marvel of adaptation, the silversword has

Opposite: A view of Haleakala Crater and Maalaea Bay from Papawai Point.

evolved to withstand the punishing extremes of climate at these altitudes of 7,000 to 10,000 feet.

Seen at a distance, it is a shimmering sphere the color of moonlight; the Hawaiians used the name *ahinahina*, the word for "gray" repeated twice. Up close, it is a rosette about 2 feet across with fine, sword-shaped leaves that are thickly covered with a lustrous silvery down. The glistening hairs reflect excess sunlight, and the rosette of leaves protects the growing point of the plant. Early explorers described the cinder cones and the crater rim as being covered with so many silverswords that they looked like snowdrifts, but by fifty years ago these plants were almost extinct. The culprits were the wild goats that ate almost everything in sight. Humans were a close second, though; souvenir hunters and hikers would uproot the shining globes and roll them downhill to see how far they would go. Only the creation of Haleakala National Park saved the silversword; National Park Service protection and the work of dedicated botanists have brought them back from a low of barely 1,000 plants in 1927 to an estimated 40,000 today.

Some other native plants that are found within the crater are the kupaoa, several alpine plants like the Haleakala geranium, and two species of *Coprosma*—one with jet black berries that are a favorite food of the Hawaiian goose.

A common plant along the crater trails is the ohelo (Hawaii's answer to the blueberry), with its shiny clusters of tasty red berries that are welcomed by thirsty hikers. A few mamane trees can be seen also, with bright yellow blossoms that are an important source of food for several native forest birds.

At the eastern end of the crater, the vegetation changes dramatically. Clouds spill over a low spot in the crater rim, and rainfall is abundant year-round, creating a lush garden of native and introduced plants. Ohia trees with their bright red blossoms, probably the most common native tree of Hawaii, flourish, as do the kolea and the mamane. A native Hawaiian raspberry, the akala, grows profusely and bears large edible berries.

The Kipahulu section of Haleakala National Park, an 8-mile valley that runs from the crater rim down to the sea, is a botanical wonderland; it is probably the largest tract of undisturbed native vegetation in Hawaii.

Botanists and biologists studying the area since 1967 have found 200 species of plants that are indigenous or endemic to Hawaii; 15 of them were previously unknown. The upper part of Kipahulu Valley is a nearly impenetrable jungle of ohia and olapa trees with a rich understory of ferns and flowers. There are at least 75 species of ferns and related plants—all but 1 native—and more than a dozen species of woody lobelias. (This section has been designated a Scientific Research Reserve, and is open only by permit to qualified scientists.)

Native Birds

Hawaii has rightly been called a "museum of evolution," and nowhere is this more evident than in its bird life. It is estimated that the more than eighty kinds of native birds that are known to have evolved before the arrival of humans in Hawaii developed from as few as fifteen original species.

One of the most remarkable Hawaiian birds, and one often seen in Haleakala Crater, is the Hawaiian goose, or nene. Although its ancestry is traced to the Canada goose, it has evolved into a species with distinctly different characteristics. It lives on high, sparsely vegetated lava flows away from water, so its feet have evolved to be only partially webbed and thus better adapted to walking on lava than to swimming. The nene was hunted almost into extinction; in 1951, it was estimated that there were only thirty-three nene in existence, and half of those were in captivity. Since then, through a concerted effort by the state of Hawaii, the National Park Service, and the Wildfowl Trust in England, a breeding and release program seems to be succeeding in reintroducing these handsome birds to their native habitat.

Even more spectacular has been the evolution of the Hawaiian honeycreepers. Scientists estimate that there are at least twenty-three species and twenty-four subspecies in Hawaii, probably all evolved from a single ancestral species. Many of these make their homes in the protected Kipahulu Valley, where a Nature Conservancy expedition in 1967 found one species that was thought to have been long extinct. The nukupuu and the Maui parrotbill would probably be extinct today if they were not protected here.

The dark-rumped petrel, or uau, which nests on the crater cliffs, is an endangered species of migratory sea bird with a strange call that sounds like the barking of a small dog. It spends March through October at Haleakala, but no one knows where it spends the rest of the year.

Birds that are easier to see at Haleakala include the apapane and the iiwi, bright red birds that are often in the tops of ohia trees, where they resemble the red ohia blooms. Also present are migratory birds, including the golden plover, which migrates to and from Alaska. Still more common along the roads are birds like the ring-necked pheasant and the chukar, both of which have been introduced.

Overleaf: Dense bamboo in Kipahulu, the lush 8-mile valley at the eastern boundary of the park.

A Drive to the Sun

The spectacular drive to the top of Haleakala Volcano is a fitting intro-
duction to the scenery at the summit. This is the only place in the
world where one can drive by paved road from sea level to an altitude
of 10,023 feet in just 37.5 miles. The drive from Kahului to Haleakala
Crater takes at least 1.5 hours, but much more time for sightseeing is
recommended.

The first part of the drive up the mountain is apt to be clear, but
clouds usually form by mid-day between the altitudes of 4,000 and
8,000 feet. (The little upland town where the clouds usually break is
named Pukalani, literally "hole to heaven.") The road zigzags up the
slopes of Haleakala, and reaches the national park boundary at 6,740
feet.

Just inside the park, at about 6,800 feet, a paved side road leads to
Hosmer Grove, with a unique collection of exotic trees planted by the
forester for whom it is named. Here flourish sugi pine and cryptomeria
from Japan, deodar from India, eucalyptus from Australia, and pine,
cedar, juniper, and spruce from North America, as well as some native
Hawaiian trees like the ohia and mamane. A short (.25 mile) nature
trail winds through the grove, and a brochure to carry along points out
the different species of trees and the native birds such as apapane, iiwi,
and amakihi that are often seen flying among them. This is a good
place to see the interplay between native and exotic plants and animals,
and is a pleasant picnic stop.

At an elevation of 8,000 feet is the trail head for the Halemauu Trail
into Haleakala Crater. It is a pleasant 1-mile walk along the first part of
this trail to the crater rim for a grand view.

At the *Leleiwi Overlook*, at 8,800 feet, is a breath-taking view of the
huge bowl of Haleakala Crater, dotted with cinder cones that range in
color from gray to orange to red. There is nothing to provide scale
until you catch sight of a tiny dot in the distance that proves to be a
hiker on one of the trails that wind among the cones. The rim is broken
on the north and south by the gaps leading to Keanae and Kaupo valleys.

If the crater is filled with clouds but there is afternoon sunshine, the
eerie "Specter of Brocken" phenomenon can sometimes be seen from
the crater rim. It is the viewer's shadow projected on the clouds and
encircled by a rainbow. (It is so named because it was first observed at
Brocken Mountain in Germany.)

At *Kalahaku Overlook*, at 9,324 feet, which can be seen on the way
down from the House of the Sun Visitor Center, are more grand crater

The 10,023-foot-high Puu Ulaula Overlook at Red Hill, the highest point on the island.

views, and also some fine examples of the rare Haleakala silversword. Between May and November, it is sometimes possible to see one or more of these dramatic plants in bloom. The silversword grows for five to twenty years without blooming, and then sends out a stalk that can reach 5 to 6 feet in height with several hundred yellow and purplish flower heads. The plant blooms only once and then dies, but each individual flower produces hundreds of seeds that are scattered by the wind.

The House of the Sun Visitor Center is on the crater rim at 9,745 feet, 11 miles from the park entrance. Again the magnificent views are the main attraction; but there is also a wealth of information, including exhibits on the geology, archeology, and ecology of the park as well as the wilderness-protection program. Park interpretive staff give talks.

From the Visitor Center, a .25-mile trail goes to the top of White Hill, past ruins of old Hawaiian sleeping enclosures.

The *Puu Ulaula Overlook* is at Red Hill, the 10,023-foot summit. The view is a breath-taking 360° panorama of the crater and, if the day is clear, of West Maui and other islands in the distance—Hawaii, Kahoolawe, Lanai, Molokai, and Oahu.

Puu Ulaula is the traditional place to view the grand spectacle of a Haleakala sunrise. It is an unforgettable sight as the first rays of the sun creep into the crater; the dark recesses of the walls come alive with a variety of changing colors, and huge multicolored cinder cones appear on the dark floor as the crater is swiftly flooded with sunshine.

Trails of Haleakala National Park

Short Summit Trails

Hosmer Grove Trail: Starts at park road, just inside park boundary, at 7,000-foot level; .25 mile; .5 hour; leads through a unique experimental planting of exotic and native Hawaiian trees; trail brochure available.

Halemauu Overlook Trail: Starts at park road at 8,000-foot level; ends at crater rim for panoramic view of Haleakala Crater with its colorful cinder cones and lava flows; 2 miles round trip; 1.5 hours.

White Hill Trail: Starts at Haleakala Visitor Center at 9,745-foot level; .5 mile round trip; .5 hour; short trail to the summit of White Hill, past stone platforms and sleeping shelters used by early Hawaiians.

Crater Trails

Halemauu Trail: Starts at park road at 8,000-foot level; ends at Paliku Cabin; 20 miles round trip; 12 hours; makes a steep 2-mile, 1,400-foot descent to the crater floor at Holua Cabin; crosses crater past Silversword Loop Trail and winds among colorful cinder cones and other volcanic features.

Sliding Sands Trail: Starts from just below Haleakala's summit cone at 10,000-foot level; ends at Halemauu Trail at cinder cone named Oili Puu; 8

Red cinders from the volcano still color many of Maui's beaches.   Fields of taro on the Keana

miles one way; about 5 hours; descends steeply to 7,300 feet in 4 miles; loose cinder trail; passes jagged cinder cones, lava blisters, and caves; hiking out of crater by Sliding Sands Trail not recommended, since easier exit is by Halemauu Trail.

Kaupo Trail: Starts at Paliku Cabin in eastern end of Haleakala Crater at 6,400-foot level; ends at Kaupo Road; 8 miles one way; about 4 hours going down; descends Kaupo Valley to park boundary at 3,800 feet; continues 5 more miles over private ranch lands.

Kipahulu Area
Waimoku Falls Trail: Starts at Oheo parking area; ends at Waimoku Falls; 4 miles round trip; 3 hours; leads up left side of Oheo stream for .5 mile to point overlooking 184-foot Mahahiku Falls; trail continues 1.5 miles through pasture land and bamboo forest.

Hawaiian Planting Area: Trail up right side of Oheo stream leads to a traditional Hawaiian farm re-created to about 1848; 1 mile round trip; 1 hour.

Oheo Trail: Starts at lower pools; ends at ocean; 1 mile round trip; 1 hour; good swimming and picnicking.
See map on pages 32–33.

Peninsula can be seen on Hana Road, which leads into the park.

Crater Day Hikes

Hikers will find 32 miles of well-marked trails winding through the spectacular, moonscape terrain of Haleakala Crater. Three main trails lead into the crater: *Halemauu Trail,* which begins at the 8,000-foot elevation of the summit road; *Sliding Sands* (or *Keoneheehee*) *Trail,* which begins near the summit at the 10,000-foot level; and *Kaupo Trail,* which is usually used as a way out of the crater down a valley to the sea.

Since all crater hiking involves a steep descent into the crater—and a stiff climb out—most day hikes are arduous. These day hikes, of varying degrees of difficulty, are suggested.

Sliding Sands Trail. Hike a short way down the Sliding Sands Trail to get a feeling of this eerie volcanic scenery. The "sands" are really volcanic cinders and ash that were expelled from cones and vents in the crater during many past eruptions. Because of the "sliding" effect, walking downhill is easy but walking uphill is very difficult, especially at this high altitude, so only a short hike is suggested. Use of this trail as an exit from the crater floor is not recommended.

Halemauu Trail, to Holua Cabin. This is not a long hike (8 miles), but it gains 1,400 feet in elevation. The Halemauu Trail descends by steep switchbacks to the crater floor, with excellent views of the multicolored cinder cones and across the crater to Koolau Gap. Along the way are native ferns (amaumaus) and pukiawe, with its tiny, evergreenlike leaves and red (inedible) berries. Holua Cabin, at the base of the cliff, is usable by reservation only, but water is usually available there. Feral goats are often seen on the cliffs behind the cabin.

Sliding Sands Trail and Halemauu Trail. This difficult, 12-mile hike is recommended for experienced hikers only, but it is immensely rewarding in spectacular scenery.

Crater Circle Hike

Sliding Sands Trail and Halemauu Trail. By far the best crater trip if time, physical condition, and reservations permit is a 2- or 3-day circle trip. Hikers enter the crater by Sliding Sands Trail and leave it by Halemauu Trail, while seeing most of the crater's features by way of the short side trails that crisscross the floor. (Obtain reservations for one or two cabins or campgrounds along the route, and arrange for transportation from the Halemauu trail head.)

The starting point for this trip is, appropriately, Haleakala's summit. The Sliding Sands Trail leaves from just below the summit cone, Red Hill. It descends into the crater over loose reddish-brown ash and cinder, with jagged rocks, spires, and pit craters in the distance.

Near the crater floor the trail passes *Puu o Pele*, a colorful cinder cone that legend says was the former home of Pele, Hawaiian goddess of fire who now lives at Kilauea Volcano on the Big Island. The grass along the trail is mountain pili, a native bunch grass.

On the crater floor, at 7,400 feet, is a trail junction; the trail to the left goes north, reaching Holua Cabin, an overnight cabin or campground stop, in 3.9 miles.

Sliding Sands Trail leads across a grassy meadow to Kapalaoa Cabin. Nene (Hawaiian geese) are frequently seen here, and the dark-rumped petrel nests on the high cliffs above.

Leaving Kapalaoa, the trail crosses a flow of the rough, blocky lava called aa. The light-colored lichen on the rock, one of the first plants to appear on new lava flows, is often called Hawaiian snow.

As the trail (now called the Halemauu Trail) rounds the cinder cone called *Oili Puu*, the lava is of the smooth, ropy type known as pahoehoe. The weather here is apt to be foggy and misty, with wetter weather ahead.

At Paliku Cabin, 9.8 miles from the start of the trail, annual rainfall averages 250 to 300 inches a year, making this the only lush spot in Haleakala Crater. Native trees and shrubs compete with introduced species of grasses. Paliku is another possible overnight stop, at either the cabin or the campground.

From Paliku, the trail doubles back to the Oili Puu junction. It crosses another aa flow and skirts a lava-rock wall that was built in the days when cattle were driven into the crater to graze on the lush grasses at Paliku. The small dark cinder cone to the left of the trail is named *Puu Nole*, or "Grumbling Hill," which suggests that it was still active after the Hawaiians arrived on Maui.

The trail skirts an old spatter vent called the *Bottomless Pit* (actually 65 feet deep). Old Hawaiian custom called for throwing the umbilical cord of a newborn child into this pit to ensure that the child would not grow up to be a thief.

Past Bottomless Pit, the trail winds through *Pele's Paint Pot*, a dazzling display of multicolored cinder cones. Differing mineral composition of the lavas and varying degrees of weathering account for the wide variety of colors.

The *Silversword Trail* leaves the main trail in a .4-mile loop, for a close look at these unique plants. At one time observers spoke of silverswords dotting all the cinder cones, but they are presently found only in isolated spots. Protected now, and with the wild goats being gradually controlled, the silversword eventually may return to its early abundance. (Please do not leave the trail to view the plants, since trampling around their bases damages the root systems.)

Just ahead are Holua Cabin and a return to the summit road 1,400 feet above by the Halemauu Trail.

Kaupo Trail. An alternative—and equally dramatic—hike begins at Paliku Cabin and leads out of the crater. This trail goes through Kaupo Gap and descends 6,000 feet to the sea in 8 miles, through gradually thickening vegetation. Passing the park boundary at 3,880 feet, the trail continues through private ranch lands to Hawaii 31. Private arrangements must be made for transportation from the trail head back to Hana or Kahului.

Kipahulu

The Kipahulu section of Haleakala National Park is not directly connected by road to the main part of the park, but can be reached in 3 to 4 hours from Kahului by the famous (or infamous) Hana road. This narrow, winding, magnificently scenic road is difficult to drive.

Kipahulu's lush tropical vegetation and cascading waterfalls are a spectacular contrast to the stark, austere views of Haleakala Crater.

Just past Hana, the road enters the national park at *Oheo,* where Oheo stream cascades through a series of pools and waterfalls of varying sizes. This is an idyllic setting—heavy, green tropical foliage, black lava, clear blue pools, and the ocean in the distance.

The road crosses a bridge between pools 4 and 5; a trail leads along the lower pools to the ocean. The pools are a delightful place for a cool fresh-water swim, but because of the danger of sudden floods from the high-rainfall area in the upper valley, it is important to leave the pools if the water level seems to be rising.

The *Waimoku Falls Trail* starts from the Oheo parking area and goes up the left side of the stream for .5 mile to an overlook where *Makahiku Falls* drops 184 feet into the gorge below. From the overlook, the trail continues for 1.5 miles across pastures and through a dense forest of exotic bamboo to lovely *Waimoku Falls.*

The *Hawaiian Planting Area* is reached from the Oheo bridge by a .5-mile trail up the right side of the stream. Here a farm, re-created to the period around 1848, cultivates taro, bananas, yams, and other crops by traditional Hawaiian methods.

Opposite: Amaumau ferns near Upper Palikea Falls in the only lush area within the crater.

HAWAII
VOLCANOES
NATIONAL PARK

Smoking Halemaumau, the inner crater of Kilauea Volcano.

HAWAII VOLCANOES NATIONAL PARK, HAWAII 96718
TEL.: (808) 967-7311

Highlights: Mauna Loa □ Kilauea □ Lae Apuki □ Kalapana Coast □ Chain of Craters Road □ Heiaus □ Holei Sea Arch □ Na Ulu Arches □ Puuloa petroglyph field □ Holei Pali Overlook □ Hilina Pali □ Sulphur Bank □ Steaming Bluff □ Thurston Lava Tube □ Tree Molds □ Kipuka Puaulu

Access: From Hilo or Kona; car rentals available.

Hours: Year-round.

Fees: None.

Parking: Throughout park.

Gas: Available at Volcano Village.

Food: At Volcano House and Volcano Village.

Lodging: Limited spaces available at Volcano House at park headquarters. Some cabins also available.

Visitor Centers: Kilauea Visitor Center near main park entrance on east rim of Kilauea Summit Caldera; Wahaula Visitor Center at Kalapana Park Entrance.

Museum: In Kilauea Visitor Center; cultural exhibits in Wahaula Heiau Visitor Center.

Pets: Permitted on leash in front country.

Picnicking: At designated sites throughout park.

Hiking: Permitted. Carry water. Topographical map advisable outside developed area.

Backpacking: Permitted with permit. Water available at each designated campground. Register at park headquarters.

Campgrounds: Limited sites available. Fires only in designated pits. Permits needed for backcountry use.

Tours: By tour companies. In English and Japanese.

Facilities for disabled: All major facilities are accessible: Visitor Centers, overlooks, restrooms, campgrounds.

For additional information, see also Sites, Trails, and Trips on pages 76–88 and the maps on pages 60–61 and 81.

VOLCANOES SHOCK THE SENSES, PRESENTING AWE-some beauty to the eye, roars and hisses to the ear, and brimstone to nose and tongue. Watching fountains of incandescent lava on a cold night can warm the body as well as the soul, bringing a subconscious awareness of power and mystery that humans can ponder, but that only nature can possess. Is it any wonder that people once conceived, and many still believe, that the Hawaiian volcanoes are homes of the beautiful and tempestuous fire goddess, Pele?

Hawaii Volcanoes National Park is 30 miles from Hilo on the island of Hawaii, known informally as the Big Island. The park includes two of the world's most active volcanoes, Kilauea and Mauna Loa; both are spectacular yet reasonably safe to watch during eruptions, and still interesting and beautiful when not erupting. The trade winds that blow from the northeast over the park, and the elevation change from sea level to over 13,000 feet, conspire to make rapid climate variations from tropical rain forests through hot deserts to often snow-covered, barren, rocky terrain well above timberline. Added to this are unusual flora and fauna that evolved in isolation and rapidly adapted to the many climatic zones. In this park of great contrasts, geologic changes occur on a human time scale. Hawaii Volcanoes National Park is an outdoor museum for everyone who is interested in geology, meteorology, ecology, scenery, and solitude. Visitors fortunate enough to experience an eruption will remember it for life; those not so lucky will still not be disappointed.

H   I   S   T   O   R   Y

Voyage Across the Pacific

Polynesians had always been a sea-faring people, but the 2,400-mile trip across the Pacific to Hawaii was an epic voyage even for them. Historians think that the first explorers sailed from the Marquesas, probably around A.D. 750, in large double-hulled canoes. They were explorers intent on settling; they brought with them coconuts and other seeds and plants, as well as fowl, dogs, and pigs to start a food supply in an unknown land.

The Hawaiian Islands as they found them were completely untouched by humans, with a unique ecology that had evolved from the immigration of relatively few species of plants, birds, and insects.

It is believed that for a time, trips were made to the Marquesas for more supplies and more colonists, but then travel between the islands

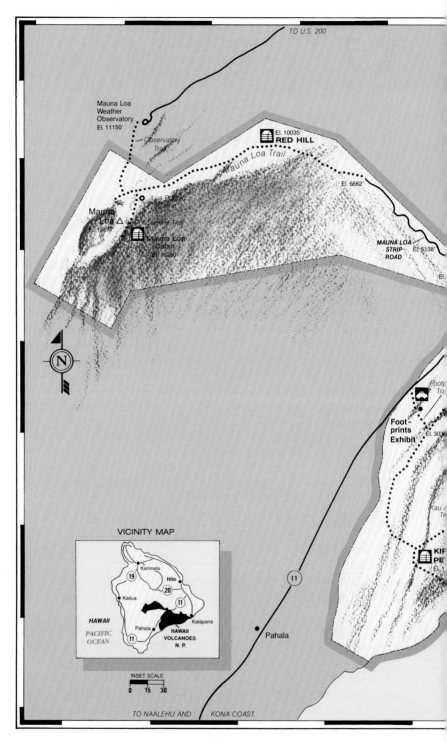

TO U.S. 200

Mauna Loa
Weather
Observatory
El. 11150'

Observatory
Trail

El. 10035'
RED HILL

Mauna Loa Trail

El. 6662'

Lua Poholo
Crater

Mauna
Loa △
El. 13677'

Summit Trail

Mauna Loa
Cabin
El. 13250'

MAUNA LOA
STRIP
ROAD

El. 5138'

El.

N

Footp
Tra

Foot-
prints
Exhibit

El. 309

Kau
Tr

KIP
PE
El. 1

VICINITY MAP

Kamuela

19

Hilo

Kailua

20

11

HAWAII

PACIFIC
OCEAN

11

Pahala

Kalapana

HAWAII
VOLCANOES
N. P.

11

Pahala

INSET SCALE
0   15   30

TO NAALEHU AND   KONA COAST

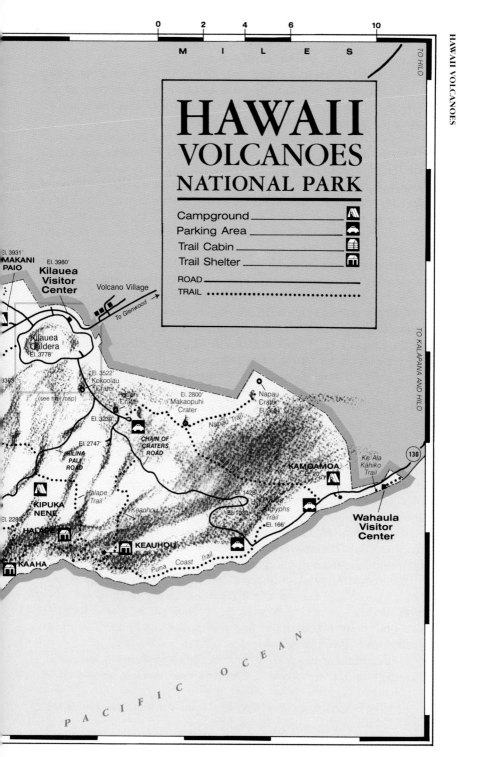

HAWAII
VOLCANOES
NATIONAL PARK

Campground _____ 🏕
Parking Area _____ 🚗
Trail Cabin _____ 🏠
Trail Shelter _____ 🏠

ROAD _____
TRAIL ••••••••••••••••••••••••••••••••

TO HILO

TO KALAPANA AND HILO

0   2   4   6   10

M I L E S

El. 3931'
MAKANI PAIO

El. 3980'
Kilauea
Visitor
Center

Volcano Village

To Glenwood

Kilauea
Caldera
El. 3778'

3363

El. 3522'
Kokoolau
Crater

(see trail map)

Pauahi
Crater

El. 2800'
Makaopuhi
Crater

Napau
Crater
El. 2584'

El. 3230'

Napau Trail

El. 2747'
HILINA
PALI
ROAD

CHAIN OF
CRATERS
ROAD

130

Ke'Aia
Kahiko
Trail

KAMOAMOA
El. 20'

KIPUKA
NENE

Halape
Trail

Keauhou
Trail

El. 1428'

El. 1030'

Petroglyphs
Trail
El. 166'

Wahaula
Visitor
Center

El. 2280'

HALAPE

KEAUHOU
El. 88'

Puna Coast Trail

KAAHA

PACIFIC OCEAN

61

seems to have stopped for several hundred years.

In about A.D. 1200, another wave of immigration took place, this time probably from Tahiti. These stronger, more aggressive people brought new gods, new customs, and new taboos (*kapus*) and imposed them on the more passive earlier settlers.

Most Hawaiian villages were in the coastal and lowland areas up to about 1,500 feet in elevation. One of the earliest, most sacred Hawaiian temples (*heiaus*) was built in the thirteenth century at Wahaula near Kalapana; its ruins are preserved today in the coastal section of Hawaii Volcanoes National Park. Nearby at Puuloa, one of the most extensive petroglyph fields in the Hawaiian Islands, Hawaiians over many hundreds of years left their record in rock carvings of images and symbols.

Early Hawaiians seldom ventured up to Kilauea Volcano, home of the greatly feared fire goddess, Pele, although ruins of what may have been two *heiaus* have been found on the crater rim.

One example of Pele's wrath can still be seen. In 1790, some of the warriors of Chief Keoua were crossing the island to confront the army of the chief's rival, Kamehameha. They had just passed Kilauea and were several miles into the Kau Desert when they were caught by a giant eruption of steam and ash and were wiped out. Footprints of the few warriors who survived were preserved in the hot ash as it dried and hardened, and they remain along the Footprints Trail in the park.

Explorers and Missionaries

The arrival of Captain James Cook in 1778 began an era of incredible change, both for the Hawaiians and for the land itself. The explorers, missionaries, and merchants who followed Cook brought a world of new objects, ideas, religions, and customs—not to mention new diseases—and Hawaiians found their lives completely reshaped.

The different plants and animals that came with each new group made tremendous inroads on the native species, causing many extinctions and near-extinctions, particularly among the birds.

The first non-Hawaiians to see Kilauea Volcano and provide a written account were missionaries William Ellis and Asa Thurston, who, with Hawaiian guides, made a circuit of the island on foot in 1823. At that time there was an active lava lake in the crater, and Ellis in his journal gives this unforgettable description:

> Astonishment and awe for some moments rendered us mute, and, like statues, we stood...with our eyes riveted on the abyss below....
> The bottom was covered with lava, and the southwest and north-

Modern travelers can still take the Tree Fern Forest Trail to Thurston Lava Tube, a popular attraction.

All dressed up for another eruption.

ern parts of it were one vast flood of burning matter, in a state of terrific ebullition, rolling to and fro its "fiery surge" and flaming billows.

Establishment of the Park

The accounts by Ellis and subsequent explorers spread around the world, making Kilauea a prime destination for adventurous travelers. It was a long, difficult trip to Kilauea Crater on foot or horseback, but the number of visitors increased every year as the volcano's fame spread.

The proposal to preserve Kilauea as a public park first surfaced in 1906, but Congress was not impressed with the idea. In 1912, the Hawaiian Volcano Observatory was established to study the two frequently active volcanoes, Kilauea and Mauna Loa; Thomas Jagger, the observatory's dynamic director, joined forces with Honolulu newspaper publisher Lorrin Thurston to press Congress to preserve this unique area as a national park. As luck would have it, in 1914 Lassen Peak in California unexpectedly erupted, and volcanoes suddenly became objects of fascination for both the public and Congress. In 1916, Congress passed only two of sixteen bills proposing new national parks; these two created Lassen Volcanic National Park in California and Hawaii National Park, which included the craters of Kilauea and Mauna Loa as well as the spectacular Haleakala Crater on Maui. (In 1961, Haleakala became a separate national park.)

Hawaii Volcanoes National Park has been extended five times since 1916 to include rain forest, desert, and the Kalapana area of the coast.

G E O L O G Y

Hawaii's Hot-Spot Volcanoes

Most volcanoes occur near the edges of the earth's great tectonic plates; typical volcanic areas are the "Ring of Fire," where the plates are converging around the rim of the Pacific Ocean, and along the mid-ocean ridges, where the plates are separating. Hawaiian volcanoes are different; they have formed near the middle of the vast Pacific plate. They have another peculiarity as well; instead of the entire Hawaiian Ridge being active, only those volcanoes that are near the Big Island at the southeastern end of the archipelago have erupted in the past few centuries. The nearly extinct volcanic islands and seamounts to the northwest become progressively older with distance from the Big Island. Loihi, a seamount whose summit is 3,000 feet below sea level, lies about 20 miles southeast of the Big Island and appears to be the youngest of Hawaii's volcanoes. The progressive aging of the Hawaiian Islands is about 1 million years for every 60-mile distance northwest of the Big Island; thus, Maui's volcanoes are 1 to 2 million years old, Oahu's about 3 million, and Kauai's about 5 million.

Snow-covered cinder cone.

Geologists offer the hot-spot theory as a possible explanation for these peculiarities of Hawaiian volcanoes. According to this hypothesis, certain locations in the earth's hot upper mantle, at depths of about 50 miles, produce abnormal amounts of molten rock (magma). This magma, being lighter than the overlying rocks, can force its way upward to the surface to form volcanoes. One of these mantle hot spots seems to be located under the southern end of the Hawaiian chain. As the Pacific plate slowly drifts over the Hawaiian hot spot, new volcanoes form at the point above the hot spot, while the older volcanoes, riding on the plate, move past the hot spot, become extinct, and slowly drift northwest in the direction of plate motion. This process of island volcanoes forming and gradually moving away has been likened to smoke signals drifting downwind from their source. This island drift is very slow, only 4 inches a year, and has not yet been directly measured. Whatever its cause, the progressive aging of the Hawaiian Islands to the northwest was recognized by the ancient Hawaiians; legend has it that Pele moved from her early home on Kauai to Oahu, then to Maui, and finally settled into Kilauea Volcano on the Big Island.

Kilauea and Mauna Loa

Most first-time visitors to a volcano expect to see a steep, cone-shaped peak, instead of a gently sloping, flat-topped mountain whose summit is a vast hole in the ground. Hawaiian volcanoes, called shield volcanoes by geologists, owe their gently sloping flanks to the relatively fluid lavas that build up these volcanoes like giant piles of candle drippings; viscous, more explosive lavas form the cone-shaped volcanoes.

Magma that builds Kilauea comes from 50 miles below the earth's surface and rises more or less continuously through conduits to a magma storage chamber located 2 to 5 miles beneath the volcano's summit. This magma chamber slowly enlarges, causing the summit region to inflate like a giant blister about 6 miles across and only a few feet high. When the pressure in the magma chamber exceeds the strength of the surrounding rocks, the rocks fracture, and magma moves toward the surface to form an eruption. Sometimes the overlying rocks fracture, and a summit eruption occurs; sometimes the rocks on the flank of the volcano are the first to fracture, and the eruption breaks out on a rift zone that is miles from the summit crater. It is even possible for the magma to move underground along a fracture but not break the surface; these shallow magma injections without eruptions are called intrusions.

When molten rock moves out of the summit magma chamber into

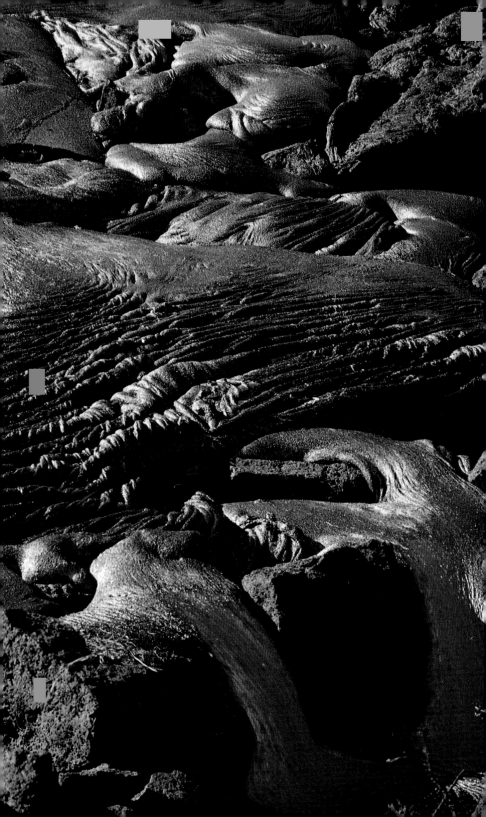

the rift zones of Kilauea, the rate at which it is drawn off often exceeds the rate at which it is being resupplied from the deeper sources. This causes the ground surface in the summit region to subside. When the magma pressure has dropped enough, the eruption or intrusion will stop. Long-lasting summit eruptions, such as the almost permanent boiling lava lakes in Kilauea's summit craters during much of the nineteenth century, are attributed to a near-balance between the slow eruption rates and the resupply to the magma chamber from greater depths.

Both Kilauea and Mauna Loa have great oval summit basins called calderas that are 2 by 3 miles across and several hundred feet deep. The calderas apparently have formed by collapse when an unusually large flank eruption on a rift zone below sea level drained a major portion of the magma chamber beneath the summit. The last time this occurred in a significant way at Kilauea was in 1790, and at Mauna Loa even earlier. Since their last major collapses, both Kilauea's and Mauna Loa's calderas have been refilling with ponded lava flows from summit eruptions. In the long life span of Hawaiian volcanoes, this cycle of caldera collapse and refill probably has occurred many times.

When William Ellis first visited Kilauea in 1823, the summit caldera was more than twice as deep as it is now. During the last 160 years, the slow but nearly continuous eruptions of the summit lava lake until 1924, and the more rapid but intermittent summit eruptions since then, have half-filled the caldera with .5 cubic mile of lava. (The most recent flows, which generally appear gray or black, occurred in 1974 and 1982.) Most recently, Kilauea's east rift zone has erupted with fairly frequent regularity throughout 1983 and 1984. During that time the eruptions have built up a major new cone more than 550 feet high.

Mauna Loa erupts less often than Kilauea, but the individual eruptions are often more voluminous. The eruption of Mauna Loa in 1950 added 600 million cubic yards to its slopes. The entire bulk of Mauna Loa, one of the world's largest mountains, is about 10,000 cubic miles. The 1975 eruption amounted to only eleven-millionths of this bulk. Mauna Loa has been formed by literally hundreds of thousands of eruptions during its 500,000-year lifetime. In the spring of 1984, the northeast flank eruption of Mauna Loa added yet another 240 million cubic yards of lava to the mountain.

Lava

When magma reaches the surface, the dissolved gases—mostly steam, carbon dioxide, and sulfur dioxide—boil away; the remaining rock is called lava. The first vents in a new Hawaiian eruption are generally fractures that are several hundreds to thousands of feet long, out of which spray curtains of incandescent lava. These linear vents soon

Carbon dioxide, sulfur dioxide, and steam escape from a fracture in Kilauea Caldera.

concentrate to one or more points along the fracture system to become the principal vents. If the magma is rich in dissolved gases, these individual vents erupt huge fountains of glowing lava, sometimes spraying to heights of over 1,500 feet. Mounds of lava fragments and spatter pile up around the vent, and pumice and Pele's hair blow downwind to form volcanic-ash deposits. Pumice consists of fragments of frothy lava glass filled with tiny gas-bubble holes, and Pele's hair is fibers of lava glass; both form by the cooling and solidifying of the drops of molten rock in the lava fountains.

Lava flows form from the fallback of lava fountains, or well out of gas-poor vents, and move slowly downslope like thick syrup. If the flows are hot and thin, often only a few feet thick, they cool to form pahoehoe (pa HOY HOY), lavas with smooth to ropy surfaces. If a flow cools and becomes more viscous while it is still moving, the surface crust of the lava breaks up into millions of jagged, blocky fragments

Overleaf: Flower petals on the lava.

69

that are rafted along on the still-moving flow. Hawaiians named these foot-slashing lava flows aa (AH AH´), a descriptive word that has become the standard geologic name for these rough, clinker-covered flows.

A distinctive feature of lava flows are lava caves, or lava tubes. These form where a thick flow crusts over to form a solid roof while the center of the flow beneath it is still moving. If the source of the flow stops, the core may continue to move downslope; the tube in which it was flowing is eventually emptied. Lava caves can be miles in length, and some have stalactites of sulfate minerals or of once-molten volcanic glass.

Hawaiian Volcano Observatory

The Hawaiian Volcano Observatory of the U.S. Geological Survey was established on the rim of Kilauea Caldera (sometimes called Kilauea Crater) in 1912 to investigate the phenomena and basic principles of volcanic activity. The observatory staff monitors changes in volcanic gases, earthquake patterns, surface uplifts or subsidences, electrical and magnetic properties, and the eruptive habits of Kilauea and Mauna Loa. Much of the current knowledge about the deep structure and volcanic processes of Hawaiian volcanoes stems from research done at this observatory.

One of the goals of the observatory is forecasting volcanic activity. By measuring the amount and rate of inflation of the summit area of Kilauea, as well as the increase in number of microearthquakes beneath the caldera—earthquakes that are too small to be felt, but still detectable by seismographs—the observatory can now estimate the probability of future eruptions on a daily, weekly, and monthly basis. Although far from precise, these forecasts are more accurate than random guesses based on the statistics of past eruptions.

N A T U R A L   H I S T O R Y

Climate and Precipitation

Hawaii Volcanoes National Park encompasses an incredible range of climate—from the warm, sunny Kalapana coast where temperatures on the glistening black lava flows average 75° F, through the upland rain forests with rainfall approaching 200 inches a year and temperatures averaging 65° F, to the severe alpine conditions at the top of 13,677-foot Mauna Loa with temperatures ranging from 11° F to 66° F.

Even at Kilauea's 4,000-foot elevation, the weather varies dramatically within a few miles. Rain clouds riding on the northeast trade winds drop as much as 100 inches of rain a year on the northeastern edge of the caldera. Clouds dissipate as they cross the caldera, and 2 miles away at Halemaumau, annual rainfall is only about 50 inches. Farther to the southwest, in the lee of the winds, it rains only 20 inches or less a year.

Hawaii's Island Ecology

The Hawaiian Islands are entircly volcanic in origin, made up of initially inhospitable lava rock. Since the islands' nearest continental neighbor is 2,400 miles away, life forms had to be highly specialized to arrive in Hawaii and to take hold in strange territory.

All life had to reach the islands by floating or swimming the ocean, by drifting or flying through the air, or by being carried on the feathers or in the digestive tracts of migratory birds. Hawaii has only two native mammals, the Hawaiian monk seal and a small bat; of those, one came by sea and the other by air.

Incredible as it is that any species survived the journey, the truly amazing story is how the few colonizing species evolved and diversified. For example, it is estimated that the more than 7,000 species of present-day native insects evolved from only about 150 colonizing species.

Native Plants

Plants that had the best chance of survival in this island environment were those whose seeds could float, such as the hala (pandanus) and the beach morning glory, both of which are prevalent along the coasts. Also ideal for adaptation were plants with tiny spores and seeds that are carried easily on the wind, so ferns and tree ferns were early arrivals. Many varieties flourish in Hawaii Volcanoes National Park; easiest to see are the handsome hapuu, a tree fern that grows as tall as 20 feet, and the amaumau, a fern whose young fronds are a reddish color for protection from the sun.

The ohia lehua is probably the most common tree in Hawaii. Similar to species found elsewhere in Polynesia, it has tiny, easily airborne seeds that not only ensured its early arrival in Hawaii, but that make it one of the first plants to become established on new lava flows. It appears in Hawaii in a remarkable variety of forms, from a scrubby shrub in dry deserts to towering giants in rain forests. All are easily identifiable by their characteristic brilliant red pompon blooms.

The best known—and most handsome—endemic Hawaiian tree is the huge acacia koa. Besides being prized for its natural beauty, its hard wood was favored by early Hawaiians for canoes and surfboards; it is used today for making furniture and lustrous bowls.

A pair of nene, native Hawaiian geese.

Other native trees to look for are the sandalwood; the mamane, with its clusters of bright yellow flowers; and the wiliwili, one of the few Hawaiian plants that is deciduous.

Common plants along roads and trails are the ti (ubiquitous throughout Polynesia) in the wet forests; the low ohelo bush, with its bright red, edible berries thought to be sacred to Pele, in the drier areas; and the naupaka and beach morning glory near the coast.

Some of the most conspicuous flowers seen in the park are those that have escaped from cultivation, such as the ginger, tritonia, fuchsia, and bamboo orchid.

Regrowth of Plants

Nature seldom provides virgin land for the study of patterns of plant growth, but a new lava flow presents just that opportunity. How fast the renewal of plant life starts on a newly erupted flow depends in large part on the rainfall; some 300-year-old lava flows on the dry side of Mauna Loa are so bare that they seem to have erupted only yesterday, while 50-year-old flows in the rain forest of Kilauea have a lush growth of new plants.

As the lava cools, cracks appear; these cracks are a good place for moisture to collect, and they also provide a bit of shade for germinating plants. In general, algae are first to arrive, with lichens, mosses, and ferns close behind. The sight of a tiny, bright green fern growing in a crack in a glistening black lava flow is a strong reminder of the tenacity of life.

A small colony of these early plants seems to improve moisture retention and makes it easier for other plants to take root. Native woody seed plants like ohia usually appear next, and exotic (non-native) plants last.

In areas where there is a heavy fall of pumice and ash during an eruption, native plants seem to be able to recover much more quickly than exotic plants. Where the temperatures of the pumice have not been too high, ohia trees have survived pumice falls up to 8 feet thick, and ohelos that have been totally buried have recovered.

Native Birds

Hawaiian birds have an astounding evolutionary history; scientists estimate that the more than seventy kinds of native birds known to have evolved before the arrival of humans in Hawaii developed from as few as fifteen original species. Unfortunately, many of those have been driven into extinction by the predators introduced by humans, by hunting, by avian diseases, and by environmental pressures of exotic plants.

The most famous native bird of Hawaii Volcanoes National Park is the Hawaiian goose, or nene, the state bird of Hawaii. Although descended from the Canada goose, it has evolved to live on high, sparsely vegetated lava flows away from bodies of water, so its feet have lost much of their webbing. A ground-nesting bird, the nene was driven almost into extinction by introduced predators such as rats and mongooses, and by hunters. By 1951, there were only thirty-three known in existence, and half of those were in captivity. A concerted effort by the National Park Service, the state of Hawaii, and the Wildfowl Trust in England to save the nene by a program of breeding and release seems to be succeeding. Groups of nene can sometimes be seen in the Kilauea area and at the end of the Mauna Loa Strip Road.

Other native birds to look for, especially in forested areas, are the wrenlike elepaio and three members of the large Hawaiian honeycreeper family: the iiwi and the apapane, both bright red birds that resemble the red blossoms of their favorite ohia trees; and the yellow amakihi, which prefer mamane blossoms.

Some introduced birds such as the mynah are common in the park, as are game birds such as the ring-necked pheasant and California quail, which live at higher elevations.

SITES, TRAILS, AND TRIPS

A driving tour of Hawaii Volcanoes National Park is best divided into two days. Ideally, the first day would be spent visiting the Kalapana coastal section of the park and then seeing the dramatic story of volcanism—ancient and recent—unfold during the drive up the spectacular Chain of Craters Road to Kilauea. After a night at Volcano House or the Namakani Paio Campground, a full day can easily be spent exploring the wonders of the Kilauea summit area.

Chain of Craters Road

The Kalapana section of Hawaii Volcanoes National Park is a 30-mile drive from Hilo, through the small towns of Keaau and Pahoa, with a stop at the famous Kaimu Black Sands Beach just before reaching the park.

One mile inside the national park boundary is the Wahaula Visitor Center, built next to one of the oldest *heiaus* on the islands, which dates from about A.D. 1250. The Visitor Center has a large relief map of the island that helps put the volcanoes in perspective, and some informative exhibits about ancient Hawaiian life. *Ke ala Kahiko Trail*, a 1.25-mile loop, follows along the sea cliffs, over rough lava by worn steppingstones, and through coastal jungle. A shorter (.25 mile) trail leads to the silent ruins of the *heiau* and circles back to the parking area.

For the next 7 miles, the road follows the coast at the top of 60-foot cliffs of craggy black lava, with bursts of white spray visible when the strong surf pounds against the rocks. There are many scenic turnouts, all worthwhile for spectacular views of the blue ocean and rugged coastline. There are no streams in this area; the land is too new, and the lava too porous, for watercourses to become established.

Two miles past Wahaula is *Kamoamoa*, a campground and picnic area in a lovely grove of old palm trees overlooking the sea; it was once the site of a Hawaiian village. At several similar locations along the road and at *Lae Apuki*, 1 mile beyond, are palm groves and archeological sites, remnants of the many villages that dotted this coastline before the destructive 1868 earthquake and *tsunami* (tidal wave generated by the earthquake) drove most of the inhabitants away.

At 6.2 miles from the park boundary is the *Holei Sea Arch*, about a 50-yard walk across the lava to the sea cliffs. It was formed by the irregular erosive action of waves on the cliffs, and is a good example of the constant interaction between the volcanoes (adding to the island)

Opposite: Gases escape from fractures in Kilauea Caldera.

and the ocean (wearing it away). The *Na Ulu* arches, formed in the same way, are 1 mile farther down the road.

Eight miles from the park boundary the road turns away from the ocean and begins to climb the massive flank of Kilauea Volcano, offering a spectacular view of the dark lava flows from the shield volcano Mauna Ulu, a new vent on the east rift zone of Kilauea. Between 1969 and 1974, when the rift erupted, these flows poured over the cliffs (*pali*) ahead, some reaching the ocean.

At 8.6 miles from the park boundary, a trail to the right of the road leads to the *Puuloa petroglyph field*. It is an easy 1-mile walk over the foot-worn pahoehoe of the old Puna-Kau trail to see these remarkable rock carvings, one of the largest concentrations of petroglyphs in Hawaii. *Puuloa* means "Hill of Long Life"; for hundreds of years Hawaiians came to this special place to carve figures, images, and symbols, most of which will probably never be deciphered. Vegetation is very scarce; a few ohia trees grow, and occasionally a noni, with its strange, many-eyed fruit.

The *Holei Pali Overlook*, about 10 miles from the park boundary, is a good place to stop for a better look at the Mauna Ulu lava flows where they poured over the cliffs. The silvery gray flows are smooth pahoehoe; the darker ones are blocky aa. In some places on the *pali*, islands of vegetation are surrounded by lava flows. These are known by the Hawaiian name *kipuka*; they occur when a moving lava flow— for reasons of topography, direction, or luck—moves around an area instead of overrunning it, leaving a green oasis flourishing in the midst of devastation. The light green trees in the *kipuka* are kukui.

About .5 mile farther on is the *Alanui Kahiko Overlook*, where part of the old Chain of Craters Road is visible between branches of the lava flow. During the Mauna Ulu eruption, 12 miles of road were covered with lava, some to a depth of more than 300 feet.

As the road climbs uphill from Alanui Kahiko, it cuts across several lava flows that are beautiful examples of the two types of lava. On the left side of the road, ribbons of glossy, iridescent pahoehoe have cascaded over a flow of dull, rough-textured aa in a fascinating juxtaposition.

The overlook at *Halona Kahakai*, 14.3 miles from the park boundary, is a good place to stop for a panoramic view of Mauna Ulu, the voluminous flows from it, and the coastline all the way to South Point. On the coastal plain below the overlook are the dark lava flows that poured down the cliffs and into the ocean between 1969 and 1974, adding 150 acres of new land to Hawaii Volcanoes National Park.

In the next 5 miles there are several fine viewpoints: *Ke ala Komo*, which has a picnic shelter on a rocky point; *Muliwai a Pele*, with a magnificent view of Mauna Loa and of the flow channel of the Mauna Ulu lavas; and *Mau Loa o Mauna Ulu*, where the road crosses a sea of pahoehoe with a fine view of steaming Mauna Ulu in the background.

At 21.1 miles from the boundary, a short (.5 mile) side road (actually a section of the old road that was cut off by lava) leads to a parking area with a closer view of Mauna Ulu and a look at the flow that closed the road. This is also the trail head for the Puu Huluhulu and Napau trails.

Just past this side road on the Chain of Craters Road is *Pauahi Crater*, typical of the deep collapse pits along the crest of the east rift zone. Drainage of magma from beneath the rift zone a few hundred years ago resulted in the formation of these craters by collapse. There was a brief eruption at Pauahi Crater in November 1979. The earlier Mauna Ulu eruption filled and buried two similar craters.

Along the Chain of Craters Road past Pauahi at about .5-mile intervals are some of the more accessible of the craters for which the road was named: *Hiiaka, Kokoolau, Puhimau,* and *Lua Manu*, where the fresh-looking lava is from a July 1974 eruption.

Between Hiiaka and Kokoolau craters, a spur road (at 22.3 miles from the park boundary) follows the edge of the Kau Desert for 8 miles to *Hilina Pali*, a steep cliff that offers a fine view of the Big Island's southeast coast. There is a picnic shelter here, and the trail head for the Halape Trail. Four miles from the Chain of Craters Road on the Hilina Pali Road is *Kipuka Nene*, a pleasant spot for camping or picnicking, and another trail head for the Halape Trail.

The Chain of Craters Road meets the Crater Rim Road at 24.6 miles from the park boundary.

Crater Rim Road

The Crater Rim Road makes an 11-mile circuit around Kilauea Caldera. The trip can begin at any of several places and can be made in either direction, but the following guide starts at park headquarters and goes counterclockwise.

At park headquarters for Hawaii Volcanoes National Park is the Kilauea Visitor Center, which has an up-to-date museum with history, natural history, and geology exhibits. Interpretive talks and movies of volcanic eruptions are presented several times each day.

Next door is the Volcano Art Center, a gallery for local artists and craftsmen, housed in the historic Volcano House, which was built in 1877.

Just beyond park headquarters, a short side road goes to *Sulphur Banks*, an area of volcanic gas seepage along a major fracture that forms an outer ring of Kilauea Caldera. The encrusting minerals include sul-

Trails of Hawaii Volcanoes National Park

Kilauea Summit Trails

Thurston Lava Tube Trail: Starts and ends at Thurston Lava Tube parking area; .3 mile round trip; .5 hour; leads through a lush fern forest and through a 400-foot lava tube; stair climb to exit tube.

Devastation Trail: Starts at Pu'u Puai Overlook parking area; ends at Devastation Trail; 1.2 miles round trip; .5 hour; boardwalk leads through the area devastated by the 1959 Kilauea eruption.

Bird Park (Kipuka Puaulu) Trail: Starts and ends at Mauna Loa Strip Road; 1.2 miles round trip; 1 hour; winds through open meadows and native forest along the slopes of Mauna Loa, one of the richest concentrations of native plants in Hawaii.

Halemaumau Trail: Starts at the Ka'auea cliff near Kilauea Visitor Center; ends at Halemaumau parking area; 6.4 miles round trip; 5 hours; self-guiding trail across the floor of Kilauea Caldera, through the lava flows of 1982, 1974, 1975, and 1954, and flows dating to before 1900.

Kilauea Iki Trail: Starts and ends at the Thurston Lava Tube parking lot; 5 miles round trip; 4 hours; drops 400 feet down into Kilauea Iki Crater; leads across the crater floor, past main vent, and ascends the Byron Ledge, where it joins the Crater Rim Trail.

Byron Ledge ('Uwe-aloha) Trail: Starts and ends along the Halemaumau Trail; 2.5 miles one way; 2 hours; climbs up Byron Ledge and then leads back down into Kilauea Caldera.

Crater Rim Trail: Starts and ends at Kilauea Visitor Center; 11.3 miles; 8 hours; leads around the Kilauea Caldera through both dense fern forest and arid wasteland; intersects other trails along the way.

Mauna Iki (Footprints) Trail: Starts and ends along Hawaii 11, 9.1 miles southwest of park; 3.6 miles round trip; 2 hours; leads along tracks of early Hawaiians preserved in volcanic ash; a branch leads to the top of Mauna Iki.

Coastal Trails

Ke Ala Kahiko Trail: Starts and ends behind the Wahaula Visitor Center in the coastal section of the park; 1.3 miles; 1.5 hours; nature walk passes through lowland forest along sea cliffs and remains of a Hawaiian village.

Puuloa Petroglyphs Trail: Starts 7.5 miles southwest of Wahaula Visitor Center on the Chain of Craters Road; 2 miles round trip; 2 hours; leads to field of petroglyphs chipped in the lava by early Hawaiians.

Mauna Loa Summit Trails*

Observatory Trail: Starts at Mauna Loa Weather Observatory, at 11,150 feet and 19 miles from Hawaii 20; ends at Summit Trail via North Pit Trail; 6 miles; 8 hours; steep and difficult; do not leave from Mauna Loa Observatory after 10 A.M.; altitude sickness likely.

*Overnight hikers must register at Kilauea Visitor Center; cabins are available on first-come basis; certain equipment needed and required; weather information is important.

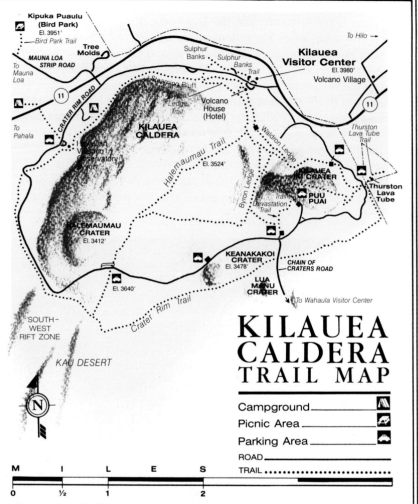

Kipuka Puaulu
(Bird Park)
El. 3951'
—Bird Park Trail
Tree
Molds
MAUNA LOA
STRIP ROAD
To
Mauna
Loa

Sulphur
Banks
Sulphur
Banks
Trail

To Hilo →

Kilauea
Visitor Center
El. 3980'
Volcano Village

11

Steaming Bluff

Byron
Ledge
Trail

Volcano
House
(Hotel)

Waldron Ledge

11

To
Pahala

KILAUEA
CALDERA

Hawaiian
Volcano
Observatory

Halemaumau Trail

El. 3524'

Byron Ledge

Thurston
Lava Tube
Trail

KILAUEA
CRATER

Thurston
Lava
Tube

Halemaumau
Trail
Devastation
Trail

PUU
PUAI

HALEMAUMAU
CRATER
El. 3412'

El. 3640'

Crater Rim Trail

KEANAKAKOI
CRATER
El. 3478'

LUA
MANU
CRATER

CHAIN OF
CRATERS ROAD

To Wahaula Visitor Center

SOUTH-
WEST
RIFT ZONE

KAU DESERT

N

KILAUEA CALDERA TRAIL MAP

Campground	◪
Picnic Area	◪
Parking Area	◪
ROAD	▬▬▬
TRAIL	••••••

M   I   L   E   S

0   ½   1   2

Mauna Loa Trail: Starts at Mauna Loa Strip Road lookout, 13.5 miles from Hawaii 11; ends at summit of Mauna Loa; 18.3-mile climb from 6,662 feet to summit at 13,250 feet (7.1 miles to Red Hill Cabin, 11.2 miles to Mauna Loa Cabin); 5 to 7 hours from Mauna Loa Strip Road to Red Hill Cabin; 10 to 12 hours from Red Hill to Mauna Loa Cabin; trail above Red Hill leads past many cinder cones and young lava flows, and into North Pit of the summit caldera; not steep, but footing is uneven and sometimes over loose lava; altitude sickness likely above 12,000 feet.

Summit Trail: Starts at Mauna Loa Trail at North Pit; ends at the summit cabin, at 13,677 feet; 2.6 miles; 2 hours one way; leads along rim of Mokuaweoweo Caldera.

See map on pages 60–61.

fur, gypsum, and hematite, and the lava bedrock has been altered to soft clays by acidic gases. The rotten-egg smell identifies hydrogen sulfide as one of the escaping gases. The ohia trees and ferns in this area have grown since the explosive eruption of Kilauea in 1790, which destroyed the vegetation around the caldera rim.

Steaming Bluff, the next turnout, is a treeless terrace between the inner and outer cliffs of Kilauea Caldera. Steam from ground water that is heated by deep, still-hot volcanic rocks escapes from many cracks. The ground a few feet down is too hot for tree roots to survive, but grasses and bamboo orchids with shallow roots cover the plain.

Ohia and koa trees are common along the stretch of the road past Steaming Bluff; ohia have dark gray-green, round leaves and rough bark;

Halemaumau with Mauna Loa in the background.

koa have paler green, blade-shaped leaves and smoother, lighter bark. Edible ohelo berries are abundant here, but Hawaiian legend advises throwing a few berries into the caldera for Pele before eating any.

Kilauea Overlook, on a short side road to the left, commands a sweeping panorama of Kilauea Caldera, and there are tables for picnicking.

Just ahead is the U.S. Geological Survey's Hawaiian Volcano Obser vatory; a few of their seismographs are visible inside the observatory window, recording earthquakes from various locations around the island. The view from the overlook in front of the observatory of Kilauea Caldera and its inner crater, *Halemaumau*, is one of the best in the park. Seen from the observatory, the steaming dome on the southeast

horizon is Mauna Ulu. The line of cones on the southwest horizon marks the southwest rift zone of Kilauea.

Beyond the observatory, the road winds down into the south end of the caldera. Vegetation begins to thin as rainfall rapidly decreases on the lee slopes of Kilauea. The ground is covered by the rocks and cinders explosively erupted in 1790. At 5 miles, the road crosses open fractures that have formed by the widening of the southwest rift as magma underground forced them open.

The desert conditions in this area are caused by low rainfall and the high acidity of the rain that does fall, which picks up the sulfur gases blowing downwind from Halemaumau Crater. When Mark Twain saw Kilauea, he remarked, "The smell of sulphur is strong, but not unpleasant to a sinner."

If the smell of sulfur dioxide is not too disagreeable, take the short trail to the edge of Halemaumau Crater for a glimpse into the inner sanctum of Pele. High lava marks on the sides of Halemaumau show the levels of molten lava lakes in the crater during 1968 and 1974. Partial drainback of these lava lakes into the magma chamber beneath Kilauea is a common ending to Halemaumau eruptions.

Just past Halemaumau, the road was covered by lava flows in 1982, and up the hill at *Keanakakoi Crater*, lava crossed the road in 1974. Rebuilding sections of roads destroyed by eruptions is a routine procedure at Kilauea.

Beyond Keanakakoi, vegetation begins to reappear. The pumice fragments that cover the road shoulders in increasing thickness fell from the great Kilauea Iki lava fountains in 1959, which reached heights of up to 1,900 feet. In another .5 mile, this pumice deposit is nearly 8 feet thick along the sides of the road. The ohia trees here were entirely stripped of their leaves and bark, and their recovery after a few years was totally unexpected.

Closer to the vent of the Kilauea Iki eruption, the thickness and heat of the pumice fall killed even the hardiest ohia trees. The *Devastation Trail* is a .5-mile boardwalk through this stark landscape.

Puu Puai Overlook, just off Crater Rim Road, is at the other end of Devastation Trail. Puu Puai is a large, barren cone of cinders just downwind from the 1959 eruptive vent of Kilauea Iki. Lavas from the same vent ponded in Kilauea Iki Crater to a depth of more than 300 feet. The solid, rocky crust of this lava lake is now nearly 200 feet thick and covers a thin lens-shaped core of still-molten rock. Several drill holes have been made in Kilauea Iki lava lake to study the way lava cools and crystallizes, and to assess the scientific feasibility of extracting energy from molten rock.

One mile farther along the Crater Rim Road, through a rain forest of giant tree ferns and ohia trees, is *Thurston Lava Tube*. The easy 20-minute walk to and *through* the lava tube is a delightful contrast of tropical jungle and mysterious cave, just 4 miles away from the barren Kau Desert.

The next turnout is *Kilauea Iki Overlook*, another view of the large cinder cone and lava lake. If hikers are on the trail that leads across the surface of the lava lake below, the grand scale of the crater and other volcanic features becomes much more apparent.

A 2-mile drive through the lush fern and ohia forest completes the circuit back to park headquarters.

Mauna Loa Strip Road

This 11.5-mile road begins about 2 miles west of park headquarters on Hawaii 11, and goes to the 6,662-foot elevation of Mauna Loa. The road is paved but narrow, and is sometimes closed during times of drought when fire danger is high.

Just after the road turns off the main highway, a short (.7 mile) loop road leads to the *Tree Molds*, formed when liquid lava cooled around tree trunks, crusting on the outside but burning on the inside. Some hollow molds are 5 feet across.

A mile and a half farther up the road is *Kipuka Puaulu* (*Bird Park*), with picnic shelters and a delightful 1-mile, self-guiding nature trail through one of the richest concentrations of native plants in Hawaii. Kipuka Puaulu is a lush, 100-acre island of vegetation surrounded by younger lava flows, with an astonishing variety of trees, shrubs, vines, and ferns. Plants along the trail are well marked, and a pamphlet with explanations keyed to the markers is available.

Here are majestic specimens of ohia and koa trees, as well as kukui, soapberry, and the rare holei tree. Tree ferns and ti are abundant, and the forest floor is thick with ground-hugging plants such as the pale violet koali (morning glory) and the introduced nasturtium and wild strawberry.

As the name of the area suggests, the treetops are alive with birds: imported birds such as the red cardinal and the Chinese thrush, and several native species such as the elepaio, the iiwi, and the apapane.

In another 1.5 miles, the Mauna Loa Strip Road passes through *Kipuka Ki*, another oasis of mature forest with magnificent old koa trees arching over the road.

The Mauna Loa Strip Road ends at the trail head for the 18-mile climb to the summit of Mauna Loa. There is a fine panoramic view of Kilauea with the ocean in the distance.

Tree molds formed when lava cooled around trees, burning them but leaving a cast.

Trails

Mauna Loa Trail. The climb to the summit of Mauna Loa is a grand adventure for well-equipped and hardy backpackers with 3 or 4 days to spend. Registration and cabin permits from park headquarters are required.

The Mauna Loa Trail begins at an elevation of 6,662 feet at the end of the Mauna Loa Strip Road, and climbs a steep 7 miles, gaining almost 3,400 feet to Red Hill Cabin, at 10,035 feet. This section of the trail leads through timberline on ancient flows of pahoehoe and aa; the silversword, native geranium, and hinahina (which has been celebrated in Hawaiian song) grow here. It is a good idea to climb slowly to get used to the altitude, since it is still 12 miles from Red Hill to the summit.

Red Hill is a large cone of red cinders on the northeast rift zone of Mauna Loa. From here, the trail follows along the rift-zone ridge of Mauna Loa and is a garden of geologic delights—young flows of pahoehoe and aa, cinder cones, spatter cones, lava tubes, and fissure vents. The trail is not so steep as it is below Red Hill, but the 3,600-foot elevation gain reaches altitudes above 13,000 feet. The scenery is moonscape, not alpine. The rugged terrain and cold, thin air require caution and good sense.

The summit of Mauna Loa is a vast caldera like that of Kilauea, totally barren and seemingly isolated from the rest of the world. The sight of the primitive summit cabin is a welcome reminder that you are still on earth. Water—often only ice—can be found in deep cracks in the lava about 200 yards beyond the summit cabin.

Only those who have climbed Mauna Loa can truly appreciate its size, and only those who have carefully planned and prepared for this arduous trek will completely enjoy the magnificent experience.

Halemaumau Trail. Probably the most exciting short hike in Hawaii Volcanoes National Park is the 3.2-mile Halemaumau Trail across the floor of Kilauea Caldera and past Halemaumau firepit. The trail starts from Volcano House, with a fairly steep descent through a lovely fern and ohia forest, past recent major rock slides from the 6.8 magnitude earthquake of November 16, 1983 to the caldera floor. The contrast when the trail suddenly leaves the forest and starts across the glistening black lava is astonishing; the caldera floor is an eerie wasteland of lava flows.

The floor is covered with overlapping flows of different ages. Some are pre-1900; but the most voluminous flows are from 1919 and 1974, and the most recent is from September 1982. The trail passes 3,000-foot-wide Halemaumau Crater, legendary home of Pele. This firepit used to contain an active lava lake, and could again in the future. The trail ends at the Halemaumau parking area; it is necessary to arrange private transportation from the parking area or retrace the trail.

Kilauea Iki Trail. Similar to the Halemaumau Trail, the Kilauea Iki Trail leaves the Crater Rim Trail about 2 miles from park headquarters and descends 400 feet into Kilauea Iki Crater. It crosses the floor of the crater, actually the cooled crust of a lava lake that ponded in the crater during the massive eruption of 1959. The "lake" still has a molten core at a depth of about 200 feet. The trail climbs up the western wall of the crater and ends at the Thurston Lava Tube parking area.

Footprints Trail. The Footprints Trail is an easy, 3.6-mile (round trip) hike in the Kau Desert, leaving from Hawaii 11 at 9.1 miles from park headquarters. This well-defined, mostly level trail provides a look at typical Kau Desert vegetation—scrubby ohia trees, ohelo, and occasional pukiawe—growing in what is mostly ash from the 1790 explosive eruption of Kilauea.

The footprints that are preserved in the hardened ash (protected now in an enclosure) are those of Chief Keoua's soldiers who were fortunate enough to escape the 1790 eruption. They and their less lucky comrades were on the way to do battle with Kamehameha.

Napau Trail. The Napau Trail offers a strenuous but rewarding 1-day hike past recent volcanic vents and lava flows, and through a fern-forest jungle on the east rift of Kilauea. The first few miles are across recent flows from Mauna Ulu. The trail goes between Mauna Ulu and Puu Huluhulu, a small, old cinder cone that has a trail to a viewpoint at the top—a nice side trip.

From Puu Huluhulu, the Napau Trail then passes Makaopuhi, the largest pit crater on the rift, and enters a thick jungle of tree ferns and ohia trees that were not covered by the recent flows. The contrast between the barren lava and the dense jungle is striking. Life in the humid tropics is tenacious and prolific; the jungle here is growing on lavas that are only 300 to 500 years old. Napau is another pit crater that is almost filled with recent flows.

The hike out and back is 14 miles, but the *Naulu Trail* provides an alternative route from Makaopuhi Crater to the Chain of Craters Road, 2 miles away at Ke ala Komo.

Halape Trail. The Halape Trail is a steep 7-mile descent of 3,000 feet from the Kipuka Nene Campground or the Hilina Pali Overlook to a small bay and beach along the rugged desert coast of Hawaii (on the south flank of Kilauea). This is a 2-day trip for sturdy backpackers, and registration and a permit from park headquarters are required.

The trail climbs down steep escarpments and benches covered with low shrubs and grass, to a shelter near the beach. Young coconut trees are growing to replace an old grove that was drowned when the land subsided 6 feet during a magnitude 7.2 earthquake in 1975.

Allow most of a day and carry plenty of water for the hot climb back to the trail head. There is an alternative 12-mile trail out along the seacoast to the Chain of Craters Road, but that route requires arranging for private transportation back to Kipuka Nene or Hilina Pali.

Opposite: In 1959 Kilauea Iki exploded, throwing lava to a record 1,700 feet into the air.

KINGS
CANYON
NATIONAL PARK

The South Fork of Kings Canyon.

KINGS CANYON NATIONAL PARK
BOX E, KINGS CANYON NATIONAL PARK, CALIFORNIA 93633
TEL.: (209) 335-2315

Highlights: Cedar Grove ☐ Frypan Meadow ☐ Roaring River Falls ☐ Mist Falls ☐ Paradise Valley ☐ John Muir Trail ☐ Manzanita Trail ☐ Viola Falls ☐ Ella Falls ☐ Sequoia Lake ☐ General Grant Tree ☐ Rae Lakes ☐ Glen Pass ☐ Fin Dome ☐ Dragon Peak ☐ Painted Lady ☐ Mount Rixford ☐ The Sphinx

Access: From Fresno, 55 miles east on California 180.

Hours: Grant Grove open year-round. Cedar Grove open from May to October.

Fees: $2/car, 50¢/person on bus. $10 Golden Eagle, Golden Age, and Access passes accepted.

Parking: At Big Stump picnic area, General Grant Tree, and Grant Grove Village.

Gas, food, lodging: At Grant Grove and Cedar Grove.

Visitor Center: At Grant Grove; open daily, 8 A.M.–5 P.M. At Cedar Grove; open daily, 8 A.M.–5 P.M., May to October.

Gift shops: At Grant Grove Village and Cedar Grove.

Pets: Permitted on leash in campgrounds and on roads, but not in buildings or on trails.

Picnicking: At Big Stump, Sunset, Columbine, at Grant Village, and at Roads End in Cedar Grove.

Hiking: Permitted. Trails leave from most campground areas and are within most sequoia groves.

Backpacking: Permitted with permit on over 700 miles of trails.

Campgrounds: At Cedar Grove and Grant Grove area, 7 campgrounds with a total of 730 sites. First-come basis. Showers available.

Tours: Many ranger-guided activities. In English.

Other activities: Horseback riding (in summer), cross-country skiing, fishing (license required), and mountain climbing.

Facilities for disabled: Most buildings and marked campsites.

For additional information, see also Sites, Trails, and Trips on pages 105–114 and the maps on pages 94–95 and 109.

WHEN CALIFORNIA 180 IS ABOUT HALFWAY TO the bottom of the Kings River Canyon, it comes to a wide viewpoint. Dead ahead, two of the deepest gorges in North America, the South and Middle forks of the Kings River, rush together, carrying between their granite ribs tumults of white water. Thousands of feet higher, rising out of the ice-sculptured ridges bordering the chasms—the one separating the Middle and South forks is aptly named Monarch Divide —are knobby peaks. Because of that dramatically elevated ground, the viewer cannot see the Sierra crest itself, 35 to 40 miles away, east and northeast. But the whole collapsing shape of the land indicates that such peaks must be there—high, frost-riven, streaked by snow, with quiet sapphire lakes caught in pale granite cups around their flanks. Just as surely as neighboring Sequoia National Park is a celebration of giant trees, Kings Canyon National Park is a celebration of the beauty and irresistible power of water in its various forms.

After reaching the narrow canyon bottom, the road turns up the South Fork toward the park boundary. When snowmelt is pouring out of the mountains during spring and early summer, the swollen stream at your elbow thunders over boulders into churning holes, then curls

The Sierra Nevada rise sharply on their eastern flank, over 10,000 feet above the valley.

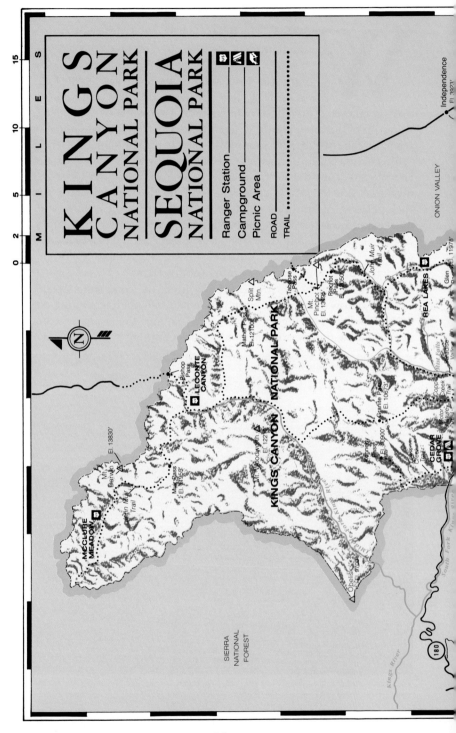

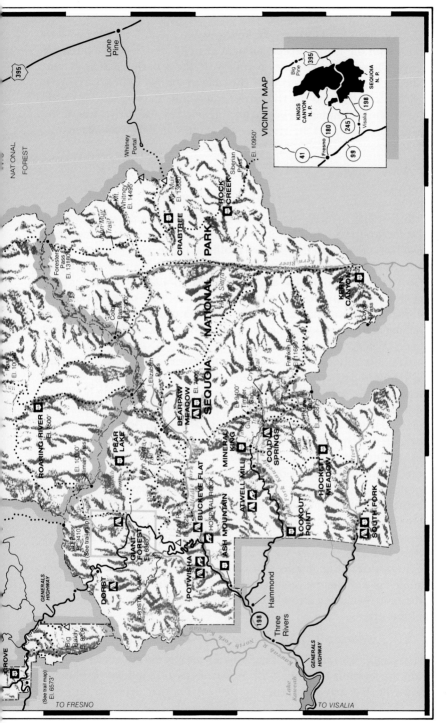

VICINITY MAP

KINGS CANYON N. P.

SEQUOIA N. P.

Big Pine

395

180

245

198

41

Fresno

Visalia

99

TO FRESNO

TO VISALIA

GROVE

GENERALS HIGHWAY

Big Baldy
El. 8209'

DORST

(See trail map)
El. 6573'

GIANT FOREST
El. 6805'

Crystal Cave

POTWISHA

Marble Fork

ASH MOUNTAIN

HOSPITAL ROCK

BUCKEYE FLAT

Moro Rock
El. 6725'

Middle Fork Kaweah

ATWELL MILL

MINERAL KING

LOOKOUT POINT

COLD SPRINGS

El. 7500'

HOCKETT MEADOW

SOUTH FORK

Three Rivers

198

Hammond

GENERALS HIGHWAY

Kaweah R. North Fork

Lake Kaweah

ROARING RIVER
El. 7600'

PEAR LAKE
El. 10000'

Tokopah Valley

High Sierra Trail

BEARPAW MEADOW
El. 7600'

Elizabeth Pass

SEQUOIA NATIONAL PARK

El. 9400'

Timber Gap Trail

Timber Gap

Franklin Pass
El. 11690'

Farewell Gap

Franklin Gap
El. 9058'

Eagle Lake Trail

Crescent Trail

High Sierra Trail

Kern River

KERN CANYON

Colby Pass
El. 12000'

Forester Pass
El. 13180'

Pass
El. 10000'

CRABTREE

ROCK CREEK

Siberian Pass

El. 10950'

Sawtooth Pass

Mt. Muir
El. 13660'

Mt. Whitney
El. 14495'

John Muir Trail

Whitney Portal

Lone Pine

NATIONAL FOREST

395

back on itself in ragged crests. Reflex waves recoil from the banks to clash with the main current; sunlight glistens on tall, erratic bursts of spray. Then, at the entrance to the park, the scouring action of vanished glaciers becomes evident. The canyon widens. Its bottom is more thickly forested, and the river loses some of its impetuosity. At Cedar Grove, good camping sites open up—a boon that the Native Americans who once occupied the area learned about hundreds of years ago.

H   I   S   T   O   R   Y

Native American Settlers

The first humans who came into these Sierra valleys were Monaches, a Paiute group who had left its homeland on the east side of the Sierra and had migrated to the western foothills. Those who found the South Fork strung their small settlements along the canyon bottom from Cedar Grove eastward to Bubbs Creek, a principal tributary. Excavations have revealed many pestles and grinding holes that were used for pulverizing acorns, hammerstones that enabled their users to crack bones containing marrow, crude stone axes, and arrowheads and knives that had been chipped out of obsidian.

The Monache soon came to rely on acorns as a staple food. After grinding hulled acorns and removing tannic acid from the meal by leaching, the cooks boiled the meal into mush by dropping hot rocks into baskets filled with water. To supplement their diet, the Monache occasionally feasted on small game animals or deer. Deer hunters often disguised themselves under buckskins and antlers in order to be able to creep close to their prey and shoot the animal with arrows whose tips were sometimes poisoned with rotted deer liver impregnated with rattlesnake venom. What they wanted but did not have, they obtained by trading during the summer with Paiutes who were still living in the Owens Valley on the far side of the Sierra. An amazing trail, laid out as nearly due east as the terrain allows, ran up Bubbs Creek to Kearsarge Pass, 11,823 feet above sea level, and then dropped steeply down the eastern side. Large numbers of obsidian flakes found at pleasant sites along the way suggest regular rest stops where the traders whiled away the time by making arrowheads out of the obsidian they had obtained in the east.

Spanish Explorers and American Trespassers

The Spanish who colonized California apparently did not get far enough into the foothills to contact the Monaches. Spain's military explorers, however, did find and name the main rivers that debouch into the

Please return to
John Muir
Martinez
Cal'.

John Muir was a leading advocate of the establishment of national parks in the late nineteenth century. This is his sketch of Kings Canyon.

Central Valley. Some of the names—Sacramento, San Joaquin, Merced —retain their original forms. Others became Anglicized. The river that Gabriel Moraga discovered on January 6, 1806, the anniversary of the day on which, it is said, the Magi first saw the infant Jesus, was named *El Rio de los Santos Reyes*. The River of the Holy Kings has since been shortened to Kings River.

During California's Mexican period, two groups of Americans who had entered the province without permission tried unsuccessfully to find ways out by crossing the Sierra in the vicinity of the Kings River country. Jedediah Smith's trappers failed in the spring of 1827 because of huge snowdrifts. John Charles Frémont had no better luck in December 1844. Although he reached an elevation of 11,000 feet somewhere along the North Fork, Frémont was finally turned back by rugged terrain and a gathering storm. After the American occupation, militiamen, pursuing Indians in 1851, saw parts of the present-day park before being halted by what they declared was the roughest country they ever had encountered. In 1858, a Paiute guided five residents of Tulare County, probably prospectors, along the Indian trail up Bubbs Creek and over Kearsarge Pass. But no really sound idea of the uplifted country emerged until after a five-man detachment of the California State Geological Survey issued a report of a sweeping reconnaissance that it had made in 1864.

Early Exploration

That was the year of California's worst drought. After riding across the Central Valley through smothering June heat, the explorers, led by William H. Brewer, climbed gratefully into the shade of the forest belt south of the South Fork of the Kings River. On hearing of a fallen sequoia tree whose hollow trunk was big enough to admit a horse and rider, they set out on foot up an almost unscalable 2,000-foot slope, dragging along one unhappy saddle animal so that they could test the assertion. True enough. Brewer rode 76 feet into the log. When he stood up in the saddle, his head still did not reach the top. Probably it was the prostrate log in the Grant Grove that is known today as Fallen Monarch.

From the tree, the small party worked out a difficult route eastward into the canyon of the Roaring River, turned up a tributary creek, and confronted a broad, pyramidal 13,570-foot peak, set with its flanking pinnacles at the northern end of the Great Western Divide. Brewer's companions named it for him. The next day, eager to solve the geographic puzzle of the interlocking headwaters of the Kings, Kaweah, and Kern rivers, Brewer and Charles Hoffman, the party's topographer, spent eight laborious hours reaching its summit. They felt well repaid. "A hundred peaks over thirteen thousand feet," Brewer wrote in his journal, "many very sharp—deep canyons, cliffs in every direction, sharp ridges almost inaccessible to man on which human foot has never trod."

Excited by speculations that there were higher peaks than Mount Brewer in that granite jungle, Clarence King and Dick Cotter set out on a six-day hiking expedition to examine them.

After picking a way through snowy basins and past lakes still half clogged with ice, King and Cotter, using lariat ropes for support, clawed their way up 14,025-foot Mount Tyndall. A partial victory only, for to the south they saw two higher peaks, Mount Williamson (14,384 feet) and Mount Whitney (14,495 feet)—names they bestowed to honor prominent contemporary surveyors.

Brewer's own concern lay farther north with massive Mount Goddard (13,568 feet), for "from it," he wrote, "we could get the topography of a large region." So north the party went. When they reached Granite Pass, they discovered that they could not get their eleven saddle horses and five pack animals down the other side into the Middle Fork, near whose headwaters dark Goddard loomed. After climbing such peaks as were close at hand, they went back to the South Fork, turned up Bubbs Creek, and followed the Indian trail into the Owens Valley. They rode north for several miles, recrossed the crest, and tried to reach Goddard's summit from that direction—only to fail by 300 feet. No matter. By that time their field maps contained enough information about the lie of the land that the central Sierra could no longer be considered one of the major unexplored regions in the United States.

Another energetic explorer of the region was the naturalist John Muir, who zigzagged through parts of it in 1873 and again in 1875. Sometimes he traveled on horseback with two or three companions. At other times he went entirely alone, walking and leading a disconsolate mule named Brownie, which found some of Muir's impulsive forays into trackless country more arduous than any pack animal should be expected to endure.

Muir claimed that he had named Giant Forest in Sequoia National Park (there is some evidence that he did not), and he showed his approval of certain sections of the Kings River Canyon—especially Cedar Grove and Paradise Valley on the South Fork and Tehipite Valley on the Middle Fork—by calling each a "yosemite," for what could be more flattering, in his mind, than a comparison with the valley farther north that he loved beyond all else?

The real significance of the trips lay in the moral fervor that they awakened in him. Muir watched lumbermen at work—lumbermen who by then knew that the wood of sequoia trees is extremely brittle. The impact of a tree's falling badly shattered all but the lowest part of the huge bole, and even the clean lumber near the base was not strong enough for heavy construction. But since sequoia wood decays slowly, it had some value for shingles, fence posts, and grape stakes. So for the quick gleaning of small profits, down the trees went, along with the more commercially valuable ponderosa and sugar pines among which they grew.

Another distressing greed was that of sheepherders, who crowded their animals onto every available grassy site, until hills and meadows could no longer function as natural reservoirs. And although Muir knew that occasional natural fires are necessary for clearing the ground so that seeds and sunlight can reach it, he deplored the wanton setting of more conflagrations than the forest could absorb merely to stimulate the growth of more grass the following year. With like-minded conservationists of the Central Valley, Muir campaigned vigorously against the despoliation, not only because preservation of trees and ground cover would conserve water that was needed by farmers, but also because respect for nature was morally right.

Establishment of the Park

The effort bore small fruit. In 1890, the General Grant Grove of big trees and another grove a little farther north were set aside in a 2,560-acre reserve called General Grant National Park. That same year, Yosemite and Sequoia national parks came into being. But no official nod was made toward the Kings River country.

Park or no, growing numbers of visitors began trickling into the South Fork by trail. (A hike from Cedar Grove up Sheep Creek will give today's tourist some notion of what the ride was like.) During the mid-1930s, a decade after Sequoia National Park had been extended eastward to the crest of the Sierra, a dazzling automobile highway was finally hewn into the South Fork from General Grant National Park. Almost simultaneously, the construction of the famed 212-mile Muir horse and hiking trail, from Yosemite National Park to the top of Mount Whitney, was completed. Popularity was immediate and led to more demands that the Middle and South Fork river systems, from mountaintops to lower canyons, be protected. (The North Fork, already littered with man-made "lakes," was not seriously considered.) In 1940, Congress obliged by creating Kings Canyon National Park, extending its northern boundary far enough along the headwaters of the South Fork of the San Joaquin River to include the magnificent ring of colorful peaks that surrounds Evolution Valley. The General Grant Grove section and adjoining groves in Redwood Canyon, although attached geographically to Sequoia National Park, were included in the new Kings Canyon unit. Exuberant expansion—roughly 450,000 acres—yet, ironically, the "yosemites" of Cedar Grove and Tehipite Valley remained outside because irrigationists and hydroelectric-power interests thought that the sites might someday be needed for reservoirs. Not until 1965 were the park boundaries redrawn to include them.

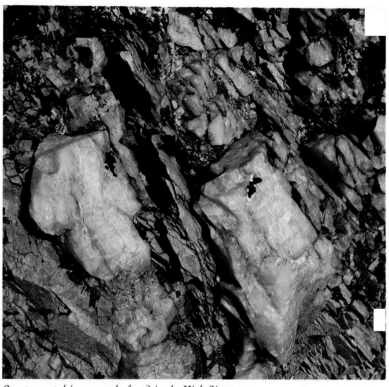

Quartz crystal is commonly found in the High Sierra.

G E O L O G Y

Continental Drift and Uplift

The light-colored granite that is so prominent a feature of the Kings Canyon scene—and of all the Sierra—is, in a sense, the result of geological trespass. The original materials of the range were indurated sediments that some 250 million years ago were bent, buckled, and thrust upward from their seabeds when the North American continental plate, drifting slowly westward across the earth's viscous mantle, collided with the much heavier, eastward-drifting plate that underlies part of the Pacific Ocean. In time, the uplifting ceased, and the hills eroded away, only to suffer the effects of another collision some 100 million years later. This time, the heavy Pacific plate was forced to slide underneath the lighter North American one. Intense frictional heat produced

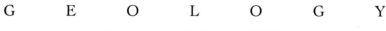

Overleaf: Sixty Lake Basin, in the northern section of the park, is a popular destination for backcountry hikers.

101

magma that pulsed upward and metamorphosed the overlying sedimentary strata: siltstone into shale, sandstone into quartzite, limestone into marble, volcanic material into schist. As the intrusive magma cooled, it crystallized into various forms of granite. Again the uplifting paused, and erosion, ever active, stripped away most—but by no means all—of the colorful, overlying metamorphic blanket.

About 60 million years ago, renewed tectonic pressures broke the eastern edge of the granite block loose from the surrounding land. But as the eastern edge lifted, the western stayed in place, like the hinged part of a trap door. As a result of the tilt, meandering streams quickened their pace and began transforming their valleys into deep, V-shaped canyons. On three more occasions the fault block was pushed higher, steepening the tilt and revitalizing the streams.

Glaciation and Erosion

The fourth and largest of these uplifts began something more than 1 million years ago and raised the Sierra crest to approximately its present elevation.

Thereafter, the Northern Hemisphere grew cold and wet. Throughout the High Sierra, except where wind swept some peaktops clean, snow accumulated to great depths. As drifts compacted into ice and weight increased, gravity tugged the masses down into the narrow canyons. Records of three such advances, each interrupted by warming trends, have been discovered by geologists. The last was halted and melted away between 10,000 and 20,000 years ago.

During the forward thrusts, each glacier picked up quantities of loose rock that studded its sides and bottom with an infinite variety of cutting points. With these "knives," and helped by glacial water that seeped into cracks, refroze, and split more fragments loose, the ice reshaped the land. It quarried huge amphitheaters called cirques into the sides of the peaks, created knife-edged ridges between them, and shaved certain exposed high points into steeples called horns. It straightened canyons by removing the ends of promontories and rounded their V-shaped bottoms into broad U's. Because the last glaciers were enormous—the one in the South Fork was 1,600 feet deep—they were able to dig farther into the main canyons than could the smaller tongues in the tributaries. The differential resulted in hanging valleys whose mouths end high above the bottom of the main gorges. Today, streams plunge down the drops in leaping cataracts that are punctuated by occasional waterfalls.

Cataracts in the high country often form the descending sections of glacial staircases. One theory that has been advanced to explain the phenomenon goes like this: if granite is fractured by many joints (vertical cracks), a glacier easily quarries out the rock between the joints, producing the precipitous slopes that form the risers of the steps. But massive granite, whose joints are widely spaced, is more resistant. The ice slides across it with little more effect than to polish the stone to almost mirror smoothness and, sometimes, to scoop out hollows that are later filled by gleaming lakes. These relatively level stretches are the treads of the stairway.

Not all erosion is glacial. Frost shatters wide stretches of closely jointed rock, creating rugged flutings in tall cliffs and repetitious ledges on gentler slopes. Colorful lichens, aided at times by weak vegetal acids in percolating water, slowly disintegrate rock into soil. More amazing are domes composed of massive granite whose surfaces, exfoliating bit by bit, finally produce huge, rounded knobs that generally rise out of the upper reaches of deep, steep-walled canyons. The most impressive one in the Kings Canyon region, and one of the most impressive in the entire Sierra, is Tehipite Dome, towering 3,000 feet above Tehipite Valley in the Middle Fork, reachable only by trail.*

S I T E S ,   T R A I L S ,   A N D   T R I P S

More than most national parks, Kings Canyon has been designed to offer its visitors a true wilderness experience. The only highway, other than those in the General Grant section, reaches 8.5 miles from the park boundary past Cedar Grove to a dead end near the junction of Copper Creek and the South Fork. All other travel must be on horses rented from the pack station at Cedar Grove, or on foot with the wayfarers' food and equipment loaded on their own backs or on the backs of burros they lead with them. Day hikes and rides range from easy jaunts along the canyon floor to more strenuous climbs beside nearby tributary creeks—Sheep, Hotel, Lewis, Deer Cove—all of them offering, here and there along the way, wonderful relief-map views of the torn and tumbled country. Longer forays into the lake-spangled headwater basins of the watershed can occupy as much time as the participants wish—or as they can carry food for.

Cedar Grove

The trails in Cedar Grove vary from short, easy walks to strenuous hikes that require careful planning. In any case, hikers should take care

*For a discussion of the natural history of Kings Canyon, see Sequoia National Park, pages 179–186.

no matter how long they are out or how far they travel. Remember that the best estimate of physical exertion is to allow 1 hour for every 2 miles on level ground and for every 1,000 feet gained in elevation.

Lewis Creek Trail. This steep former sheep trail climbs through an area that still is recovering from the Lewis Creek fire of October 1980. Along the first 1.3 miles to the junction with the Hotel Creek Trail, dry chaparral vegetation is returning. The next 1.6 miles leads through a charred forest of yellow pine to Comb Creek and then on to the Lewis Creek crossing. Frypan Meadow is 1.6 miles beyond; the wildflowers that bloom in July and August make this 7,800-foot-high meadow a photographer's delight.

Hotel Creek Trail. The Hotel Creek Trail passes through an experimental forest-restoration area where burning was started in 1969; the cascade on Hotel Creek is a short distance beyond. The trail then climbs rather steeply by way of switchbacks to the top wall of the canyon, a total of 5.5 miles from the trail head. It is an 80-foot climb to the cascade, and a 1,200-foot ascent to the valley view.

Don Cecil Trail. The Don Cecil Trail to Sheep Creek and Lookout Peak passes through a forest of ponderosa pine, incense cedar, white fir, and black oak. Before arriving at Sheep Creek (1 mile), which was named by early sheepherders, look back (north) at the 11,000-foot Monarch Divide. This ridge separates the drainage areas for the Middle and South forks of the Kings River. Lookout Peak is 5 miles ahead. Just beyond the peak is Summit Meadow (outside the park boundary), which presents a fine display of wildflowers in the summer.

River Trail. The short, easy River Trail is one of the most attractive hikes in the park; it leads both to the Roaring River Falls (.5 mile) and to Zumwalt Meadow (1.6 miles). During years of heavy runoff, the river races through the gorge and over the falls with a tremendous roar; but the falls are impressive at any time. Keep in mind that from the falls viewpoint, only about 80 feet, or one-third, of the falls is visible. The river trail to Zumwalt Meadow leads off to the left just before the falls viewpoint.

Zumwalt Meadow Trail. Zumwalt Meadow was named for D. K. Zumwalt, an attorney for the Southern Pacific Railway Company, who

Opposite: The General Grant Tree, 267 feet tall and 107.6 feet in circumference, is a major attraction of the park.

Trails of Kings Canyon National Park

Cedar Grove Area

Lewis Creek Trail: Starts on main road, 2 miles down canyon from Sentinel Campground entrance; 11 miles; 6 to 8 hours; 3,200-foot ascent; passes through charred remains of 1980 fire; Frypan Meadow, at 7,800 feet, is filled with wildflowers in July and August; carry water.

Hotel Creek Trail: Starts .25 mile down canyon from pack station; .25 mile round trip to the cascade (80-foot ascent); 5.5 miles (4 to 6 hours) round trip to valley view (1,200-foot ascent); passes through an experimental forest-restoration area begun in 1969.

Don Cecil Trail: Starts on main road, .25 mile up canyon from Sentinel Campground entrance; 2 miles round trip to Sheep Creek (600-foot ascent); 12.2 miles round trip to Lookout Peak (3,900-foot ascent); passes through ponderosa pine forest; magnificent views of 11,000-foot Monarch Divide; wildflowers abundant; strenuous climb beyond Sheep Creek; carry water.

River Trail: Starts at Roaring River Falls parking area; easy 1 mile round trip (.5 hour) to the falls; 3.2 miles round trip (2 to 3 hours) to Zumwalt Meadow; wide variety of trees and shrubs.

Zumwalt Meadow Trail: Starts at Zumwalt Meadow parking area; 1.5 miles round trip (1 to 2 hours) to meadow; 2.2 miles round trip (2 to 3 hours) to Roads End; easy walk along river, across a suspension bridge, through a forest, and on to the meadow.

Copper Creek Trail: Starts and ends at Roads End long-term parking area; 7 miles round trip; 6 to 8 hours; 2,800-foot ascent; one of the more strenuous trails in Cedar Grove area; switchbacks and steep climbing lead to the northern portions of the Kings Canyon backcountry; carry water.

Paradise Valley Trail: Starts at Roads End short-term parking area; 8 miles round trip (6 to 8 hours) to Mist Falls; 14 miles round trip (14 to 16 hours) to Paradise Valley (1,500-foot ascent); hot and dry first 2 miles to Bubbs Creek bridge, where right-hand branch leads off to Sphinx Creek and the backcountry; links with John Muir Trail at Upper Woods Creek.

Grant Grove Area

Manzanita Trail: Starts at far end of Visitor Center parking area; ends at Park Ridge; 3.3 miles round trip; 2 hours; 800-foot ascent; climbs up Manzanita Hill and back along the Azalea Trail; first section in forest; steep in places.

Park Ridge Trail: Starts at the Panoramic Point parking area; ends at fire lookout tower (manned May to October); 4.7 miles round trip; 3 hours; 200-foot ascent; easy trail that provides magnificent views of Hume Lake in Sequoia National Forest and the San Joaquin Valley.

Dead Giant Loop Trail: Starts and ends at extreme end of General Grant Tree parking area; 2.2 miles round trip; 1.5 hours; 400-foot ascent; easy trail that first goes downhill along an old road through forest of sequoia, fir, and pines, to the Dead Giant and the Sequoia Lake Overlook; 6-mile loop trail at end affords a view of the lower Kings Canyon and remnants of the 1955 fire, which destroyed 13,000 acres of forest.

Sunset Trail: Starts across the main highway from the Visitor Center (take trail going to left below highway, skirting Sunset Campground); 6 miles round trip; 3 to 4 hours; 1,400-foot ascent; leads to Viola and Ella Falls, and to Sequoia Lake; return by same trail or follow old road to General Grant Tree parking area.

General Grant Tree Trail: Starts and ends at Visitor Center or at the General Grant Tree parking area; 2.3 miles round trip; 1.5 hours; easy walk to the famous tree named after the Civil War general and president; passes the Michigan Tree, which fell in 1931.

North Grove Loop Trail: Starts and ends at extreme end of the lower General Grant Tree parking area; 1.5 miles round trip; 1 to 1.5 hours; easy walk that follows old one-way road through grove of giant sequoias and sugar pines. **See map on pages 94–95.**

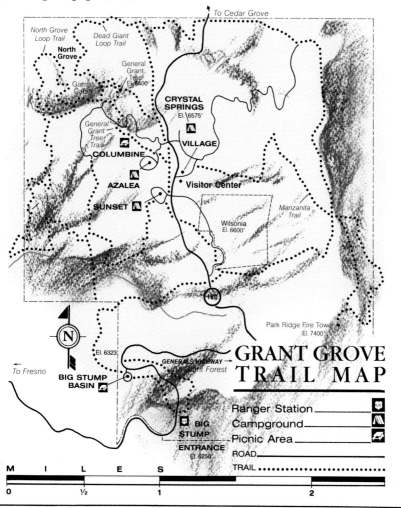

was responsible for having this land set aside as a forest reserve in the early 1900s. It is .75 mile from the Zumwalt Meadow parking area to the meadow, and 1.1 miles to Roads End. After an easy walk along the river, hikers will reach a suspension bridge across the South Fork and should turn left after crossing the river. The trail climbs onto the talus slope above the meadow for some magnificent views. A return loop trail goes around the meadow.

Copper Creek Trail. The Copper Creek Trail is one of the most strenuous in the Cedar Grove area. By a series of switchbacks, it climbs steeply into the Kings Canyon backcountry. After 1 mile, hikers will have excellent views of the glaciated Kings Canyon, Bubbs Creek Canyon, and Zumwalt Meadow. This is superb backpacking country.

Mist Falls and Paradise Valley Trail. The Mist Falls and Paradise Valley Trail is one of the most popular trails in the park. Thousands of backpackers travel this route to the high country in the summer. The trail is hot and dry for the first 2 miles to Bubbs Creek Bridge, where the trail splits. The right branch goes off 2 miles to Sphinx Creek and on into the backcountry. The main trail continues straight ahead for 2 miles to Mist Falls and for another 3 miles to Paradise Valley. Look for the many small cascades and waterfalls on Glacier and Gardiner creeks across the canyon. Once at Paradise Valley, the trail is on an easier grade than the 1,500 feet climbed thus far; it meanders through the valley, linking up with the John Muir Trail at Upper Woods Creek.

Grant Grove

The Grant Grove trails do not lead to the backcountry; instead, they are just a few minutes' walk from the road and turnoffs and take visitors into an area of solitude and beauty. There are many trails; just a few of them are described here.

Manzanita Trail. The Manzanita Trail is a 3.3-mile, 2-hour round trip that leads from the Visitor Center parking area up Manzanita Hill to Park Ridge and back by the Azalea Trail. Azaleas abound along the trail, as does manzanita, a shrub identified by its smooth red bark, roundish thick leaves, and small applelike berries. The Azalea Trail meets a tributary of Sequoia Creek a short way downhill, and from there leads to a connector trail to the South Boundary. The hiker then crosses the Wilsonia Road and heads back to the Visitor Center.

Opposite: Muir Hut was built in the early 1930s by the Sierra Club to provide refuge to hikers on the John Muir Trail.

Bullfrog Lake.   *Rae Lakes Basin.*

Park Ridge Trail. The 4.7-mile Park Ridge Trail begins at the Panoramic Point parking area and leads first to the point, .25 mile from the trail head, for an excellent view of the valleys and mountains to the east; in the foreground is Hume Lake in Sequoia National Forest. A little farther along the trail there is a view of the San Joaquin Valley and, if the sky is clear, the Coast Range 100 miles to the west; the elevation at this point is about 7,540 feet. The fire tower at the end of the trail is operated from May to October; permission must be obtained to ascend. Hikers must retrace their route from the tower.

Dead Giant Loop Trail. The Dead Giant Loop Trail is an easy, 2.2-mile, 1.5-hour round trip that begins at the extreme end of the General Grant Tree parking area and proceeds downhill along an old road to a meadow, off of which a short trail leads to the Dead Giant, a large sequoia felled some years ago. The trail continues to the left to Sequoia Lake Overlook, from where there is an excellent view of the lake. The lake, now the location of YMCA camps, was constructed around 1890 as a millpond to supply water for the flume to carry lumber to the San Joaquin Valley. A short distance back up the ridge, the return trail turns to the right. Off to the left of this ridge can be seen the lower Kings Canyon. From here the trail leads back to the road and the parking area.

Sunset Trail. The Sunset Trail is 6 miles round trip, takes about 3 to 4 hours, and is strenuous; but the rewards are many. It leads through an open and varied forest of firs, pines, and oaks to Viola Falls, Ella

Falls, and Sequoia Lake. The trail begins across the main highway from the Visitor Center, skirts the Sunset Campground, branches to the right .25 mile later, and then winds downhill. After about 1.25 miles, it intersects with the South Boundary Trail. Hikers follow the South Boundary Trail for .25 mile to Viola Falls, sometimes called Laughing Waters Cascades. In the spring and early summer the falls are spectacular with water from snowmelt. Ella Falls is about 1 mile farther along the trail toward Sequoia Lake. The old park road leads from the lake to the General Grant Tree parking area, where another trail returns to the Visitor Center.

General Grant Tree Trail. The General Grant Tree is one of the most popular and famous landmarks in the park, and it is located only a short distance from the Visitor Center. The round-trip walk is a little over 2 miles, and it takes only 1.5 hours. The trail begins at the Visitor Center, passes through Azalea Campground and Columbine picnic area, and leads to the self-guiding loop trail around the General Grant Tree. Cassette recorders with a 30-minute taped message about the trees may be rented at the Visitor Center.

North Grove Loop Trail. The pleasant 1.5-mile North Grove Loop Trail begins at the end of the lower General Grant Tree parking area and follows an old one-way road through a beautiful grove of giant sequoias, sugar pines, white firs, and dogwoods. Just to the right of the first junction, an unpaved road leads downhill to a meadow where many giant sequoias grow. The trail follows the road to the left up the paved road to the parking area.

High Country

The 43-mile hike to the Rae Lakes—considered by some to be as beautiful a spot as any in the High Sierra—and back begins at Roads End. Although the walk can be completed in 5 days, it is well to allow 2 or 3 more for loitering—fishing, sketching, or just sitting still. And remember to obtain permits at the ranger station. This is one of the most popular hikes in the High Sierra; for the sake of the land and the enjoyment of the campers, the National Park Service has placed limits on the number of visitors who can start the hike each day and has restricted camping at most campgrounds to a single night.

From the parking area, walk 2 miles—hot, dry miles late in the summer—to the bridges that lead across the South Fork to the steep, deep trench of Bubbs Creek. The trail climbs along the north side of the impetuous creek, sometimes high on the wall above it. The character of the forest changes: soft-needled firs now, slender lodgepoles and

Jeffrey pines, and occasional aspens, their white trunks gleaming against the darker background. Past avalanche chutes carved into granite and sudden meadows spangled with wildflowers. Reaching the Muir Trail is always exciting—there is no more famous pathway in the West. You swing left along it, still climbing. The forest thins out; the foxtail and white-bark pines grow gnarled. Fat, golden-hued marmots interrupt their sun baths long enough to whistle as you approach; pikas scurry with their harvests of grass among the talus boulders; gray and black Clark's nutcrackers scold like the raucous jays they resemble. And still the switchbacks climb and climb, leveling out only occasionally to skirt small tarns and gentle meadows. Thin sheets of water slide like moving glass over low granite ledges, beside white marsh-marigolds and maroon shooting stars.

Glen Pass, nearly 12,000 feet high, opens the way to the Rae Lakes and a stupendous view. From there, knee-jarring switchbacks lead down to the scooped-out hollows, rimmed with thin stands of trees, that hold the lakes. On still mornings they are shining mirrors for the striking thumb of granite called Fin Dome and for Dragon Peak, Painted Lady, and Mount Rixford, whose colored bands of metamorphic rock, called roof pendants, somehow escaped the erosive forces that elsewhere stripped bare the intrusive granite.

From the lakes the return to the South Fork is by way of the tilted trench of Woods Creek, as profound as the one that encases Bubbs Creek. The descent of the South Fork brings you to the magnificent, 3-mile-long "yosemite" of Paradise Valley. Then the trail begins to pitch downward again; toward Mist Falls, the glacier-sharpened point of the Sphinx comes into view, its huge flanks smoothed and grooved by rock-studded masses of ice that may return eons hence to finish their work.

Here is another of those spots where it is good to sit still for a moment and contemplate the riddle of an older sphinx, though more recently named, than the one beside the Nile. Earth cycles: new roots finding energy in decay; the ceaseless circulation of water from sea to land and back again; mountains raised up and worn down to provide materials for more uplifts. These are old mysteries that are often forgotten during the day's distractions, but they grow fresh again when you regard as monumental a carving as the Sphinx or as tiny a thing as a drop of dew. Part of the Park Service's task is to maintain that freshness amid increasing hordes of people. It is not an easy dilemma to resolve, but perhaps it can be done if the land receives from all its visitors the one boon it needs most—respect.

Opposite: Cascading streams are a characteristic sight of Kings Canyon.

LASSEN
VOLCANIC
NATIONAL PARK

Lava formations from the 1914 eruption of Lassen Peak frame Mount Shasta.

LASSEN VOLCANIC NATIONAL PARK
MINERAL, CALIFORNIA 96063
TEL.: (916) 595-4444

Highlights: Emerald Lake □ Hot Rock □ Lake Helen □ Chaos Jumbles □ Horseshoe Lake □ Juniper Lake □ Hot Creek Valley □ Badger Flat □ Summit Lake □ Hat Lake □ Nobles Pass

Access: From Red Bluff, 40 miles east via California 36. From Redding, 40 miles east via California 44. From Susanville, 65 miles west via California 36.

Hours: Open year-round; park roads and trails open June through September. Park road closes during winter, but ski area (near Mineral) is open Thanksgiving to mid-April.

Fees: $1/car.

Parking: Throughout park.

Gas: At Manzanita Lake Camper Service Store.

Food, lodging: In park, Drakesbad Guest Ranch.

Visitor Center: At Manzanita Lake (temporary) and southwest entrance.

Gift shops: At Manzanita Lake and southwest entrance.

Pets: Permitted on leash in front country, but not permitted on trails.

Picnicking: At designated sites throughout park.

Hiking: Over 150 miles of trails. Boil water.

Backpacking: Permitted with permit. Boil water.

Campgrounds: Tents permitted from May to October. Fires only in designated areas.

Tours: In English. Full schedule of interpretive programs.

Other activities: Skiing, swimming, boating, and fishing.

Facilities for disabled: Restrooms and Visitor Center.

For additional information, see also Sites, Trails, and Trips on pages 131–139 and the map on pages 120–121.

WITHOUT ANY WARNING…A HUGE COLUMN OF black smoke shot upward with a roar…and in an instant the air was filled with smoke, ashes, and flying rocks from the crater. They all ran for their lives." This eruption of Lassen Peak, described by B. F. Loomis, happened on June 14, 1914, surprising a party of local lumbermen who were standing at the crater's very edge. One hid behind an overhanging ledge; another slid down a steep snowbank; and a third had the misfortune of being hit by a block that gashed his shoulder and broke his collarbone—the only known injury during the entire seven years of Lassen's activity.

Small explosive eruptions of Lassen Peak began on May 30, 1914, and continued with varying intensity until 1921. The activity climaxed on May 22, 1915, with a major explosive blast that leveled 3 square miles of forest, and held the attention of the fascinated American public for the next few years while the eruptions waned in intensity. Until the eruption of Mount St. Helens in 1980, Lassen Peak had been the only volcano in the forty-eight contiguous United States to erupt in the twentieth century. Although Lassen's eruption was a significant one, the remote location and low population density forestalled disaster, and the final result was a fortunate one: the inclusion of this wild and beautiful area into the national park system.

Lassen Volcanic National Park is 200 miles north-northeast of San Francisco. Its 106,000 acres of volcanic terrain lie east of the northern end of the Central Valley of California and comprise the southern end of the Cascade Range, which stretches from northern California through Oregon and Washington into southern British Columbia. With elevations in the park ranging from 5,300 feet to the 10,457-foot summit of Lassen Peak, the winters are cold with deep snowfalls, and the summers are cool and dry. Besides its volcanic and thermal-spring attractions, Lassen is a lovely wilderness of coniferous forests and mountain meadows, worthy of a visit for a day or for a full summer. Destruction and creation, two of the many faces of nature, can both be witnessed here.

H I S T O R Y

American Indians

Several tribes of American Indians lived in the Lassen area, hunting in the higher country in the summer and migrating to lower surrounding lands in the winter.

The Yana tribes lived southwest of Lassen Peak along the streams

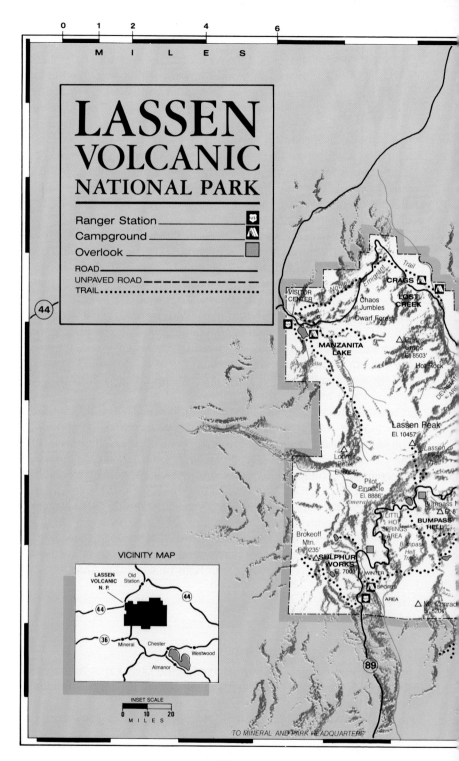

MILES
0 1 2 4 6

LASSEN
VOLCANIC
NATIONAL PARK

Ranger Station _____ US
Campground _____ 🏕
Overlook _____ ⬛

ROAD_____
UNPAVED ROAD — — — — —
TRAIL •••••••••••••••••••••

44

VISITOR
CENTER

Emigrant Trail
Nobles
Emigrant

CRAGS
LOST
CREEK

Chaos
Jumbles
Dwarf Forest

MANZANITA
LAKE

Manzanita Lake

Chaos Crags
El 8503'

Hot Rock

DESOLATION AREA

Lassen Peak
El 10457

Lassen
Peak Trail

Loomis
Peak
El 8668'

Pilot
Pinnacle
El 8886'

Emerald Lake

Bumpass
△ El 8

BUMPASS
HELL

LITTLE
HOT
SPRINGS
AREA

Bumpass
Hell Trail

Brokeoff
Mtn.
El 9235'

SULPHUR
WORKS
El 7000'

WINTER

SPORTS

AREA

△ Mt. Conrad
El 6204

VICINITY MAP

LASSEN
VOLCANIC
N. P.   Old
Station

44

44

36   Mineral   Chester

Westwood

Almanor

89

INSET SCALE
0   10   20
MILES

TO MINERAL AND PARK HEADQUARTERS

120

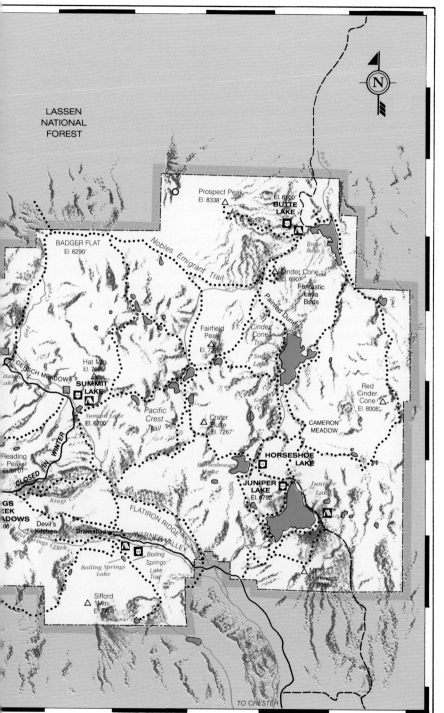

LASSEN
NATIONAL
FOREST

N

Prospect Peak
El. 8338'

El. 6100'
BUTTE
LAKE

BADGER FLAT
El. 6290'

Nobles Emigrant Trail

Butte Creek

Butte Lake

Cinder Cone
El. 6907'

Fantastic
Lava
Beds

Fairfield
Peak
El. 7272'

Cinder
Cone
Trail

Painted Dunes

Snag
Lake

Hat Mtn.
El. 7635'

DERSCH MEADOW

Hat
Lake

SUMMIT
LAKE

Summit Lake
El. 6700'

Pacific
Crest
Trail

Crater
Butte
El. 7267'

Grassy
Creek

Red
Cinder
Cone
El. 8008'

CAMERON
MEADOW

Reading
Peak
El. 8701'

CLOSED IN WINTER

Horseshoe
Lake

HORSESHOE
LAKE

JUNIPER
LAKE
El. 6792'

Juniper
Lake

GS
EEK
ADOWS
00'

Kings Creek

FLATIRON RIDGE

Devil's
Kitchen

Drakesbad

WARNER VALLEY

Hot Springs Creek

Boiling
Springs
Lake

Boiling Springs
Lake Trail

Mt.
Harkness
El. 8045'

Sifford
Mtn.
El. 7408'

TO CHESTER

that lead into California's great Central Valley, subsisting mainly on the abundant acorns from the foothill oak trees. By about 1900, the settlers and ranchers who were moving into the area had dispersed or killed most of the Yana, and the survivors had been driven into hiding in remote mountain valleys. In 1911, years after the last Yana had been seen, a young Indian who was almost dead from starvation was found wandering in the outskirts of the town of Oroville. He spoke a dialect that none of the local Indians could understand, and gradually an incredible story began to unfold. This Indian, whom anthropologists named Ishi, was the last survivor of the Yahi tribe of the Yana, and probably the last American Indian to live by purely Indian ways. His appearance in "civilization" was an act of desperation when he could no longer survive alone.

Anthropologists found a gold mine of information preserved in Ishi, and were able to piece together much that had been either unknown or misunderstood about American Indian culture. Ishi came to believe that the whites were "smart but not wise, knowing many things including much that is false." Nature remained for him the ultimate truth.

Indian tribes other than the Yana made more gradual transitions to coexistence with settlers, and some of their stories have been assimilated into local folklore. The Atsugewi, some of whom still live north of the park, have a legend about a warrior chief who dug his way into

Tourists visit Hot Rock, not long after it was deposited by mudflows following the 1915 eruption. The boulder, now cool, is still there.

Eruptions of Lassen Peak were common from 1914 through 1917.

Lassen Peak to recover his abducted lover. Impressed by his power, the mountain spirits invited him to marry his beloved and live with them inside the peak. The storm clouds that sometimes are seen above the volcano are said to be smoke from the warrior chief's peace pipe.

The Maidu tribes, who lived south of Lassen in the area that is now covered in part by impounded Lake Almanor, had an explanation for the earthquakes that often are felt in this volcanic region; they believed that the world was anchored in a great sea by five ropes, and that earthquakes occurred when the gods were angry and tugged on the ropes. The Atsugewi also have an earthquake legend: one time the shaking of the ground was so bad that people who lived on flat land became sick, and people who lived in the canyons were buried by rocks falling from the cliffs. It is possible that this legend had its origin in the great avalanche that formed Chaos Jumbles about 300 years ago.

The Indians knew Lassen Peak by several names, including Water Mountain, Little Shasta, Broken Mountain, Mountain-ripped-apart, and Fire Mountain. This last and most forthright has a good ring to it in its original—Amblu Kai.

Early Explorers

The Spanish and the Americans conferred their own names on this "unnamed" mountain. Don Luis Arguello, one of the early governors of Spanish California, called the mountain San José; explorer Jedediah Smith called the landmark St. Joseph; and Charles Wilkes on his 1841 map altered this name to Mount St. Joseph.

About this time the man for whom the peak was eventually named appeared on the scene. Peter Lassen, a Danish blacksmith, was lured to California by immigrant fever in the years just before the gold rush. He was given a large tract of land east of the Sacramento River by the Mexican government, established a ranch there, and set himself up to guide parties to California by way of his "Lassen's Cutoff."

Unfortunately, Peter Lassen was something less than a natural woodsman, and the route he chose was circuitous and extraordinarily difficult. He used the now-Lassen Peak as a landmark, but occasionally mistook Mount Shasta for Lassen, making the trip even more hair raising than usual. Some of his emigrant parties almost starved, and others were aroused to fury when they realized that their guide was frequently lost. Local legend has it that one outraged party forced Lassen at gunpoint to climb the peak that now bears his name to get his bearings. When the groups eventually reached Peter Lassen's ranch, however, his kindness and hospitality generally won back their admiration.

Establishment of the Park

As more and more settlers moved into the region, the need for lumber increased. By 1907, lumbering was threatening the magnificent forests of the Lassen area; to protect it, Lassen Peak and Cinder Cone were set aside as national monuments. Lassen Peak was assumed to be extinct, but the eruptions of 1914 and 1915 created so much nationwide interest that in 1916 the area was given full national park status.

G E O L O G Y

Ancient Volcanism

The geological story that is still evident in the surface rocks began about 2 to 3 million years ago with the growth of the first of three ancient volcanic centers in the Lassen area. Geological mapping in progress by Michael Clynne identifies these three ancient centers as Dittmar Volcano in the southeastern part of the park, Tehama Volcano in the southwestern corner of the park, and Maidu Volcano to the southwest of the park (near the town of Mineral). None of these once-massive volcanic peaks is still visible as an obvious volcanic cone; explosion and collapse, and the ravages of over 1 million years of waxing and waning glacial erosion, have torn these volcanoes into rugged mountains and valleys. Only by careful mapping of the remaining volcanic rocks can their majesty be reconstructed in the mind's eye of geologists.

The youngest of the three ancient volcanoes was Mount Tehama. Its main cone-building stage, from a vent in the vicinity of the present Sulphur Works thermal-spring area, lasted from about 600,000 to 350,000 years ago. Mount Tehama was a strato-volcano, so called because its cone was built up of layers of lava and volcanic ash. Mount Fuji in Japan is the archetypal strato-volcano, but there is no way of knowing if the cone of Mount Tehama, probably 11,000 feet high, was as strikingly symmetrical as that of Mount Fuji.

Manzanita Lake, which was formed by an avalanche that blocked Manzanita Creek, reflects 10,457-foot Lassen Peak.

Following its long buildup, Mount Tehama exploded and collapsed into a 3-mile-wide basin called a caldera. Glacial erosion has destroyed much of the shape of this caldera, but the remnant peaks—seen today as Brokeoff Mountain, Mount Diller, Pilot Pinnacle, and Mount Conard—mark its rim.

Thick flows and domes of viscous lava then poured from the northern and western flanks of collapsed Mount Tehama; they now form the high western peaks of Lassen Volcanic National Park. These silica-rich volcanic rocks, infamous for their explosive behavior, erupted during the last 250,000 years. They issued from many vents, the youngest and most prominent of which are Lassen Peak (11,000 years old) and Chaos Crags (only 1,100 years old). The last major glaciation had ended about 14,000 years ago, and Lassen Peak and Chaos Crags owe their well-preserved shapes to the fact that they were formed after that time.

Lassen Peak and Chaos Crags are interesting volcanic features called lava domes, great upwellings of viscous lava that is so sticky that instead of flowing away from the vents, it forms huge mounds at the surface over the conduits that delivered it from below.

Modern Eruption

The 1914 eruption of Lassen Peak was just one of thousands of volcanic eruptions that have occurred in the Lassen area in the last million years. But it was unique in having been witnessed by many observers and carefully documented by the pictures of B. F. Loomis and other photographers.

Bert McKenzie, a resident of Chester, California, reported the first explosion of steam and volcanic ash that rose several hundred feet over the peak on the late afternoon of May 30, 1914. The next day a forest ranger climbed to the summit and found that a small new crater, about 30 feet across, had been blown open on the inside wall of Lassen's 1,000-foot-wide and 360-foot-deep summit crater. More than 170 steam explosions during the next year blasted out old volcanic debris, enlarging the active crater until it encompassed the entire former crater.

Almost a year after the steam explosions had begun, molten rock reached the surface and overflowed the crater, tumbling in a deep-red sheet down the western side of Lassen Peak. Some of this same lava apparently also flowed or avalanched down the eastern side of the peak, rapidly melting the snow. The melt water mixed with loose volcanic ash from previous eruptions to form large mudflows that moved as far as 30 miles down the valleys of Lost Creek and Hat Creek. Mudflows

Opposite: Bumpass Hell is the most active thermal area in the park.

are floods of water that is so laden with sediment that it has the consistency of wet cement; they are dense enough to transport huge boulders and knock down trees. Mudflows are much more destructive than are floods of clearer water, for when the crest recedes, the mud and rocks remain, filling homes, fields, and entire valleys. Miraculously, the few inhabitants along Lost Creek and Hat Creek, warned by barking dogs and upstream neighbors, escaped the Lassen mudflows, and no one was hurt.

The largest explosive eruption occurred on May 22, 1915. A huge mushroom cloud, 7 miles high and seen as far away as Sacramento, formed over Lassen Peak. The cloud was accompanied by a lateral blast of hot gas and lava fragments that blew down a swath of forest 1 mile wide and 3 miles long on the eastern side of Lassen Peak. The devastated area is still visible, but a young forest is now growing there and will eventually heal the scar. Smaller explosive eruptions continued through 1916 and ended in 1917; steam "puffs" were occasionally seen until 1921, but since then Lassen Peak has remained dormant.

Thermal Springs and Future Eruptions

Ground water that is heated by hot rocks in the volcanic conduits keep several thermal-spring areas warm to boiling: Sulphur Works, Devil's Kitchen, Hot Springs Creek, Boiling Springs Lake, Terminal Geyser, and Bumpass Hell—an area named for an old-timer who had the misfortune to break through the crust of a hot spring and badly burn his leg. Although these thermal features at Lassen are not as large and spectacular as those in Yellowstone National Park, they indicate that much of the southern part of the park and the area beyond it may be a large geothermal system with underground steam contained in the pores and cracks of subsurface rocks. The thermal-spring areas, with some steam jets as hot as 318° F, are simply surface leakages of this vast underground steam reservoir. If geothermal power were to be developed south of the park, it could affect the thermal features within the park. The dilemma of economic development versus preservation of nature will probably soon raise its horns.

The central and eastern areas of Lassen Volcanic National Park are a rolling tableland of older lava flows with a few well-preserved volcanic forms like Hat Mountain, Crater Butte, and Fairfield Peak. Cinder Cone, a 700-foot young volcano in the northeastern corner of the park, has erupted basaltic lava and ash several times over the past 400 years; its latest eruption, which occurred in 1850 and 1851, lit up the night sky so brightly that the glare was reported by witnesses 40 miles away. Several of the small, beautiful lakes that decorate the Lassen landscape, especially in the eastern part of the park, were formed by lava flows and glacial deposits that dammed the stream drainages.

What is next in volcanic activity in the Lassen area? Probably a long wait followed by renewed eruptions at or near Cinder Cone. Eruption of a new lava dome near Chaos Crags is another reasonable possibility. Only one thing is certain: nature will continue to create violence, majesty, and beauty in this volcanic wonderland.

NATURAL HISTORY

Climate and Precipitation

Lassen Volcanic National Park is located at the junction of the Sierra Nevada Range to the south and the Cascade Range to the north. Both ranges are noted for their heavy winter snowfalls—up to 30 feet or more from the moisture-laden Pacific storms. In the summer, the Pacific storms are often blocked by a high-pressure area off the coast of California, and summer weather is generally dry except for occasional thunderstorms. The temperature is strongly affected by altitude, which ranges from 5,300 to 10,457 feet. The highest elevations are cold in summer and severely cold in winter; the lower areas are warm on sunny summer days, cool on summer nights, and cold in winter.

Flowers and Trees

Volcanic rocks slowly disintegrate into rich soils that support lush vegetation, and Lassen is a showcase of the results. Some of the higher elevations are above timberline, but the rolling tableland of the central and eastern areas of the park is covered by majestic coniferous forests and lovely mountain meadows with as elegant a display of wildflowers as can be found anywhere in the Cascade Range.

From May to October, flower watchers can follow the melting snowpack up the mountainsides as nature progressively uncovers its gardens. Brilliant red snow plants push through the edges of the retreating snow, followed by fawn lilies (dogtooth violets), alpine shooting stars, Columbia monkshood, and a profusion of other early flowers. The lavish display of blooms along the roads and trails changes as the seasons progress, and the moisture-loving corn lilies and monkey flowers give way to lupine, pussy paws, and the ubiquitous mountain mule-ears in drier locations. Lassen has several hundred species of wildflowers, and some can be seen until the snow falls again.

Lassen's forests are made up of trees that are native to the Sierra and

Although bears live in the park, they are shy and restrict themselves to the backcountry.

Cascade ranges. Fine stands of Douglas fir, incense cedar, and ponderosa pine grow at lower elevations, while red fir and lodgepole pine flourish in the higher forests. Nearer to timberline are beautiful groves of mountain hemlock—a tree much admired by John Muir—and gnarled specimens of the white-bark pine.

Perhaps the most unusual and least-recognized plants at Lassen are the algae that grow in the hot-spring waters between 125° F and 196° F. Millions of these microscopic organisms provide a spectrum of colors that can be seen in the thermal-spring areas.

Wildlife

Fishing is good in the backcountry lakes, since most are accessible only by trail or an occasional dirt road. Rainbow, Loch Leven, and brook trout are available to the patient fisherman. The lakes are also havens for migratory birds; in the fall, it is not unusual to see large numbers of waterfowl, including Canada geese and wood ducks, on their way to wintering grounds. These and all other animals are protected in the park, of course, and some have become quite tame. Black-tailed and mule deer, fox, marten, marmot, chickaree, and black bear are often seen, and begging chipmunks can hardly be avoided.

SITES, TRAILS, AND TRIPS

Lassen Park Road

The summer visitor to Lassen Volcanic National Park can see many of the main features in one day, although that is just an appetizer for a longer stay. A 34-mile highway (closed in winter) climbs and winds around the southern, eastern, and northern sides of Lassen Peak.

From the south, at the junction of California 36 and California 89, the Lassen Park Road (California 89) climbs 4.9 miles to the entrance station and ski area at 6,650 feet. The road is kept open only this far in winter.

At 6 miles and 7,000 feet, the road passes *Sulphur Works* thermal-spring area, near the center of the eroded volcano Mount Tehama. Prowling off the boardwalks or well-trodden trails around the steaming cracks, hot springs, and mud pots can lead to painful and sometimes crippling burns. The thin crust of apparently firm ground may give way into scalding mud beneath. With a little caution and common sense these hazards can be avoided, and the sights to be found far outweigh the risks. The rotten-egg smell is caused by hydrogen sulfide gas, and the yellow, pink, and white clays are formed by the breakdown of volcanic rocks in the hot, acidic springs.

At 6.8 miles, there is a fine view of 9,235-foot Brokeoff Mountain across the valley to the west.

At 7.8 miles, a striking view of Lassen Peak appears to the north.

Emerald Lake, at 10.7 miles and 8,000 feet, fills a small glacially eroded basin. Large rainbow trout can be seen, but fishing is prohibited in this high alpine lake.

The start of Bumpass Hell Trail is at 11.1 miles. Bumpass Hell is Lassen's most interesting thermal-spring area and well worth the 3-mile round-trip hike.

Lake Helen, at 11.3 miles and 8,164 feet, is a beautiful glacial lake that is often still partly frozen in early summer. The trail that zigzags up Lassen Peak can be seen across the lake to the northwest.

The Lassen Peak Trail parking area, at 12.4 miles, is the start of a strenuous but worthwhile climb of 2,000 feet along a 2.5 mile (one way) rocky trail.

The highest point on the highway is 12.4 miles from the junction of California 36 and California 89. Snowbanks may last all summer at this 8,512-foot elevation. The highway next winds down the southeastern slopes of Lassen and Reading peaks.

At 14.5 miles and 8,000 feet, Prospect Peak, a shield volcano (so named for its gently sloping sides) can be seen to the far northwest.

Trails of Lassen Volcanic National Park

Forest Lake and Brokeoff Mountain Trail: Starts at road marker 2; ends at Brokeoff Mountain; 7.4 miles round trip; 5 hours; 2,600-foot ascent; steady uphill climb for 2 miles; rugged mountain scenery; wildflowers are abundant every season; excellent views of other peaks, including Mount Shasta.

Mill Creek Falls Trail: Starts at Southwest Campground; ends at the highest waterfall in park; 4.6 miles round trip; 2.5 hours; 600-foot ascent, but first descends about 300 feet; rather steep climb for 1,000 feet; wildflowers and birds in abundance.

Ridge Lakes Trail: Starts at Sulphur Works parking area; ends at several small lakes in a cirque below the rim of Mount Tehama Caldera; 2.2 miles round trip; 2 hours; 1,000-foot ascent; passes through red fir and white pine forests; the striking leopard lily is found on this trail.

Sulphur Works Trail: Starts and ends at east end of parking area; .3 mile; .5 hour; one of the easier trails in park to the thermal area; a few steep places but no substantial ascent; mineral deposits stain the formations yellow, red, green, and orange; one of the largest fumaroles in the park is found at Sulphur Works.

Bumpass Hell Trail: Starts at Bumpass Hell parking area, road marker 17; ends at Bumpass Hell; 3 miles round trip; 3 hours; 500-foot ascent; spectacular mudpots, fumaroles, and boiling springs in most active thermal area in park; outstanding views of other peaks and high mountain meadow flowers; trail guide available.

Lassen Peak Trail: Starts at Lassen Peak parking area; ends at summit of Lassen Peak; 5 miles round trip; 4.5 hours; 2,000-foot ascent; the view from the summit is worth the arduous climb up a 15 percent grade, from 8,500 feet to 10,400 feet; recent volcanic activity; mountain hemlock and white-bark pine mark the timberline; trail guide available.

Kings Creek Falls Trail: Starts at road marker 32; ends at Kings Creek Falls; 3 miles round trip; 2.5 hours; 700-foot ascent; flowers in bloom all summer; this is one of the few places in the park where mountain ash is found.

Summit Lake to Echo and Twin Lakes: Starts at Summit Lake; ends at Lower Twin Lake; 8 miles round trip; 6 hours; uphill 500 feet in first mile, then descends 500 feet to lake; excellent trail for viewing wildflowers, trees, and birds; deer commonly seen along trail.

Summit Lake to Horseshoe Lake via Upper Twin Lake: Starts at east side of Summit Lake; ends at Horseshoe Lake; 14 miles round trip; 12 hours; 700-foot ascent; a major trail to the eastern section of the park; crosses two bridges; several lakes along the way; typical of park flora and fauna; a good day hike through pine and fir forests and meadows.

Summit Lake to Cluster Lakes: Starts and ends at east side of Summit Lake; 10.5 miles; 7 hours; leads to Bear Lakes, Cluster Lakes, and Upper and Lower Twin Lakes.

Cinder Cone, in the northeast near Butte Lake, was last active in 1853.

Paradise Meadow Trail: Starts at road marker 42; ends at Paradise Meadow; 3 miles round trip; 3 hours; .5 mile steep ascent of 600 feet; best area in park for midsummer wildflowers; lush meadow with many birds and deer.

Pacific Crest Trail: Starts at Little Willow Lake; ends at Badger Flat; 19 miles round trip; 16 hours; 1,000-foot ascent; trail crosses park north to south.

Cinder Cone Trail: Starts and ends at Butte Lake Campground; 5 miles; 3 hours; 800-foot ascent; loop trail around one of the most perfectly formed cinder cones in the United States; excellent view of other nearby peaks; trail guide available.

Butte Lake to Snag Lake: Starts and ends at Butte Lake parking area; 3.5 miles; 5 hours; 100-foot ascent; example of recent volcanic activity; hike can be extended an additional 3 miles and 3 hours to the south end of Snag Lake; portion of trail winds along the base of a large basalt lava flow.

Horseshoe Lake to Snag Lake: Starts and ends at Horseshoe Lake ranger station; 6 miles; 3.5 hours; 600-foot ascent; trail touches south end of Snag Lake; remains of a drowned forest can be seen along edge of lake.

Juniper Lake to Snag Lake: Starts and ends at Juniper Lake ranger station; 6 miles; 4.5 hours; 1,000-foot ascent; trail passes through ponderosa pine forest most of way; wide variety of wildflowers in July and August; remains of an early settler's cabin in Cameron Meadows.

Boiling Springs Lake Trail: Starts and ends at Warner Valley picnic area; 3 miles; 2 hours; 200-foot ascent; trail crosses a meadow and passes through a mixed coniferous forest and steam vents and mudpots along the lake's shoreline; trail guide available.

Devil's Kitchen Trail: Starts and ends at Warner Valley picnic area; 3 miles; 2.5 hours; 300-foot ascent; an excellent trail for those interested in biology and geology; very active thermal area, one of the more important in the park. **See map on pages 120–121.**

Passing through Kings Creek Campground, at 16.8 miles and 7,400 feet, the road leads through fine stands of red fir and some mountain hemlock. By *Summit Lake*, at 21.3 miles and 6,700 feet, red fir is still prominent, and lodgepole pine and western white pine begin to appear.

Dersch Meadows, north of the road at 22 to 24 miles and about 6,500 feet, is a good area to see deer and many varieties of wildflowers.

Hat Lake, at 24.2 miles and 6,450 feet, was formed by the mudflow eruption of May 19, 1915, and is now rapidly filling with sediments and becoming a new meadow. At 24.7 miles, the devastated area on the eastern and northeastern flanks of Lassen Peak becomes clearly visible. Now an area of young forest and brush, this was a 3-square-mile stand of mature forest that was destroyed by the mudflows of May 19 and the steam blast of May 22, 1915. Some of the downed trees can still be found, all pointing away from the blast, which originated high on the eastern summit of Lassen Peak.

A solitary snowshoer makes his way toward Lassen Peak.

Hot Rock (long since cooled), one of many boulders seen at 26.7 miles along Lost Creek, was carried there by the 1915 mudflows.

From 28 to 30 miles, the road passes through white fir, Jeffrey pine, sugar pine, ponderosa pine, and incense cedar. *Nobles Pass*, at 31.5 miles and 6,000 feet, was an important way through the mountains for an old emigrant trail between the Black Rock Desert in Nevada and Shasta City, California, a cutoff from the Humboldt Trail across Nevada to northern California.

From 32 to 33 miles, the road crosses *Chaos Jumbles*, a large rock avalanche that fell about 300 years ago from a group of lava domes called Chaos Crags, which formed only 1,100 years ago.

Just as volcanism has created much of the fascinating scenery of the Lassen area, it also poses future hazards to the park. Although the risks are vanishingly small to any one person at any one moment, they do concern the National Park Service in its interest for the collective safety of all visitors over many years. Geologists Dwight Crandell and Donal Mullineaux, who warned in 1975 that Mount St. Helens might erupt violently before the end of the century, have evaluated the volcanic hazards at Lassen Volcanic National Park. Their principal concern is the Chaos Jumbles area. This avalanche covered a tract of about 2 square miles and reached downhill for 3 miles. It dammed Manzanita Creek to form *Manzanita Lake*. It is not known if the rockslide was triggered by a steam explosion, a major earthquake, or some other cause. Because of the possibility of another avalanche, which could occur without any warning, the Manzanita Lake Visitor Center was closed in 1975. A new Visitor Center is to be built just outside the northwestern corner of the park in Lassen National Forest.

The chance of renewed explosive eruptions in the Chaos Crags area is also a potential hazard. They probably would not occur without some premonitory signs such as earthquake swarms or ground-surface displacements. Such symptoms in the Lassen area are now being monitored by seismographs and tiltmeters by the U.S. Geological Survey. These instruments can detect the microearthquakes and slight bulging of the ground surface that often precede volcanic eruptions. The combination of volcanic monitoring and awareness of the hazards should help to ensure the safety of visitors to this magnificent park.

At 34.3 miles, the Lassen Park Road ends at the junction of California 89 and California 44.

Other Roads

Four dead-end, dirt roads lead to various backcountry areas in the park. The road to Drakesbad, a starting point for pack trips, begins from Chester, California, 19 miles southeast.

Horseshoe Lake and *Juniper Lake* in the southeastern portion of the park can also be reached by dirt road from Chester. (Between Horseshoe and Juniper lakes, the road is closed to motorized vehicles.)

Hat Creek Valley and *Badger Flat* in the north central portion of the park are accessible by a dirt road (also closed to vehicles) that turns north from the Lassen Park Road near Hat Lake.

The dirt road to Butte Lake Campground and the trail head to Cinder Cone in the northeastern corner of the park is reached by 29 miles of paved road (California 44) that circles north of the park from its junction with California 89.

Opposite: Kings Creek meanders through Kings Creek Meadows in the south of the park.

Clusters of arrow-leaf balsam root, with 9,235-foot Brokeoff Mountain in the distance.

Trails

Bumpass Hell Trail. Bumpass Hell Trail leads through stands of mountain hemlock and white-bark pine to the largest and most spectacular thermal-spring area in the park. The 3-mile (round trip) trail climbs and descends several hundred feet, and is usually open by July 1. The hot and boiling springs, steam vents, and mud pots are leaks from a major underground reservoir of steam that is heated by the molten roots of the volcanoes. Colors in the thermal springs come from both living algae and chemical decomposition of volcanic rock.

Cinder Cone Trail. Cinder Cone Trail begins at Butte Lake ranger station, and the 5-mile round trip takes 3 to 4 hours. The last eruption of Cinder Cone was in 1850 and 1851, and the deposits are still vividly fresh. The climb up the loose cinders gains an altitude of about 800 feet. All cinder cones look like giant anthills. The larger fragments thrown out by the exploding volcanic vents fall nearby and create steep cones of loose debris that surround the summit craters. Rugged lava beds near the base of Cinder Cone are partly covered by volcanic ash, forming a colorful area called the Painted Dunes. Butte Lake and Snag Lake were formed by the lava flows from Cinder Cone, which dammed the natural stream drainages. The summit of Cinder Cone provides fine views of a variety of nearby volcanic peaks.

Lassen Peak Trail. Lassen Peak Trail begins from the Lassen Park Road at 8,500 feet and climbs a steep but steady grade to the summit of Lassen Peak at 10,457 feet, the highest point in the park. The trail is usually open by July 1, but snowbanks often persist all summer. Four hours round trip (5 miles) is about the average time needed to hike this rocky but spectacular trail. Mountain hemlock and white-bark pine are common near the trail head, but much of the trail is above timberline. The gray to tan rock that forms Lassen Peak is called dacite. It erupted about 11,000 years ago, forming a steep dome of lava that was too viscous to flow away from its vent. Much of the broken lava lies in talus piles that tumbled down the steep dome as it pushed upward. The darker rock at the summit and high on the western slope of the peak is the dacite that erupted in 1915. The panorama from the summit on a clear day is superb (if there is any indication of a thunderstorm, it is best to retreat from the lightning-scarred mountaintop): looking north to Chaos Crags and turning clockwise, you can see Prospect Peak, Cinder Cone, the distant ranges in Nevada, Dyer Peak and Lake Almanor, the distant Sierras near Lake Tahoe, Brokeoff Mountain, Loomis Peak, the Trinity Alps in the distance, and, 75 miles to the northwest, 14,161-foot Mount Shasta—the next major Cascade volcano.

Boiling Springs Lake Trail. Boiling Springs Lake Trail begins just west of the campground on the dirt road to Drakesbad Lodge. It is an easy 2-hour (3-mile) round trip that ascends only 200 feet, yet travels through backcountry forest and meadow to a most interesting thermal-spring area. Boiling Springs Lake is small, and is heated to a fairly steady 125° F by underwater hot springs and steam vents. There is also an extensive area of mud pots along the shore. En route to and from the lake are stands of incense cedar, Douglas fir, white fir, ponderosa pine, and sugar pine. This trail is generally open by June 15, and wildflowers are abundant as melting snow waters the meadows.

Other Trails. Other trails in Lassen Volcanic National Park add up to well over 100 miles in length. A few, such as the short trails at *Manzanita Lake* and *Sulphur Works*, are often open by May 15. One or two, such as the steep trail to *Brokeoff Mountain*, may not be open until July 15. However, most of the thirty-five other trails—some with such intriguing names as *Devil's Kitchen, Bathtub Lake, Paradise Meadow, Widow Lake*, and *Crystal Lake*—are generally open by June 15 or July 1.

REDWOOD
NATIONAL PARK

REDWOOD NATIONAL PARK
1111 SECOND STREET
CRESCENT CITY, CALIFORNIA 95531
TEL.: (707) 464-6101

Highlights: National Tribute Grove □ Stout Grove □ Jedediah Smith Redwoods State Park □ Del Norte Coast Redwoods State Park □ Prairie Creek Redwoods State Park □ Saddler Skyline Trail □ Fern Canyon Trail □ Tall Trees Grove □ Enderts Beach □ False Klamath Cove

Access: U.S. 101 runs through the park, north and south. From Grants Pass, Oregon, U.S. 199 to north boundary of park.

Hours: Daily, 24 hours, year-round.

Fees: None, except for use of shuttle bus: $2/adult, $1/senior citizen, 50¢/child under 16.

Parking: At Crescent City Visitor Center (about 50), Hiouchi ranger station (about 30), and Orick ranger station (about 15).

Gas, food, lodging: In Crescent City, Klamath, and Orick.

Visitor Centers: Crescent City Visitor Center, Hiouchi ranger station, and Orick ranger station offer exhibits, talks, and audio-visual program.

Pets: Permitted, except on trails and in backcountry.

Picnicking: At designated sites throughout park.

Hiking: On designated trails throughout park. Treat water before drinking.

Campgrounds: At Jedediah Smith, Del Norte, Prairie Creek, and Gold Bluff; primitive sites at Enderts and Redwood Creek. No hookups, but disposal stations available.

Tours: Tall Trees Grove tour in English.

Other activities: Horseback riding, swimming, and fishing (license required).

Facilities for disabled: Booklet entitled *Access National Park* available.

For additional information, see also Sites, Trails, and Trips on pages 156–163 and the maps on pages 144–145 and 161.

THROUGHOUT REDWOOD NATIONAL PARK AND THE state park system within it, wilderness prevails: dense, moist forest; three major streams; and abundant wildlife. More than 1,000 species of plants and animals are found within the park's 106,000 acres in coastal northern California. The coast redwood, *Sequoia sempervirens*, dominates, but its cathedral-like forests support and are in turn supported by dozens of other trees, shrubs, flowers, and associated understory.

Wildlife that can be seen along the park's 100-mile trail system includes such majestic creatures as the Roosevelt elk, black bear, and deer. Beaver and porcupine are here, too, and offshore is the domain of whales, porpoises, seals, and sea lions. Myriad animals, large and small, inhabit the park's tidepools.

Elk herd off Gold Bluffs Beach in the Prairie Creek area. These elk now survive only in some areas of northern California, Oregon, and Washington.

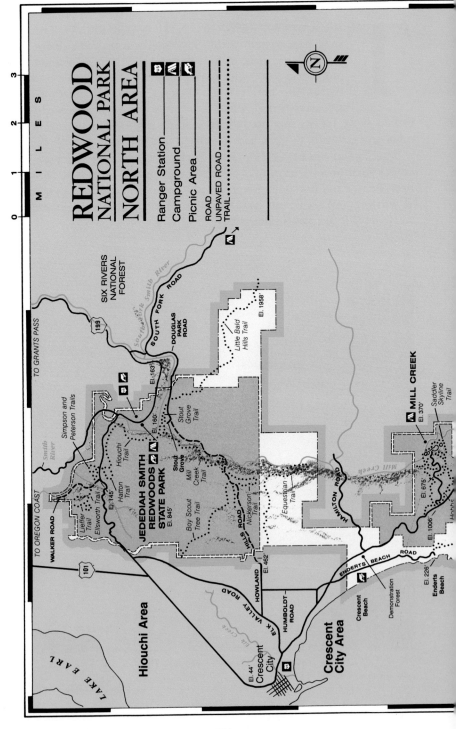

REDWOOD
NATIONAL PARK
NORTH AREA

Ranger Station
Campground
Picnic Area

ROAD
UNPAVED ROAD
TRAIL

MILES
0 1 2 3

TO GRANTS PASS

SIX RIVERS NATIONAL FOREST

South Fork Smith River

199

SOUTH FORK ROAD

DOUGLAS PARK ROAD

El. 163'

El. 1958'

Little Bald Hills Trail

Smith River

Simpson and Peterson Trails

Hiouchi Trail

Stout Grove Trail

El. 160'

Hatton Trail

Ellsworth Trail

Leiffer Trail

El. 145'

JEDEDIAH SMITH REDWOODS STATE PARK
El. 845'

Stout Grove

Mill Creek Trail

Boy Scout Tree Trail

Nickerson Trail

Equestrian Trail

MILL CREEK
El. 370'

Saddler Skyline Trail

Mill Creek

El. 675'

El. 1006'

Hobbs

TO OREGON COAST

WALKER ROAD

101

HOWLAND HILLS ROAD

El. 462

ELK VALLEY ROAD

Mill Creek

HUMBOLDT ROAD

HAMILTON ROAD

ENDERTS BEACH ROAD

El. 226'
Enderts Beach

Demonstration Forest

Crescent Beach

Hiouchi Area

LAKE EARL

Crescent City

El. 44'

Crescent City Area

144

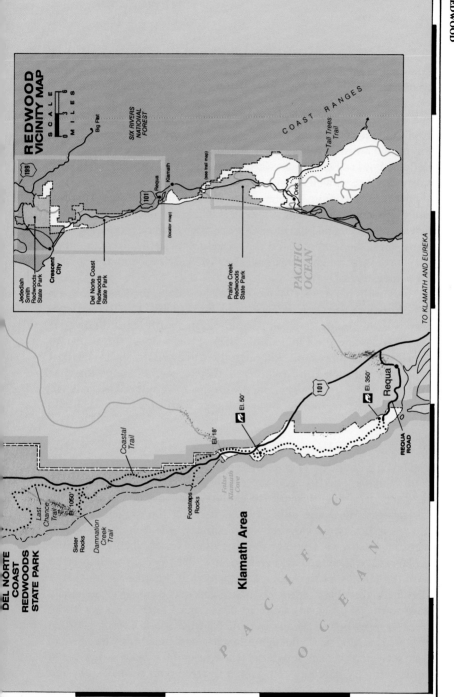

REDWOOD
VICINITY MAP

SCALE

0   3   6

M I L E S

Big Flat

SIX RIVERS
NATIONAL FOREST

199

Jedediah
Smith
Redwoods
State Park

Crescent
City

Requa

Klamath

(see trail map)

Del Norte Coast
Redwoods
State Park

101

(locator map)

C O A S T   R A N G E S

Tall Trees
Trail

Orick

Prairie Creek
Redwoods
State Park

PACIFIC
OCEAN

TO KLAMATH AND EUREKA

DEL NORTE
COAST
REDWOODS
STATE PARK

Last
Chance
Trail

El. 1050'

Sister
Rocks

Damnation
Creek
Trail

Coastal
Trail

Footsteps
Rocks

El. 18'

False
Klamath
Cove

El. 50'

101

El. 350'

Requa

REQUA
ROAD

Klamath Area

P A C I F I C

O C E A N

Native Americans

The earliest inhabitants of Redwood National Park were three groups of Indians: the Yurok, the Tolowa, and the Chilula. They maintained several dozen villages and a well-ordered society along streambanks and on the seacoast of the region. For these original residents, the environment easily fulfilled most needs. The forests provided timber for frame houses, canoes, and implements. Their canoes, usually hollowed-out redwood logs, were quite efficient and could be paddled safely offshore as well as on local streams and rivers.

Fish, mostly salmon, supplemented the Indians' main diet of acorns, and there was an abundant supply of shellfish and deer. Seaweed satisfied salt requirements, and mussels were taken from tidepools. For additional meat, hunters imitated the barking of seals in order to entice their prey. And when a whale was occasionally beached, it was time for a special feast.

The Yuroks maintained numerous villages along the Klamath River, which, then as now, was an excellent source of fish. The Tolowa territory was the Smith River, in present-day Jedediah Smith Redwoods State Park, while the Chilula built their settlements in the Redwood Creek Basin farther south. Although the three groups spoke different languages and their cultures differed, they frequently joined together for social activities. Wars among the groups were not unknown, however, nor were the Indians always at peace with later white explorers and settlers.

Early Explorers

Beginning with the party of Joao Rodrigues Cabrilho, a Portuguese navigator commissioned by Spain for New World exploration, a succession of Spanish and English maritime explorers sailed past the Humboldt coast beginning in the mid-1500s. Because of the rugged coastline, however, they could view redwood country only from afar. The first white to actually walk through the present-day park probably was Bruno de Heceta, a Spaniard, who arrived in 1775. Heceta was impressed with the fertility of the soil, and remained in the area for nine days. Credit for the coast redwoods' actual discovery, however, generally goes to the Franciscan missionary Fray Juan Crespi, who saw these trees six years before Heceta, but much farther south. Crespi recorded that the redwood was "the highest, largest and straightest" tree he had ever seen, and that "although the wood resembles cedar somewhat in color, it is very different." He named the tree *palo colorado*, or "red tree" in Spanish. It was not until the 1800s that white explorers came again, occasionally trading for food and furs with the local Indians. There were no permanent settlements on the north coast, and after its original discovery of California, Spain virtually ignored its holdings in the western part of the New World.

Overland Explorers and Settlers

In April 1828, the famed explorer and mountain man Jedediah Smith led a party of twenty men westward from California's north Central Valley. He was determined to reach the Pacific. It was an arduous journey; for days the men beat through thick underbrush and tangled forest in driving rain. But Smith succeeded in reaching the redwood region, crossing the Smith River on June 20, 1828. The next white

A traveler in earlier times takes the Howland Hill Road from Crescent City to Gasquet, California, through what is now the park.

figure of note was Dr. Josiah Gregg, who passed through the area in 1849; members of his party later built the first tiny settlements in the Humboldt coast area.

The discovery of gold at Gold Bluffs Beach in April 1850 touched off an immigration boom that still has not subsided. Copper and silver also were found in the region, but their mining was a short-lived enterprise. In still later years, the area now within Redwood National Park was host to a succession of humanity with widely divergent goals: settlers, farmers, dairymen, fishermen, trappers, military servicemen of two world wars. Traces of their tenure are preserved and marked within the park.

The Loggers

Logging began in what is now Redwood National Park in 1850, and had reached an annual harvest measured in millions of board feet by the turn of the century. As developing technology replaced hand equipment with power tools for cutting, hauling, and processing the huge redwood logs, the rate of decline of these magnificent trees accelerated. Not only were the trees disappearing, but as the tempo of logging increased through the housing boom that followed World War II, road after road was slashed through the virgin wilderness, coastal roads were built, and settlers supporting the timber industry began to clear other forests for their communities. From 1947 through 1958, logging rose to a peak of more than 1 million board feet per year throughout the entire redwood region. Clear-cutting removed thousands of old-growth, virgin trees. Indeed, by 1960 so many trees had been cut that some mills were forced to shut down because of the shortage of easily available timber.

Establishment of the Park

The establishment of Redwood National Park in 1968 was the culmination of several efforts over many years to preserve and protect some of the remaining stands of magnificent coast redwoods, the world's tallest trees, which occur naturally only in coastal northern California. In 1902, Big Basin Redwoods State Park was created south of San Francisco, formally bringing the state of California into the effort for the first time. In 1908, Congressman and philanthropist William Kent donated Muir Woods, north of San Francisco, to the federal government; the grove of virgin redwoods, named for naturalist John Muir at Kent's request, is a national monument.

For half a century, various conservation groups, notably the Save-the-Redwoods League, campaigned for protection of old-growth forests,

The Dobeer Donkey steam engine. Logging was a prime activity in the region, which is now the park, for a century preceding its establishment in 1968.

and more state parks were added to the system. Aided by a grant of $64,000 from the National Geographic Society, and at the instigation of the Sierra Club, the National Park Service conducted an inventory of remaining California coast redwoods in the early 1960s. The report, released in 1964, galvanized public action: from an original 2 million acres of primeval redwoods in the state, only about 300,000 acres remained, and only 50,000 of these acres were protected within the state park system. In 1968, President Lyndon B. Johnson signed the act that established Redwood National Park.

It soon became apparent, however, that the original boundary of the park did not include enough land to ensure adequate watershed protection for Redwood Creek or Mill Creek; the areas were threatened with damage as a result of logging and other activities. With this in mind, Congress approved the Redwood Park Expansion Act, which President Jimmy Carter signed on March 27, 1978. The act added 48,000 acres to the park, for a total of 106,000 acres, and thus helped to ensure that logging and other activities outside the original boundaries would not further endanger the lofty trees. It also provided for a massive rehabilitation program for cutover lands already damaged.

G E O L O G Y

The geology of Redwood National Park is complex, and only recently have scientists begun to fully understand what they term its "scrambled" nature. The major geologic feature is the Franciscan Formation, which consists of the muddy sandstones, igneous rocks, and metamorphic rocks that underlie most of coastal northern California. Very few fossils are contained in this formation. The origin of the rocks dates to 100 million years ago, when a gigantic collision began to occur between the sea floor of the eastern Pacific and the edge of the North American continent. The accumulation of sediments was greatly deformed and reshaped during this collision.

As "the squeeze" slowly pushed sediments upward, it formed the present Coast Range, which bisects Redwood National Park from north

"Sea stacks," small rock islets, are a common sight off the coast of Redwood.

to south. The range rises from sea level to a maximum altitude of 3,097 feet. Gently rounded summits are found in some parts of the range; in others, steep-sided drainages have been created by uplift and erosion of less-resistant rocks. The uplift continues even today.

The oldest rocks in the park are those in the Kerr Ranch Schist. The schist forms the base for most of the southern portion of the park, and outcrops may be seen along Redwood Creek Trail and stream. Geologists are uncertain about the age of these rocks, but it is believed that they are older than rocks formed during the Coast Range Orogeny (episode of deformation that leads to the formation of a mountain range), and possibly older than 135 million years. Soils developed from rocks of the Kerr Ranch Schist appear reddish because they contain oxidized iron. Such soil is seen frequently along U.S. 101 just west of the Orick gateway.

River flood plains are evident in the park, and may extend upstream for several miles. They are formed during periods of heavy rainfall, which causes rivers to overflow and spill silt, sand, and gravel. River waters erode downward through underlying rock to carve canyons and river terraces from the remnants. Tall Trees Grove on Redwood Creek in the southern area of the national park is one of the best places to view both terraces and flood plains. Ancient river terraces may rise as high as 100 feet above the present stream level upstream from the grove. Another good example of a flood plain is where the Klamath River empties into the Pacific Ocean near Requa.

The growth and melting of glacial ice less than 2 million years ago also has affected the landscape of Redwood National Park. The glaciers did not reach the park itself, but wave-cut benches, or terraces, common in the park's 35-mile-long seacoast, are evidence of glacial action. They were formed during periods of wave erosion, and in some respects they are similar to terraces that are now developing below offshore waters of northern California.

The shoreline also includes rock sections and sandy beaches. In some places, small rock islets—called "sea stacks"—rise just beyond the surf. Seaside lagoons, such as Freshwater Lagoon, can be seen in the southern section of the park. Several thousand years ago, the sea level rose and drowned stream valleys. Wave action then built large sand bars across small outlet streams and formed the present-day lagoons.

Cliffs along some beaches are composed of river sediments that were deposited as an ancestral delta of the Klamath River about 2 million years ago. Older Franciscan rocks form a rocky shoreline in other places. Sand is delivered to the beaches from the erosion of waves and from inland sources.

N A T U R A L   H I S T O R Y

Climate and Precipitation

Cool summers with frequent coastal fog, and mild but wet winters: that best describes the annual weather cycle in Redwood National Park. The climate is ideal for the coast redwood; in fact, without the summer fog and winter rains, the species probably could not survive because these trees consume great quantities of moisture daily.

The park rarely experiences extreme heat or cold. The January mean temperature is 47° F near the coast, while in August it is 57° F. There is a more pronounced temperature variation inland.

The climates of both southwestern Oregon and northwestern California are determined largely by a weather system that originates in the North Pacific. In spring and summer, a massive semipermanent system called the Pacific high dominates atmospheric circulation; in autumn, the high weakens and is pushed about by low-pressure fronts moving in from the Gulf of Alaska. Rainfall, fog, ocean winds, and wave patterns are controlled by the pressure systems and by the effect of the southward-flowing California Current, which parallels the seacoast.

Trees and Other Plants

Redwoods such as those found in Redwood National Park, which are living links to the Age of Dinosaurs, once were distributed over vast regions of the earth. Together with the longer-living sequoia of mountainous eastern California and a smaller cousin found only in China, they and their ancestors grew as far north as the Bering Sea, and in Europe and Asia. But even the hardiest of these trees could not withstand the influence of sheets of ice that moved south in the ice age, and the coast redwood's retreat drove it to its present last stand in a 450-mile-long strip of coastal California.

There are more than 1,000 species of plants and animals in Redwood National Park, but a single species literally towers over them all. It is the awe-inspiring, reddish-barked, long-living giant that John Muir called "the king of its race."

The coast redwood is the world's tallest tree. Average mature trees reach a height of 200 to 250 feet, a diameter of 10 to 15 feet, and an age of between 400 and 800 years (individual trees can live up to 2,000 years). The world's tallest tree grows on the banks of Redwood Creek: when it was measured in 1964, it was 367.8 feet tall.

Coast redwoods grow both from cone seeds and from sprouts gener-

Opposite: Redwoods are the world's tallest trees, commonly reaching between 200 and 250 feet, with many individuals much taller.

Sea otter.

ated on injured or fallen trees. (Sprouting is a rare characteristic among conifers.) The mature tree produces seeds almost every year; compared with the height of the full-grown tree, the seeds are almost infinitesimal; 120,000 seeds weigh 1 pound. The redwood is a tree that resists fire, fungus diseases, and insect damage. Its surprising durability and resistance to rot is a major reason why it is a lumberman's dream; few other trees combine so many commercial advantages.

The root system of the redwood is broad and shallow; despite the tree's great height, the species surprisingly has no taproot but manages to remain upright during its long life with only a shallow support.

The redwood shares its forest domain with a variety of other trees, shrubs, and flowers. The trees include Douglas fir (the redwood's closest rival in size), tanoak, the distinctively reddish-barked madrone, and western hemlock. Where redwoods grow close to the coast, they are usually protected from wind and salt spray by the Sitka spruce.

Bleeding hearts, several species of ferns, and myriad herbs carpet the forest floor. Perhaps the most distinctive flower is the redwood sorrel, or oxalis, with its cloverlike leaves; the leaves fold up like tiny umbrellas when exposed to sunlight. Salal (with its leathery green leaves and purple summer fruit), salmonberry, and huckleberry also are found in profusion. In May and June, rhododendrons and azaleas burst forth in glorious color.

Grasses are the predominant plant of the prairie-meadows, which are bordered by trees such as the Douglas fir. On the prairie, too, is the

Douglas iris.   Young bobcat.

hazel (a favored basket material of the Indians), exquisite irises, native blackberries, thistle, and lupine.

Wildlife

The most imposing land mammal in Redwood National Park is the Roosevelt elk, which was once widely distributed from Mount Shasta to California's Central Valley. The elk shares its forest and prairie habitat with many other mammals, including deer, bobcat, beaver, otter, raccoon, porcupine, fox, and mountain lion. Shrews may be seen scampering through the forest in search of prey; the Douglas squirrel, or chickaree, feeds on the cones of both the redwood and the Douglas fir. The park's three major rivers are prime suppliers of trout and several species of salmon, for which the region is famous. Smelt, silverside perch, herring, and flounder tempt anglers in seaside lagoons.

The largest mammal of all is the California gray whale. It is not a resident, however, but only a seasonal visitor en route from the Arctic to Mexico during winter. Offshore, too, on a more regular basis, are porpoises, seals, sea lions, and, on rare occasions, sea otters.

Redwood National Park is a bird lover's paradise. More than 350 species of birds have been recorded in the region. Many are migrants that follow the Pacific Flyway during spring and fall, and more than half are associated with water: gulls, cormorants, and brown pelicans are examples. Inland birds include jays, crows, hawks, owls, bald eagles, falcons, and myriad songbirds.

155

Three California state redwoods parks, each with its special features and visitor attractions, lie within the boundary of Redwood National Park. There are almost sixty-three trails within the combined park systems, facilitating access to the various ecosystems of forest, meadow, stream, and seacoast.

Where to begin? One of the park's three Visitor Centers—in Crescent City, Hiouchi, and Orick—is best; each is a good place to gather detailed information and advice for a venture through redwood country.

Unlike trails in some national parks, which may require days to traverse, those in Redwood National Park are generally short, and the effort required is minimal. Some longer loops are formed by joining shorter trails.

Jedediah Smith Redwoods State Park

Located along the scenic Smith River off U.S. 199 north of Crescent City, this 9,200-acre park is indeed tall-timber country, home of some of the finest preserved stands of coast redwoods. Howland Hill Road, a historically important gravel artery, meanders through the hushed groves, which include the 5,000-acre National Tribute Grove dedicated to men and women who served in the two world wars. The park's largest measured redwood—16 feet in diameter, 340 feet high—is in Stout Grove. Thick stands of other Pacific Northwest trees, as well as flowers and shrubs, can best be seen by hiking this park's fine system of trails.

Two of them, *Lieffer* and *Ellsworth*, combine for an excellent 1.3-mile, 1-hour sampling of Jedediah Smith. Together they form a moss-laden path through big maple and old-growth forest with plenty of benches for resting. The trail head is on the left side of Walker Road, .4 mile from U.S. 199.

Chinese gold mines are thought to have been operating in the 1800s along *Boy Scout Tree Trail*, which extends 3.7 miles from a trail head on Howland Hill Road and forks after 3 miles. Enclosed in a mature redwood forest, the right fork leads to the Boy Scout Tree, while the left leads to Fern Falls, where the chattering of wrens pleases the ear.

Huckleberries, trillium, and rhododendrons brighten *Hiouchi Trail* in summer; this 2-mile, 1.5-hour walk starts at the Jedediah Smith Campground or at the U.S. 199 turnout south of Hiouchi Bridge. The murmur of Smith River is always within earshot.

Little Bald Hills Trail, 4.5 miles long, is an old road that takes the visitor through several open meadows that once were the site of a ranch.

Hugged by pines and firs, the trail is excellent for birdwatching, and begins just east of Stout Grove.

The *Stout Grove Trail* is an easy 30-minute walk that leads to its namesake, Stout Grove, where fishing and swimming in summer provide a restful change from a day of exploring old-growth forests. It is accessible from Howland Hill Road.

Another popular loop in Jedediah Smith is the combination of the *Simpson* and *Peterson* trails. Each is less than 1 mile long and leads the visitor through stands of virgin redwoods featuring large burls. There are many fern species along the trail, and skunk cabbage is abundant in the creek drainage.

Del Norte Coast Redwoods State Park

Covering 6,400 acres south of Jedediah Smith, Del Norte Coast Redwoods State Park borders the Pacific Ocean and is noted for both its wide variety of foliage and wildlife and its scenic marine vistas. It is thickly forested in old-growth redwoods, and its western boundary slopes to the sea with easy access to beachcombing and tidepool exploring. Here the visitor can well appreciate the dramatic variety of northern California's seacoast: rocky offshore islets, wave-eroded cliffs, long stretches of lonely beaches sprinkled with driftwood. In the spring, Del Norte sports a dazzling display of rhododendrons, some growing 30 feet high, as seasonal precipitation creates a rain-forest effect.

One of the most popular trails in this park is *Damnation Creek Trail*, which leads northward along the coast for 2.5 miles from U.S. 101 near False Klamath Cove. Heavily forested in old-growth redwoods, it descends steeply to a small rocky beach that is ideal for studying local marine life. The trail winds through a spruce forest on its way to the sea. Near the trail head, hikers cross a paved road that once was U.S. 101.

A longer trail, 6-mile *Last Chance Trail*, offers exceptional bird-watching opportunities and photographic vistas of the redwood seacoast. It begins at the end of Endert's Beach Road in the Crescent City area of the national park. Spruce is prominent here, as are redwood and alder that extend to coastal bluffs.

Named after Hobbs Wall Company, a major logging firm of the late 1800s, *Hobbs Wall Trail* provides evidence of timbering in its heyday in the form of logging cables and machine parts. The redwoods seen here are of the second-growth variety—trees that have grown up since their virgin predecessors were felled for industry. The 3.7-mile trail

Overleaf: Coast redwoods, such as these in Del Norte State Park, grow both from cone seeds and from sprouts.

Trails of Redwood National Park

There are more than sixty hiking trails in the Redwood National Park complex, many of which are in the state-park areas. Highlighted here are those within the boundaries of the national park.

Enderts Beach Trail: Starts at Crescent Beach Overlook, end of Enderts Beach Road in north area of Redwood National Park; ends at beach; .6 mile; .33 hour; features tidepools, primitive camping, and picnic areas.

False Klamath Cove Trail: Starts at Wilson Creek picnic area, Lagoon Creek picnic area, or False Klamath Cove turnout in north area of Redwood National Park and Del Norte Coast Redwoods State Park; ends at Klamath Cove; .5 hour; tidepools, surf fishing, driftwood collecting, and birdwatching.

Coastal Trail (DeMartin Prairie section): Starts at Wilson Creek picnic area or Damnation Creek trail head; ends at bluffs overlooking ocean; 5.5 miles; 4 hours one way; runs through Del Norte Coast Redwoods State Park.

Coastal Trail (Hidden Beach section): Starts at Lagoon Creek picnic area or Klamath Overlook (Requa), in north area of Redwood National Park; ends at Requa Hill; 4 miles; 2 hours; whale watching, berry collecting, birdwatching, and listening to sea lions offshore; not level, but not difficult walk above the sea.

Coastal Trail (Flint Ridge section): Starts at Flint Rock Head Overlook or Douglas Memorial Bridge; 4.5 miles; 3 hours one way; old-growth redwoods; connects loop of Coastal Drive.

Lost Man Creek Trail: Starts at Lost Man Creek picnic area; ends at Bald Hills Road, in south area of Redwood National Park; 10 miles; 8 hours one way; near trail head is site of National Park dedication as a World Heritage Site.

Redwood Creek Trail: Starts at Redwood Creek trail-head parking area, off Bald Hills Road (take Bald Hills Road off U.S. 101 and drive 2 miles north of Orick); ends at Tall Trees Grove; 8.2 miles; 5 hours; wildlife photography, swimming, backcountry camping allowed on stream bars; foot bridges are removed from September 30 to May 30; suggested loop starts with morning shuttle-bus pickup at trail head (summer only), then to Tall Trees Grove via bus and hike to parking area; do not drink this water or any other creek water without purifying or boiling.

Lady Bird Johnson Grove Nature Loop Trail: Starts and ends at Lady Bird Johnson parking area, 2 miles up on Bald Hills Road, south area of Redwood National Park; 1 mile; .5 hour; leads through old-growth redwoods along an old logging road; steep drive to parking area not recommended for trailers or large recreational vehicles; site of national park dedication.

Tall Trees Trail: Accessible only in summer months by shuttle-bus system; shuttle starts at Redwood Information Center and drops off passengers at Tall Trees trail head, where they can hike to Tall Trees Grove and back; option to return to vehicles via Redwood Creek Trail; 1.2 miles; round-trip time from information center via bus is 3 to 4 hours; total time, including hike back to vehicle, is 8 hours; bus fee charged; mature redwood forest including the Tall Trees Grove on alluvial flat formed by Redwood Creek; buses tour through extensively logged area where forest rehabilitation can be seen; steep grades.
See map on pages 144–145.

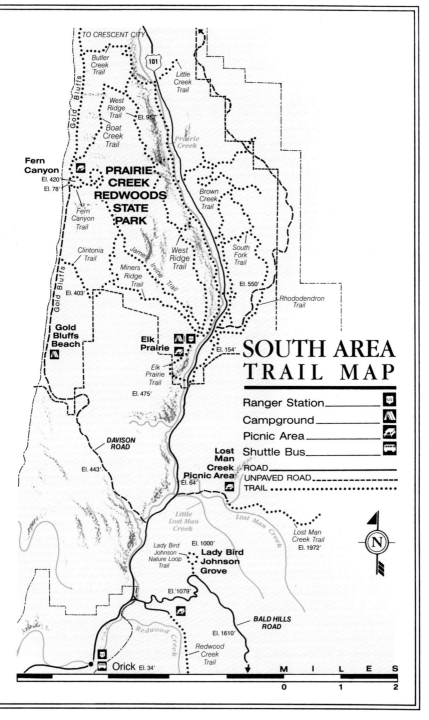

TO CRESCENT CITY

Butler
Creek
Trail

101

Little
Creek
Trail

Gold Bluffs

West
Ridge
Trail

El. 957'

Boat
Creek
Trail

Prairie
Creek

Fern
Canyon
El. 420'
El. 78'

**PRAIRIE
CREEK
REDWOODS
STATE
PARK**

Brown
Creek
Trail

Fern
Canyon
Trail

Clintonia
Trail

James Irvine Trail

West
Ridge
Trail

South
Fork
Trail

Miners
Ridge
Trail

El. 550'

Gold Bluffs

El. 403'

Rhododendron
Trail

**Gold
Bluffs
Beach**

Elk
Prairie

El. 154'

Elk
Prairie
Trail

El. 475'

**DAVISON
ROAD**

El. 443'

**Lost
Man
Creek
Picnic Area**
El. 64'

SOUTH AREA
TRAIL MAP

Ranger Station
Campground
Picnic Area
Shuttle Bus
ROAD
UNPAVED ROAD
TRAIL

Little
Lost Man
Creek

Lost Man Creek

Lost Man
Creek Trail
El. 1972'

Lady Bird
Johnson
Nature Loop
Trail

El. 1000'

**Lady Bird
Johnson
Grove**

El. 1079'

**BALD HILLS
ROAD**

El. 1610'

Redwood Creek

Redwood
Creek
Trail

Orick El. 34'

MILES
0 1 2

N

161

begins at one of three trail heads and takes about 3 hours to hike.

The Mill Creek Campground entrance station is the trail head for the 20-minute, 1-mile *Nature Loop Trail,* which provides a hurry-up, short glimpse of a redwood forest if one is indeed in a hurry. Madrone trees—with bright red bark that recalls that of manzanita—are scattered throughout Redwood National Park, and some of the best examples are along this trail.

Douglas fir and a young redwood forest, plus huckleberries and bird life, make *Saddler Skyline Trail* an especially enjoyable walk. The 1.5-mile trail begins either between campsites 7 and 8 at Mill Creek Campground or on the Nature Loop Trail, and can be leisurely walked in 1 hour.

Prairie Creek Redwoods State Park

Covering 12,500 acres, Prairie Creek Redwoods State Park is composed mostly of old-growth coast redwoods and is the southernmost of the state parks within the boundaries of Redwood National Park. Many of its redwoods exceed 300 feet in height. They are hardy survivors of logging activities that doomed many of their centuries-old relatives in the past century. Two herds of Roosevelt elk roam in Prairie Creek. It was near this park, at Lady Bird Johnson Grove, that Redwood National Park was dedicated in 1968 to culminate a half-century of conservationists' efforts. Prairie Creek has 75 miles of trails, including the *Revelation Trail* for the blind. Visually disabled visitors may "see" the park's features both on signs and in a Braille handbook that is available at park headquarters.

Fern Canyon Trail is a .7-mile streamside loop through Fern Canyon, where delicate five-fingered ferns cling to 50-foot-high canyon walls. In summer, the trail requires only about 1 hour of easy walking; in winter, the creek is often impassable, but the canyon is still visible by looking down from the rim. The trail runs up to a prairie that once was a mining settlement.

Redwood National Park

Redwood Creek Trail is one of the major trails in Redwood National Park. Extending 8.2 miles, it is not a trail for the visitor in a hurry, since at least 5 hours are necessary to fully appreciate what it offers. The walk can begin just off Bald Hills Road north of Orick or, less strenuously, from a trail head to the Tall Trees Grove, reached in summer only by shuttle bus. Wildlife viewing, photography, and swimming are popular activities. A highlight is the Tall Trees Grove, where the world's tallest living thing was discovered in 1964. Backcountry camping is allowed

Agate Beach at Patrick's Point State Park is on the coast highway south of Redwood.

on stream bars, but permits, available at the trail head, are required.

Coastal Trail extends from Enderts Beach, in the Crescent city area, to Gold Bluffs Beach, at the southern end of Prairie Creek Redwoods State Park. (Eventually, it will be a link in a series of trails along the coast between Canada and Mexico.) It wanders high above the sea through spruce and alder forests that entice the berry collector, bird-watcher, and wildflower lover. From this elevated vantage point, the hiker often can hear the barking of sea lions offshore and, in winter, see the telltale spouts of migrating California gray whales.

Boat Creek Trail, 2 miles long, follows a creek through a steep canyon that was logged during World War II to provide spruce wood for airplane building. Vistas of the coast are seen by hikers as they walk through old-growth redwood groves.

Beach Trips

Those with an affinity for the ocean will find many sites in Redwood National Park to their liking. Enderts Beach, for instance, is one of the finest for tidepool exploring on the northern California coast. Depending on the state and height of the tide, thousands of marine organisms can be seen, each within its special "niche," or zone. Just north is 3.5-mile Crescent Beach, which is noted for its excellent opportunities for surf fishing, driftwood collecting, clamming, sandcastle building, and birdwatching. There are fine tidepools, too, at False Klamath Cove, while at Gold Bluffs Beach can be found some of the largest numbers of elk in the park.

SEQUOIA
NATIONAL PARK

These huge sequoia trees cover 5 square miles of Giant Forest.

SEQUOIA NATIONAL PARK
ASH MOUNTAIN, THREE RIVERS, CALIFORNIA 93271
TEL.: (209) 565-3341

Highlights: General Sherman Tree □ Huckleberry Meadow □ Squatter's Cabin □ Washington Tree □ General Lee Tree □ Moro Rock □ Monarch Lakes □ Crystal Lake

Access: From Visalia, 35 miles east via California 198.

Hours: Daily, year-round. Some park roads closed during winter.

Fees: $2/visit; Golden Eagle pass accepted. Camping, $6/night.

Parking: Throughout park.

Gas: At Lodgepole and Three Rivers.

Food: At Giant Forest and Three Rivers; general store at Lodgepole in summer.

Lodging: At Giant Forest.

Visitor Centers: Ash Mountain Visitor Center offers visual program, permits, books, and maps. Lodgepole Visitor Center offers audio-visual program, natural history and history exhibits, permits, books, and maps.

Pets: Permitted on leash in developed areas. Not permitted on trails.

Picnicking: At designated sites throughout park.

Hiking: Trails available.

Backpacking: Permitted on over 700 miles of trails with permit. Water available but must be treated.

Campgrounds: At Potwisha, Buckeye, Lodgepole, Dorst, Cold Springs, and Atwell Mill. Fires are permitted in pits only. Showers at Lodgepole.

Tours: In summer, free naturalist-guided walks are given daily. In winter, free snowshoe walks are given weekends and holiday periods. In English.

Other activities: Horseback riding, skiing, fishing (license required), and wilderness hiking (permit required).

Facilities for disabled: Restrooms, campgrounds, picnic areas, and campsites at Potwisha and Lodgepole.

For additional information, see also Sites, Trails, and Trips on pages 186–194, the map in Kings Canyon National Park on pages 94–95, and the map on page 189.

O N A CLEAR SUMMER DAY IN 1861, HALE D. Tharp and his two grown stepsons, John and George Swanson, dismounted from their horses at the base of a massive granite dome perched on the high north rim of the Middle Fork of the Kaweah River—the protuberance later would be named Moro Rock—and began to climb. One motive was the human urge to stand high. Beyond that was a quest for orientation. The trio had spent the greater part of this 1861 trip, and of earlier ventures as well, zigzagging out of the immense canyon of the Kaweah's Middle Fork into a forest of conifers that were gigantic beyond their previous imagining. Now they felt a need to fit the marvels they encountered into a coherent whole, here on the rough western slope of the southern Sierra Nevada.

Since that day, uncounted thousands of other people have made the same 300-foot ascent of Moro Rock's back side. It is easier now—concrete steps are guarded by steel handrails. But the view from the bald summit, 6,725 feet above sea level, remains as overwhelming, *on clear days*, as when Tharp and the Swanson brothers first saw it.

Scarcely 12 miles to the east rise the snow-streaked peaks of the Great Western Divide, some of them more than 12,000 feet high. (The Great Western Divide is a spur of the main Sierra Nevada.) From the snow streaks on the divide, converging streams plunge into the Kaweah's Middle Fork. By the time the combined waters have roared past the canyon wall on which Moro Rock sits, they have dropped to an elevation of 4,000 feet—a descent of 1.5 miles in the span of a glance. And still the river has to descend another 3,000 feet before emerging into California's San Joaquin Valley.

At first that dramatic panorama holds the viewer in thrall. Then, slowly, ecological variations wrought by changes in altitude command attention. At one end of the spectrum are the pastel colors of the wild oats and chaparral of the foothills; at the other, the pale rock of the barren summits. In between, rolling north and south along the waist of the Sierra, is the dense, dark-green canopy of what naturalist John Muir called "the grandest and most beautiful" coniferous forest in the world. Rising here and there out of that canopy are the huge, rounded tops, some decorated with snags as arrogant as spikes on a helmet, of the bulkiest trees now alive: the giant sequoias, or, in botanical terms, *Sequoiadendron giganteum*.

Overleaf: Sunset Rock, west of Giant Forest, is famous for its view of the San Joaquin Valley.

Native American Settlers

Hale Tharp, the first non-Indian to view the magnificence of this land, had brought his family to the foothills near the lower Kaweah River in 1856, looking for cattle range. About 2,000 Indians, he said later, were living in the district. They were Potwishas, a subtribe of the Monaches, or Western Monos, whose homeland had once lain at the eastern base of the Sierra. At some time between A.D. 1000 and 1500, small groups of Monaches had drifted west. Over the course of many years, they scattered. One subgroup, the Tubatulabals, settled beside the turbulent, southward-flowing Kern. From that new homeland they ranged, on occasion, as far up the river as its headwaters in the vast horseshoe of peaks formed by the Great Western Divide and the outliers of Mount Whitney—at 14,495 feet the highest point in the lower forty-eight states, and since 1926 a part of Sequoia National Park.

Others of the nomads moved north from the Kern along the western base of the mountains. Avoiding the heart of the San Joaquin Valley, which was occupied by Yokut Indians, they settled in extended family groups near the points where the Tule, Kaweah, and Kings rivers break from the mountains. Though all were Monaches—that is, Monos who had moved west—the different groups were given different names, probably by the Yokuts: Potwisha, Woksaki, and Wobonuch.

In their new homes, they were introduced to the staple food of most California Indians—acorns. The nuts existed in such quantities that long wanderings in search of sustenance were no longer necessary. After carrying home a harvest in baskets on their backs, the women hulled the acorns, put the kernels into small holes in slabs of flat-lying foothill granite, and pulverized them with stone pestles. As many as fifty grinding holes, arranged close together so that the women could work in company, have been found at Hospital Rock beside the Middle Fork of the Kaweah River in Sequoia National Park. The pulverizing finished, the meal was dumped into a small basin of sand lined with grass. It was then covered with cedar boughs that acted like spreading screens, and water was poured through to leach away the acorns' bitter tannic acid. The product was then ready for boiling into mush or baking into cakes.

The Indians also feasted on dried manzanita berries, rats, rabbits, squirrels, and occasional deer. Instead of making temporary houses out of brush and gnarled piñon sticks, as did the Monos east of the mountains, the Monache groups built semipermanent homes by erecting a conical frame of willow poles and covering it with strips of cedar bark. Temperature rather than the availability of food controlled group movements. Winter was the time for congregating along the lower edges of the foothills, where snow seldom fell. But summer could be hot in the foothills, and then the families sought the shade of the forest belt, where deer abounded. Long before Europeans had reached California, the Monaches, and undoubtedly the Yokuts, were familiar with the ruddy-barked sequoia trees that were scattered grandly among other conifers.

Trade kept the Monos east of the mountains in touch with the Monaches to the west. The eastern Indians seem to have been the most active, carrying with them on their journeys pine nuts, the dried larvae of flies taken from the alkaline lakes of their homeland, salt, rabbitskin blankets, and obsidian; the last was in demand for making arrowheads and cutting tools. These goods were exchanged for acorn meal, shell beads, deerskin, and arrow shafts of strong, straight tule. Some of this trade extended to the Yokuts as well.

Mostly the merchants traveled by way of Walker Pass, but during the few weeks in summer when the high country was free of snow, venturesome traders clambered up one side of the mountain crest and down the other. Enough traces of their passing have survived to show that the land's native inhabitants had begun using the high mountain trails and passes of the southern Sierra centuries ago.

American Settlement

The Spanish, who made their first settlement in California in 1769, knew none of this. Only rarely did they and the Mexicans who suc-

The entrance to the park at the turn of the century.

ceeded them venture far enough inland to glimpse in the distance the long white line of mountains they named Sierra Nevada. Later, when American trappers, explorers, and, finally, settlers were seeking the Pacific, the rugged loftiness of the southern Sierra deflected them down toward Walker Pass or to other low crossings well to the north. Thus the foothill Indians were able to continue their ways with no more knowledge of what was happening than they could glean from rumors told beside smoky fires.

The gold rush ended the isolation, even though the only placer diggings in Monache land were shallow gravels along the lower Kern. But miners needed food. Farmers drifted into the fertile San Joaquin Valley, and in 1850, some of them founded the town of Visalia not 30 miles from the Potwisha villages along the Kaweah. In 1856, Hale Tharp followed with his herd of cattle.

He got on well with his Indian neighbors. Wondering about cool summer range for his animals and eager to see the huge red-barked trees that the Indians talked about, Tharp persuaded two of them to guide him, in the summer of 1858, to their favorite flower-jeweled, forest-girt meadows. The group probably started from the Indian village at Hospital Rock (so named because the Potwisha had treated one of Tharp's stepsons there) and zigzagged upward, much as the modern road does, past Moro Rock and into what is now known as the Giant Forest: 18,657 massive trees (8,411 of them over 1 foot in diameter at breast height) scattered with an array of tall firs and pines across 3,200 cool acres, the most extensive grove of big trees—or series of groves, depending on how one defines *grove*—in the world.

Tharp's initial trip was followed by a longer one in 1860. The next year—the year he and his stepsons climbed Moro Rock—he established a squatter claim to the area by pasturing horses in the vicinity of Crescent Meadow. But he did not take cattle up the rough hill until 1869, after he had hewn a trail wide enough to accommodate livestock. Needing living quarters while he watched the animals, Tharp found a huge log that had been hollowed out by fire and capped its cavernous end with a shed fitted with a door and window!

The Native Americans of the area fared less well. Following a clash with Visalia settlers in 1859, fragmented groups of Monaches—those who had not succumbed to measles and smallpox introduced by the invaders—fled across the Sierra to join their relatives in the Owens Valley. There they became allies of the Monos and other Paiute groups that were waging a fierce guerrilla war against miners who were pushing into the Coso Mountains, southeast of Owens Lake, where silver had been discovered in 1860. To protect the miners, the army on July

4, 1862, established Camp Independence in the Owens Valley. Hoping to shorten travel time between Visalia and Camp Independence, an entrepreneur named John Benjamin Hockett obtained a franchise to build a toll trail. Reporting to the county supervisors that he had completed the task during the summer and fall of 1863 at a cost of $1,000, Hockett prepared to collect tolls. Alas for hope. The army found his work substandard and took over maintenance of the trail in 1864.

One of the users of the Hockett Trail that summer was young Clarence King of the California State Geological Survey; King was afire with ambition to scale Mount Whitney, recently named for his boss, Josiah Whitney. (King later became the first head of the far bigger U.S. Geological Survey.) Because of his penchant for wandering into cul-de-sacs, he failed in the attempt. When he tried again in 1871, he got lost in swirling clouds and, without realizing the mistake, landed on Mount Langley. So the actual first ascent of the tallest peak in the conterminous United States was made on August 18, 1873, by three fishermen who had been camping in the upper Kern River Canyon. An agitated Clarence King refused to believe their reports until he had once again followed the Hockett Trail into the high country, and on September 19, 1873, stood belatedly and dejectedly on the peak that he thought he had conquered two years before. One month later, another famous Sierra figure, John Muir, reached the top alone after pioneering a difficult route out of Owens Valley.

By the time Whitney had been scaled, lumbermen were edging into the lower parts of the forest belt. Sheep ranchers were keeping pace. Large numbers of sheep were held on the winter grazing and spring lambing grounds of the southern half of the San Joaquin Valley. There was not enough summer grass to go around, however, and more and more ranchers looked toward the mountains. But the owners did not like the hard, dirty, lonesome work of herding, and so they imported expert Basque workers from the Pyrenees of Spain and France. These herders, most of whom intended to return home after making a stake, had no interest in protecting the land. To keep the animals from getting lost in the forest, they herded them in tight bands, with the result that they trampled out even more grass and tree seedlings than they ate. The herders also set fire to the underbrush so that increased sunlight would produce thicker crops of grass the following year. Inevitably some of the fires swirled out of control.

John Muir wrote articles excoriating the practices—he called sheep "hoofed locusts"—and Clarence King reported angrily, after his 1873 ride along the Hockett Trail, that the once lovely Kern plateau had

been devastated: "The indefatigable shepherds have camped everywhere, leaving hardly a spear of grass behind them." No remedies followed; it was not the American way, in those days, to check the exploitation of natural resources.

Establishment of the Park

When a change in policy did come, it was related to what at first was regarded as fraud in the acquisition of timberland. In October 1885, fifty-three members of a San Francisco-based socialistic group filed claims to several plots of timberland in the Kaweah River's watershed. Notice of the filings was published in the Visalia *Delta*, as required by law. So many simultaneous claimings by men from the same city (several used the same street address) roused the suspicions of the *Delta*'s editors, for timber companies, anxious to sidestep the laws that limited the amount of public land they could acquire, often hired out-of-work panhandlers to make the entries and then transfer title.

Giant Forest Administrative Building, circa 1922.

Apprised by the paper of the activity, the government withdrew several key townships—a township contains 36 sections, or 23,040 acres—from entry pending investigation. The colonists took the situation in stride. They had acted in good faith, and nothing in the nation's land laws prevented like-minded groups from working as associations on community projects. Confidently they went ahead with their plans to ship timber all over the world and to develop from the proceeds a flourishing settlement that would show the superiority of communal societies over capitalistic ones. On its part, the government did nothing to investigate the colony.

All this took place at a time when conservationists, led by George Stewart of the Visalia *Delta*, were agitating for a national park that would protect the valley's watersheds by ending ruinous grazing and lumbering practices. John Muir brought his trenchant pen to the crusade; the American Association for the Advancement of Science joined the fray. More weight came from the Southern Pacific Railroad, which wanted, in addition to tourist traffic to the proposed park, an assured supply of water for the many acres of grant land it hoped to sell to incoming farmers. But when President Benjamin Harrison finally signed, on September 25, 1890, a congressional bill creating Sequoia National Park—the second in the nation, after Yellowstone—the agitators were dismayed. They had dreamed of an Eden-like reserve extending from present Yosemite National Park south to the Kern and from the foothills to the Sierra crest. What they received was far less, what amounted to about 50,000 acres located along the watershed of the Kaweah's South Fork far from Giant Forest and even farther from Mount Whitney and its adjoining 14,000-foot peaks.

No one can prove what happened next, but apparently a Southern Pacific land agent approached some of California's delegation in Washington and showed them the light. A pending bill to create Yosemite National Park was revised in such a way as to create small (2,560-acre) General Grant National Park and enlarge Sequoia National Park to roughly 160,000 acres. None of this land touched the high country—but it did deprive the Kaweah colonists of many of their claims without recompense and without a hearing. No other marked change came until the creation, in 1916, of the National Park Service under the direction of Stephen Mather. As an early-day visitor to the area, Mather knew that Sequoia National Park embraced about 4,000 acres of private holdings that might at any day be logged over or subdivided for summer cabins. When government appropriations fell short of the amount needed to purchase the tracts, Mather sought funds from private sources. Gradually the geographic integrity of the park was achieved.

In 1926, years of agitation for a park that would include at least some of the high country east of the original reserve bore fruit, and the boundary was rolled east to the Sierra crest. A last expansion resulted years later; to prevent the building of a major access road through one corner of the park and to protect a pair of redwood groves as well as an important jumping-off point into the wilderness, Congress in 1978 placed the area within the jurisdiction of Sequoia National Park. Thus a unit that had begun life embracing about 50,000 acres had grown almost sevenfold in eighty-eight years, clear indication of the doggedness that characterized the efforts of many Americans to preserve the remnants of their nation's once wild lands.*

---

*For a discussion of the geology of Sequoia, see Kings Canyon National Park, pages 101–105.

Whitebark pine is able to grow in the high altitudes of the Sierra Nevada.

Mt. Whitney towers 14,495 feet above the autumn trees at Lone Pine Creek.

N A T U R A L   H I S T O R Y

The Sierra Nevada is a classic fault-block mountain range. Powerful movements in the earth's crust, occurring intermittently during many millions of years, thrust its eastern edge upward more than 2 miles—a phenomenon strikingly visible in the erosion-clawed escarpment that lines the section of the Owens Valley that is directly opposite Sequoia and Kings Canyon national parks. Westward, the tilted Sierra block, incised by enormous canyons, drops gently toward the Pacific. These geographical circumstances make the growth of a belt of big trees, sequoias among them, all but inevitable.

Climate and Precipitation

Beginning in October or November and continuing until May, a sequence of massed storm clouds float out of the North Pacific to deluge the California coast. The densest portion of them strikes the northern part of the state, but strong flankers swing southward. As the oncoming front is forced upward by the Coast Range, the water vapor cools and rain begins. The obstacle is not very high, however; the storm passes easily over it and then sags again, growing warm enough to reabsorb the water droplets as vapor. As a consequence, the San Joaquin Valley lies in a "rain shadow," where precipitation is slight.

Immediately beyond the valley, the Sierra slope forces the cloud cover to rise much higher than before. Again precipitation falls as rain in the oak and chaparral belt of the foothills and as snow in the higher elevations. Then, at an elevation of 8,000 to 9,000 feet, intensity tapers off, for the clouds have dropped the bulk of their freight. Dry winds howl, and the high, cold plateaus and basins above timberline are actually deserts, although drifts piled by blizzards and evaporating slowly because of the cold tend to disguise the reality.

Latitude adds another element to the equation. The southern foothills are warmer on average than the northern. Tree lines are higher. Evergreens start growing at an elevation of about 1,200 to 1,500 feet near Lassen Peak, but at 2,500 feet or so in the south. Arctic-zone timberline conditions appear at about 8,000 feet on Lassen Peak, but at about 11,000 feet on the Kings-Kern Divide near Mount Whitney.

Then add this: winter storms from the Pacific are relatively warm. When their rain turns to snow—generally at 4,000 or 5,000 feet in Sequoia National Park—it is moist and heavy, not the insubstantial powder of the peaktops. It clings stickily to the trunks and boughs of the conifers and presses the latter sharply downward, giving the forest belt an extraordinary whipped-cream appearance that delights cross-country skiers. Thermometers seldom dip to 0° F at Giant Forest, and the 10 to 20 feet of snow on the ground are an ideal insulator. The porous soil beneath the blanket absorbs enough water to last throughout the dry, warm summer that follows, and the impervious granite beneath the soil is frequently close enough to the surface to keep that moisture within reach of even the sequoias' shallow roots. Thus, because of equitable year-round temperature and adequate moisture distribution, the Sierra forest belt has produced, in addition to the giant sequoias, some of the tallest sugar pines, lodgepole pines, and red firs ever recorded.

Watch the beginning of nature's annual surge as you drive, in the spring, from park headquarters at Three Rivers to Giant Forest. The new leaves of the willows, sycamores, alders, and occasional cottonwoods that line the Middle Fork of the Kaweah River shine like sequins. Gnarled oaks and matted chaparral cover the hillsides. A bend in the deepening canyon opens a sudden view of the Great Western Divide, its peaks still covered with snow. Down here a different white appears —plump, creamy fingers swaying at the tip of almost every branch of the big, sprawling bushes called California buckeye, and tall, candle-straight yucca marching like white-uniformed acolytes up a rocky ridge toward the dome of Moro Rock.

The road leaves the stream to twine upward along the steep, arid, south-facing canyon wall. Soon the first ponderosa (yellow) pines appear, sunlight glowing on long, green needles and on thick, orange bark, which on the trunks of mature trees is divided into massive plates separated by deep black or brown grooves. Then, still higher, as the land flattens somewhat, appears a mixture of other conifers—sugar pines, incense cedars, white firs, a few red firs, and, most prominently, the commanding, cinnamon-red boles of the sequoias.

Sequoiadendron giganteum

They are giants indeed, relics of the Age of Dinosaurs. Once they grew throughout northern Europe and North America, but environmental changes slowly strangled them. Ten million or more years ago, only a few survivors remained in what is now southern Idaho and western Nevada. They, too, seemed doomed, for the gradual rise of the Sierra Nevada was draining water from Pacific storms and creating more aridity to the east than the ancestral sequoias could tolerate. Yet somehow, in the geologic nick of time, seeds managed to reach the moist western slope.

Tiny seeds. The ones we know today are paper thin and no bigger than a little fingernail. About 90,000 of them weigh 1 pound. Even so,

Clockwise from top left: Snow plant; mountain lion; hairy woodpecker; golden-mantled squirrel.

it is not difficult to find a few by brushing your hand across unlittered soil near a big tree. The thin black line that contains the embryo divides the seed into two tannish "wings." Under propitious conditions, those wings can carry a sequoia embryo as much as .33 mile from its birthplace. Could similar seeds have been blown across relatively low Sierra passes 10 million years ago? Or did birds and small animals, which today pay scant attention to the seeds, act as carriers in ancient times? No one knows.

No one knows, either, the extent of the ancient relocated forest of *Sequoiadendron gigantea*. Today the trees are scattered in groves of varying size over a span of 260 miles. Most are clustered in the southern Sierra at elevations of 5,000 to 7,000 feet. They favor "platforms" on or near the tops of the heavy-shouldered ridges that rise between profound canyons. This is a very different environment from that of the coastal hills of northern California, where another redwood (*Sequoia sempervirens*) flourishes within sound of the surf. Although thinner than the Sierra tree, mature coast redwoods are taller and grow in dense stands of their own kind. *Gigantea*, by contrast, are always mixed, very sparsely, with a retinue of other species.

Because reproduction is difficult and uncertain, *Sequoiadendron gigantea* generate floods of seeds. In a normal year, a mature tree produces about 2,000 cones the size and shape of a hen's egg. These bright green cones hang on the upper branches of the tree for several years. Meanwhile, more keep coming along—and some drop, too—so that it is not unusual for a medium-sized sequoia to hold 15,000 or more cones at once. Each cone contains an average of 200 seeds. Three big trees standing close together are potentially able to put 1 million seeds on a single acre in a year.

The seeds sometimes are released by the larvae of a minute beetle that chews through a cone in such a way as to cut its water supply; the scales then dry and shrink, freeing the seeds. But the indefatigable sower is a small and frantically energetic squirrel. The chickaree has a bushy tail, a brownish back, a light-colored belly, and a white ring around each bright, black eye. Although chickarees prefer pine nuts and disdain sequoia seeds, they do relish the inside fibers of sequoia cones, which they store in great numbers for winter use. After scampering up a tree and tearing open a few cones for breakfast, scattering seeds the while, the animals start a frenzied clipping; one observer tells of 538 cones, severed by a single squirrel, plumping to the ground in 31 minutes. The cones are carried one by one to storehouses, where more seeds will be strewn about during winter banquets.

About 75 percent of a cone's seeds are viable when shed. If living embryos fall onto a spot where full sunlight dehydrates them quickly or if they land in dry duff, they perish—the fate of more than 98 percent of them. Those that survive are the few that land on dampish mineral soil that recently has been disturbed by the falling of a tree, by logging or road-building activities, or by fire, which by burning away the organic matter in the topsoil creates, for a short time, tiny cavities that act as refuges. Fire also eliminates the forest's understory of brush and smaller trees, white fir in particular, that otherwise would cut off the sunlight that the seedlings need once they have sprouted. Indeed, fire is so beneficent that when conditions are favorable, the National Park Service itself starts fires to improve the forest ecology.

Except for characteristic tiny, overlapping, pointed leaves that cling tightly to each twig, a young sequoia bears scant resemblance to a mature tree. The numerous branches of the younger tree point downward; its shape is sharply conical. But as competition for sunlight increases, the lower branches die and fall off, exposing 100 or more feet of the magnificent trunk that so rivets the attention of park visitors. Now the bulky crown may be lopsided because fire scars have cut off part of the sap supply or because lightning has killed a huge upper branch, leaving behind a hoary snag. Also, many of the high branches twist about and grow upward, reaching for the sun. The cone shape vanishes, and what is left is a gnarled embodiment of serene power.

The essence of this impression does not come from height alone. Although the General Sherman Tree in Giant Forest is 274.9 feet tall, many coast redwoods stand higher. Although the Sherman's circumference at the ground is 102.6 feet, a genus of cypress in Mexico is much bigger around. Age? Bristlecone pines live 1,500 years longer than the General Sherman's estimated age of 2,500 to 3,000 years. But because there is relatively little taper in the Sherman's trunk, it emerges as the bulkiest living thing on earth; its great bole alone weighs an estimated 1,385 tons—a truly remarkable figure because sequoia wood is light, 13 pounds per cubic foot, compared, for example, with the 53 pounds of a live oak. Any living object that is capable of sustaining such overwhelming volume is bound to be regal.

Amazement increases when one realizes that although the giant's root system may reach out more than 100 feet from the trunk, it goes down only 3 feet or so. To keep standing, the tree must be well balanced. Hence the marvelous straightness of most of them. Further buttressing is provided by a basal swelling that time carves into knobs that look like elephant feet. Eventually, though, imbalance comes. Every old se-

Overleaf: Manzanita bush in Giant Forest.

183

quoia has lived through many blazes—thanks to the resistant qualities of its thick, resin-free, and tannin-filled bark—but eventually fire is likely to eat away enough substance of some of them to weaken the whole. Floods will undercut. Snow will overweigh one side or the other. If the ground is soggy at the time, and if gales roar across the ridges, there may be a thunderous toppling. Then silence. And a shattered trunk—sequoia wood is very brittle—whose pieces will be almost as long in decaying as the tree was in reaching its prime.

S I T E S ,   T R A I L S ,   A N D   T R I P S

Giant Forest

All who know the sequoias agree that no other grove of trees on this planet is so beautiful and awesomely impressive as the Giant Forest; and, some say, only the words of John Muir, who saw them in the waning days of the nineteenth century, can describe them. Although he spoke eloquently, even Muir failed to capture the majesty that is revealed to each visitor, who, when encountering a sequoia for the first time, is stunned by its magnificence. One must find his or her own way to accept what nature has done here. And along the almost 40 miles of footpaths in the 5 square miles of Giant Forest there is no better place. An excellent trail folder with map is available from the Sequoia Natural History Association.

Hazelwood Nature Trail. The Hazelwood Nature Trail is an easy, 1-mile loop that wraps up the whole story of the sequoias for those with little time or some physical disability. Trail-side exhibits lead the visitor over gentle grades through excellent stands of the giant trees. The trail begins and ends opposite the Giant Forest Lodge registration office and takes about 1.5 hours.

Huckleberry Meadow Loop Trail. The 5-mile Huckleberry Meadow Loop Trail goes through the central portion of the Giant Forest, which begins near the lodge, and leads to some of the lesser-known features of the park: Huckleberry Meadow; the historic Squatter's Cabin; and the 250-foot-tall Washington Tree, one of the finest examples of a truly giant sequoia. The trail is marked by purple-lettered signs and takes about 3 hours to complete.

Crescent Meadow and Log Meadow Loop Trail. The gentle meadows of Sequoia National Park are as much a part of the whole picture as the

Crescent Meadow is in the southeastern corner of Giant Forest.

trees, and the Crescent Meadow and Log Meadow Loop Trail is one of the easiest trails that reveals these treasures. A 2- to 3-hour walk around the two meadows offers wonderful views of giant sequoias, the oldest pioneer cabin in the park, and, in the right season, blankets of wildflowers. The 1.8-mile trail begins and ends at the Crescent Meadow parking area and is marked by orange-lettered signs.

Congress Trail. Take a folder with you; you can buy one at the trail head. This is a fascinating place, filled with trees with interesting names, not the least of which is the famous General Sherman Tree and its companion, the General Lee Tree. There are others: Lincoln, McKinley, and the House and Senate Group. The Congress Trail is easy, a 2-mile loop, and it takes about 2 to 3 hours to enjoy. Follow the yellow-lettered signs.

Trail of the Sequoias and Circle Meadow Loop Trail. The 6-mile Circle Meadow Loop Trail explores the east portion of the Giant Forest and visits Log and Circle meadows as it wanders through some of the finest giant sequoia stands. Green-lettered signs lead off the Congress Trail to Crescent Creek and the open, grassy Log Meadow. Allow 4 hours for some moderately difficult hiking.

Trails of Sequoia National Park

Giant Forest Area

Hazelwood Nature Trail: Starts and ends at south side of Generals Highway, opposite the Giant Forest Lodge registration office (follow purple-lettered signs); 1 mile; 1.5 hours; an easy loop trail that wanders on gentle grades through great stands of giant sequoia; trailside exhibits.

Huckleberry Meadow Loop Trail: Starts and ends at south side of Generals Highway, opposite the Giant Forest Lodge registration office (follow purple-lettered signs of the Hazelwood Nature Trail for approximately .5 mile to the junction of the Hazelwood, Alta, and Soldiers trails; then follow blue-lettered signs); 5 miles; 3 hours; loop trail through the central portions of the Giant Forest to the Squatter's Cabin, and Huckleberry and Circle meadows, past the 250-foot-tall Washington Tree and other sequoias nearly 300 feet tall.

Crescent Meadow and Log Meadow Loop Trail: Starts and ends at Crescent Meadow parking area (follow orange-lettered signs); 1.8 miles; 2 to 3 hours; begins on a short section of the High Sierra Trail, then follows the fringe of Crescent Meadow to Tharp's Log and Chimney Log.

Congress Trail: Starts and ends at General Sherman Tree (follow yellow-lettered signs); 2 miles; 2 to 3 hours; ascends gently into Alta Plateau section of Giant Forest, past the President, Chief Sequoyah, General Lee, and McKinley trees, as well as the House and Senate groups.

Trail of the Sequoias and Circle Meadow Loop: Starts and ends at General Sherman Tree (follow yellow-lettered signs of the Congress Trail for .7 mile to the junction of the Congress, Alta, and the Trail of the Sequoias; then follow green-lettered signs); 6 miles; 4 hours; steady, moderate climb to Crescent Creek in the Giant Forest; at first junction past the creek (about 1 mile), trail branches off and meets the Circle Meadow Loop, at an elevation of approximately 6,700 feet, which passes the historic Tharp's Log and Chimney Tree.

Moro Rock and Soldiers Trail Loop: Starts and ends at Giant Forest Village (follow red-lettered signs); 4.6 miles; 3 to 4 hours; loop trail to the granite dome Moro Rock; spectacular views from the summit, 300 vertical feet up Moro Rock; trail changes name and returns by the Soldiers Camp, where the United States Cavalry lived in 1913.

Mineral King Area

Timber Gap Trail: Starts at Sawtooth Pass parking area; 4 miles round trip; 1,400-foot ascent; climbs steadily on an old mining route into a dense red fir forest and then onto an open slope; wildflowers are in abundance in the summer.

Crystal Lake Trail: Starts at Sawtooth Pass parking area on Timber Gap Trail (junction with branch to Crystal Lake is 3.2 miles from Monarch Lakes trail head); 9.8 miles round trip; 3,000-foot ascent; trail through the remnants of the old Chihuahua Mine and into an avalanche-prone basin; some steep climbing through foxtail pine and over broken talus to Crystal Lake; magnificent views of Mineral Peak and Rainbow Mountain.

Eagle Lake Trail: Starts at Eagle-Mosquito parking area; 6.8 miles round trip; 2,200-foot ascent; leads past Eagle Basin and the mysterious Eagle Creek, and through a boulder field to Eagle Lake.

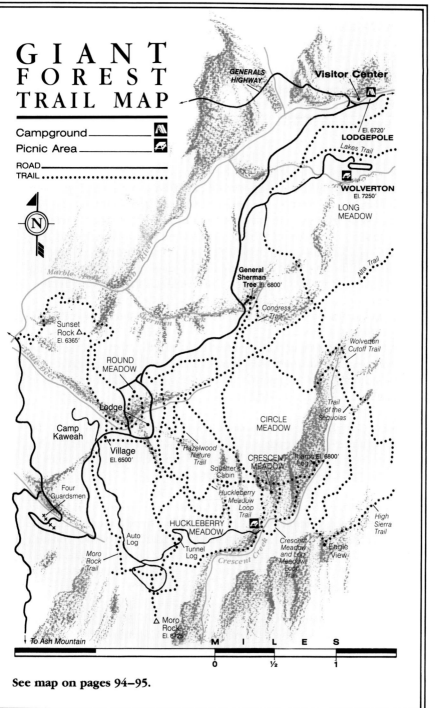

GIANT FOREST TRAIL MAP

Campground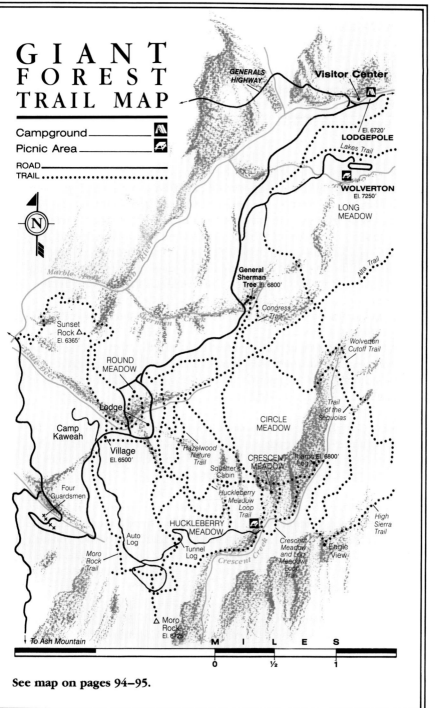
Picnic Area

ROAD
TRAIL ··············

N

GENERALS HIGHWAY

Visitor Center

El. 6720'
LODGEPOLE
Lakes Trail

WOLVERTON
El. 7250'

LONG MEADOW

Marble Fork Kaweah River

General Sherman Tree El. 6800'

Congress Trail

Alta Trail

Sunset Rock △ El. 6365'

Sherman

Little Deer

Wolverton Cutoff Trail

ROUND MEADOW

Trail of the Sequoias

Lodge

CIRCLE MEADOW

Camp Kaweah

Village El. 6500'

Hazelwood Nature Trail

CRESCENT MEADOW

Tharps Log El. 6800'

Squatter's Cabin

Four Guardsmen

Huckleberry Meadow Loop Trail

High Sierra Trail

Auto Log

HUCKLEBERRY MEADOW

Tunnel Log

Crescent Creek

Crescent Meadow and Log Meadow Loop Trail

Eagle View

Moro Rock Trail

↓ To Ash Mountain

△ Moro Rock El. 6725'

M I L E S

0   ½   1

See map on pages 94–95.

Moro Rock and Soldiers Trail Loop. Beautiful groves of giant sequoias and an exciting climb up Moro Rock highlight this 3- to 4-hour, 4.6-mile loop trail. From Moro Rock summit, to which there is a 300-foot vertical climb, there are spectacular views of the foothills of Sequoia National Park, the town of Three Rivers, the San Joaquin Valley, and, if there is no smog, even the Coast Range, over 100 miles to the west. Follow red-lettered signs that begin just west of the cafeteria at Giant Forest Village.

Mineral King

The Mineral King area of Sequoia National Park gets its name from the optimism that spurred the mining investments here in the late 1870s. For a few short years, this quiet mountain valley promised to become the answer to dreams of wealth—rich silver ore as limitless as that taken from Nevada's great mines. Nearly a decade later the dream had vanished, but the greatest treasure, which most of the miners missed completely, was still there. Nearly lost a second time, when recreation developers almost added their scars to the landscape, Mineral King is now an integral part of Sequoia National Park, and its trails reveal some spectacular scenery.

All trails in the Mineral King area begin at 7,500 feet. Hiking at this altitude can be extremely dangerous. All trips should be gauged to the least fit member of the party. A trail folder with excellent information is available.

Timber Gap Trail. The 4-mile round-trip Timber Gap Trail begins at the Sawtooth Pass parking area and climbs a total of 1,400 feet through a dense red fir forest to Timber Gap. At the gap are views of the valley of the Middle Fork of the Kaweah River.

Monarch Lakes Trail. The Monarch Lakes Trail leads through Ground Hog Meadow, 1 trail mile and 920 vertical feet from Mineral King, and then through a long series of switchbacks in the climb to the Monarch Lakes. At the higher levels, the trail goes through Sawtooth Pass, which offers one of the most magnificent views in the southern Sierra. The total elevation gain in this 4.2-mile one-way hike is 2,580 feet.

Crystal Lake Trail. The Crystal Lake Trail ascends 3,000 feet along the 4.9 miles that lead from the Sawtooth Pass parking area to the termination at the Southern California Edison dam site. The trail branches from the Monarch Lakes Trail 3.2 miles from the trail head; it is easy to miss. There are campsites on the terrace just below Crystal Lake. Al-

Kaweah River Canyon as seen from the summit of Moro Rock, 6,725 feet above sea level.

though there is no trail beyond this point, a short scramble up the bluffs to the northeast leads to Little Crystal Lake.

Franklin Lake Trail. When hikers reach Franklin Lake, they are at an elevation of 10,327 feet, in the "High Sierra." The Franklin Lake Trail begins at the Eagle-Mosquito parking area, fords the Kaweah River, and then follows an old road and some short switchbacks to Farewell Gap. From the gap, the lake route leads through the prospecting country of an 1870s mining operation, across Franklin Creek, and on to a rock and masonry dam built in 1904/05. The hike is 5.4 miles, and the total elevation gain is 2,527 feet.

White Chief Trail. During midsummer the White Chief meadows are filled with wildflowers, just one thing that makes this hike so attractive. The steep but very scenic trail to White Chief Canyon begins at the Eagle-Mosquito parking area and terminates some 3 miles later at the old White Chief Mine. Although it becomes increasingly faint, the trail continues another mile above the mine until it disappears in the giant glacial cirque that forms the head of the canyon. The total distance is 4.1 miles, and the elevation gain is 2,200 feet.

Eagle Lake Trail. The Eagle Lake Trail follows the same route as the White Chief Trail for the first mile, then branches to the right toward Eagle Canyon. In early summer, the canyon is abundant with flowers —lupine and snow plant in shady areas, and orchid, leopard lily, Indian paintbrush, and shooting star in the meadows. Surrounded by mountain crests, Eagle Lake is a typical glacially formed lake called a tarn, and it is spectacular. The distance is 3.4 miles, and the elevation gain is 2,200 feet. Along the way, the trail passes Eagle Creek sink hole, where the creek literally disappears; where the water goes, no one really knows for certain.

Mosquito Lake Trail. Take the right-hand trail about 1 mile from the White Chief and Eagle Lake trail head. The Mosquito Lake Trail is a 3.4-mile hike up and over Miner's Ridge and down to Mosquito Lake 1. There are four other lakes, but no real trail to them; a steep climb leads to lake 2, but there is no elevation change from there on. The distant lakes are excellent for brook and rainbow trout fishing. The total elevation gain to lake 1 is 2,200 feet.

High Country

Some of the most spectacular hiking trails in all the national parks are found in the high country of Sequoia National Park. For the sturdy and dedicated, there are no better.

High Sierra Trail. For good reason, one branch road and several winding forest trails converge on lovely Crescent Meadow in the southeastern corner of Giant Forest. For here is the starting point of the spectacular High Sierra Trail, which ultimately joins the even more famous John Muir Trail on Wallace Creek, 49 miles away. Add another dozen miles for the push to the top of Mount Whitney, and the young in limb and heart are able to take in, on foot or on horseback, a full cross section of the park. Popularity is such that limits have had to be placed on daily use.

Construction of the trail began in 1928, two years after the park's boundaries had been rolled east to include the Sierra's crest. The need for extensive blasting and the placing of suspension bridges across reverberating chasms delayed completion until 1932. The engineering returned high rewards. One lofty point after another opens sweeping panoramas. Environments change constantly as the trail slants across slopes matted with slow-growing chinquapin and red-barked manzanita, and then dips into the forested bottoms of the glaciated troughs of the

A fallen sequoia in Giant Forest.

Big Arroyo and the awesome Kern. Avalanche chutes scar the steep granite sides of the Angel Wings. There are meadows and lakes, and creeks where gray water ouzels flit across the glinting water before disappearing into a curtain of spray. The song of canyon wrens cascades; clumps of red penstemon burst out of unlikely cracks in the rock.

Tree species change with altitude. Among them are Jeffrey pines, which resemble ponderosas but favor higher places; soaring sugar pines, whose cones, up to 18 inches long, dangle like ornaments from the tips of the uppermost branches; lodgepoles as straight as if they had been set by a plumb line; and massed red firs that cast a cathedral shade. Near timberline the forest thins, and the junipers, foxtail pines, and white-bark pines are often cruelly deformed, flattened, and stripped of much of their bark and foliage by the arctic weather.

High Country. The long rumple of peaks on the Kern-Kaweah Divide looks like a sea of choppy water turned to stone. The somber colors of lofty Black Kaweah contrast strikingly with the pale granite of most of the other summits. Somewhere on almost every peak is a horseshoe-shaped cirque, the rims of its sheer walls often sculptured by erosion into formidable spires. The steely sheen of ice-scoured stone, the vast tongues of talus and scree—it would be a forbidding land were it not for the paternoster strings of bright turquoise lakes and the dwarfed flowers that bloom in a frenzy of exuberance to complete their life cycles within the six or seven weeks allowed them.

There are signs of trouble, too. Although venturesome backpackers can work their way across country to seldom-visited glens, most campers cling to the trails and gravitate toward familiar campsites. Meadows suffer, especially from horses. Some swales have been closed to grazing, and a few to any camping. To preserve the last bits of timberline wood—and to do away with ugly circles of smoke-blackened rocks —campers must use only gas stoves in some areas at higher altitudes. To halt the steady degradation of water purity, visitors must camp well back from streambanks and lakeshores. But the main defense has to be the consideration and cooperation of those who love the backcountry enough to want to keep it as free as possible from the pressure of their own numbers.

Worse things may be lying in wait. A century ago, travelers in the San Joaquin Valley used to exclaim over the view of the mountains. That view is seldom visible now, except after winter rains. To understand why, shift viewpoints. On a day of summer atmospheric inversions, look from the top of Moro Rock down the Middle Fork of the Kaweah River. The murk that obscures the canyon has in it some dust and smoke from agricultural activities, but most is smog that has leaked out of the San Francisco–Oakland region to mingle with fumes generated by the valley's own cities. Prevailing winds sweep the miasma inexorably up the Sierra's gentle slopes. Concern is growing about the possible effect of acid rain on the trees. Ponderosa pines are particularly vulnerable; characteristically, the enduring sequoias seem more resistant.

But they are so very rare. They make up less than 1 percent of the southern belt of mixed conifers. Perhaps that is why they take on an air of individuality for those who spend time with them—rapport is difficult to achieve with a crowd. But with them you can sit still and let the scope of their grandeur unfold slowly, which is the only approach it will yield to. You may even sense a timeless wisdom there. Having so narrowly escaped extinction themselves, the sequoias have much to say to us now.

YOSEMITE
NATIONAL PARK

YOSEMITE NATIONAL PARK, P. O. BOX 577
YOSEMITE NATIONAL PARK, CALIFORNIA 95389
TEL.: (209) 372-4461

Highlights: Yosemite Valley □ Half Dome □ Yosemite Falls □ Bridalveil Fall □ Indian Cultural Museum □ Happy Isles □ John Muir Trail □ Mariposa Grove □ Tuolumne Meadows □ Tioga Pass

Access: From Merced, 81 miles to Yosemite Valley via California 140. From Fresno, 94 miles to Yosemite Valley via California 41.

Hours: Daily, year-round.

Fees: $3/visit (private, noncommercial vehicle); 50¢/person in bus, on horseback, foot, or bicycle.

Parking: At Yosemite Valley and Mariposa Grove; in summer, at Glacier Point, Wawona, Crane Flat, and Tuolumne Meadows.

Gas, food, lodging: Year-round at Yosemite Valley. Gas year-round at Wawona. Other areas during summer.

Visitor Centers: Yosemite Valley Visitor Center offers information, maps, exhibits, backcountry permits, park publications, orientation slide program, and films. Tuolumne Meadows Visitor Center (summer only) offers information, maps, books, and exhibits. Big Oak Flat entrance information station.

Museums: In Yosemite Valley Visitor Center, Happy Isles Nature Center; also Indian Cultural Museum nearby, Hill's studio at Wawona, and Sequoia Ecology Museum at Mariposa Grove.

Gift shops: Several in Yosemite Valley; also at Wawona, Glacier Point, Mariposa Grove, and Tuolumne Meadows.

Pets: Permitted on leash in developed areas, but not allowed in public buildings and wilderness areas, and on trails. Kennels available.

Picnicking: At designated sites in Yosemite Valley and other areas of park.

Hiking: Throughout park. Water available in some areas, but must be purified.

Backpacking: Throughout backcountry except where prohibited.

Campgrounds: Many sites throughout park. Yosemite Valley, reservations required in summer. Tents and trailers; showers.

Tours: Guided walks, hikes, and bicycle tours.

Other activities: Horseback riding, skiing, swimming, boating, fishing (license required), and mountain climbing.

Facilities for disabled: Parking, some lodging, restrooms, Visitor Center, some trails, special interpretive programs, and sign-language interpreter in summer.

For additional information, see also Sites, Trails, and Trips on pages 217–232 and the maps on pages 200–201 and 224–225.

Y OSEMITE VALLEY, ONCE SEEN, IS NEVER FORGOTTEN. It is one of the few places in the world where the scenery seems to be in perfect, harmonious balance: the towering granite cliffs and domes surrounding a grassy valley floor; the dark forests and shining rocks; the movement of water everywhere, falling from the cliffs in rushing waterfalls and flowing through the length of the valley in the Merced River—and all touched with sunlight and shadow. There is no temptation to rearrange the elements—to move a waterfall or readjust a pinnacle—the scene has the memorable beauty of completeness.

Yosemite Valley is also a living place; most of the geological forces that shaped it are still at work, and the changing seasons bring a constant renewal of grass, trees, and flowers.

But Yosemite Valley is only a small part—less than 1 percent—of Yosemite National Park's 1,189 square miles. In the park's backcountry the scenery may not be as concentrated, but it is no less magnificent. There are dense forests and glowing fields of wildflowers, alpine meadows and lakes, deep canyons and snow-capped peaks, and groves of centuries-old giant sequoias.

The grandeur of the scenery is reason enough to visit Yosemite, but there are millions of years of history here too. It is almost impossible to spend any time at Yosemite and not wonder what powerful natural forces could have shaped and sculpted the great rocks. Some colorful theories have been proposed over the years; Galen Clark, the first

Water plummets down glacier-made Vernal Fall throughout the year, even during the summer.

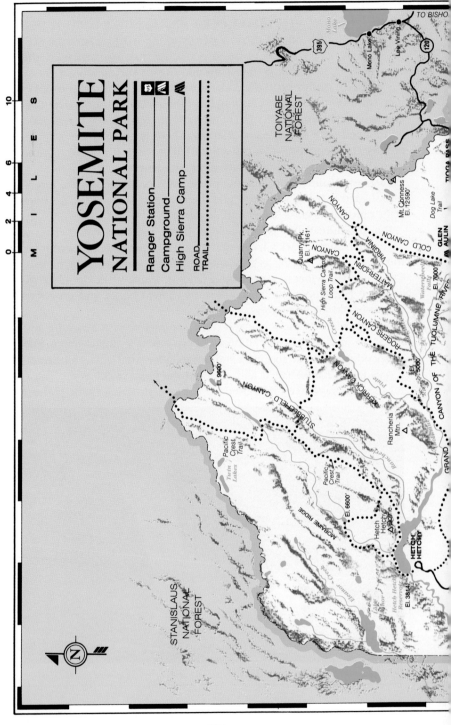

YOSEMITE
NATIONAL PARK

Ranger Station
Campground
High Sierra Camp

ROAD
TRAIL

MILES

0   2   4   6   10

N

STANISLAUS
NATIONAL
FOREST

TOIYABE
NATIONAL
FOREST

Mono
Lake

Mono Lake

Lee Vining

395

120

TO BISHO

TIOGA PASS

Mt. Conness
El. 12590'

Dog Lake
Trail

GLEN
AULIN

COLD CANYON

VIRGINIA CANYON

CANYON

Quarry Pk.
El. 11161'

High Sierra Camps
Loop Trail

MATTERHORN CANYON

Creek

Waterwheel
Falls

ROGERS CANYON

El. 7000'

El. 5000'

CANYON OF THE TUOLUMNE RIVER

GRAND

KERRICK CANYON

Piute

El. 9600'

STUBBLEFIELD CANYON

Rancheria
Mtn.

Pacific
Crest
Trail

Twin
Lakes

Creek

Pacific
Crest
Trail

MORAINE RIDGE

El. 6600'

Eleanor Creek

Lake
Eleanor

Hetch Hetchy
Reservoir

Hetch
Hetchy
Dome

HETCH
HETCHY

El. 3814'

200

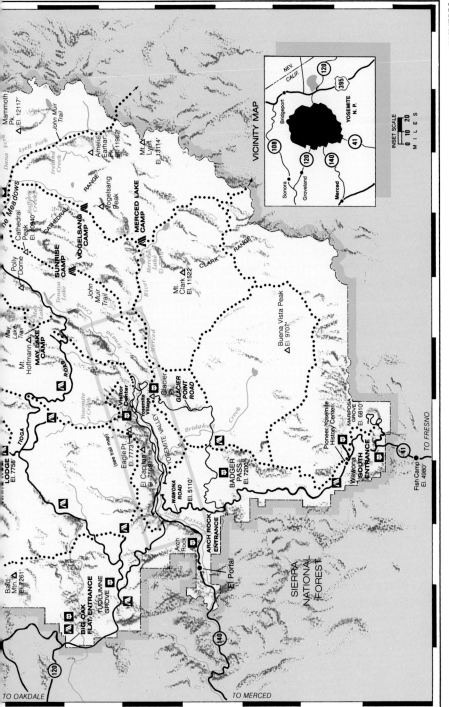

Guardian of the Yosemite Grant, thought that the domes were "great, frozen gas bubbles." Scientific thought has refined Yosemite's geological history since then, but it is still a fascinating story, as are Yosemite's natural history and human history. As John Muir, conservationist and celebrant of Yosemite, said, "This one noble park is big enough and rich enough for a whole life of study and aesthetic enjoyment... its natural beauty cleanses and warms like fire, and you will be willing to stay forever in one place like a tree."

H   I   S   T   O   R   Y

Indians of Ahwahnee

The first humans to live in the Yosemite region probably arrived more than 4,000 years ago, crossing the Sierra from the Great Basin country to the east of the mountains. Over the centuries, Miwok-speaking people from central California gradually moved into the area, living in villages along the Merced River and in Yosemite Valley itself. They called the valley Ahwahnee, loosely translated as "deep grassy valley," and themselves, the Ahwahneechee.

These early Indians were hunter-gatherers, dependent mainly on the valley for food, shelter, and other needs. In late spring and summer they moved into the high country to hunt for deer, and carried on trade with Mono Lake Paiutes across the mountains.

A staple of the Ahwahneechee diet was the acorn of the black oak. Women collected acorns and stored them inside free-standing granaries (*chuck-ah*) woven from branches of deerbrush, grapevine, and conifer. When needed, the acorns were removed from the *chuck-ah*, shelled, pounded into a fine flour, leached repeatedly to remove the bitter tannin, and cooked into soup, mush, and cakes.

A delicacy was the *ka-cha-vee*, a small insect larva collected by the millions by Mono Lake Paiutes and traded to the Ahwahneechee. Mushrooms, camas and brodiaea bulbs, and greens of miner's lettuce, bracken fern, and clover were gathered and eaten in season. To this diet was added rainbow trout that the men speared or trapped in the Merced River, deer and other large wildlife killed with bows and arrows, and squirrels, flickers, and other small animals caught with snares.

The Ahwahneechee cold-weather shelter was the *umacha*, a cone of poles overlaid with bark from incense cedar trees. In warm weather,

---

Opposite: President William Howard Taft, behind driver, and conservationist John Muir, to Taft's left, visit Mariposa Grove in 1909.

the Ahwahneechee slept outdoors. Using earth, brush, grapevine, poles, and cedar bark, the men also built sacred meeting lodges (roundhouses) and sweathouses. Authentic models of these structures stand today behind the Visitor Center in Yosemite Valley.

The Mariposa Battalion

The first documented entry of non-Indians into Ahwahnee took place in 1851, although the valley may have been seen from the rim in 1833 by members of the Joseph Walker trapping party. The discovery of gold in the Mother Lode Country of the Sierra foothills had brought thousands of miners and prospectors into what had been for centuries Indian land. Bands of Indians had taken to raiding nearby trading posts in retaliation for this invasion, so in the spring of 1851, the state-sanctioned Mariposa Battalion was sent into Yosemite Valley to rout the Indians and move them to a reservation. The expedition was a failure; the Indians easily eluded the battalion. Other expeditions were dispatched to the valley, and several skirmishes later, most of the Ahwahneechee were taken to a reservation on the Fresno River. Although some Indians later returned to Yosemite, their lives had been irrevocably changed.

Establishment of the Park

The Mariposa Battalion may not have been particularly effective against the Ahwahneechee, but its visit was to change Yosemite forever. The descriptions that the soldiers brought back of the incredible natural wonders of the valley aroused the curiosity and excitement of the public, and within a few years the first trickle of what was to become a flood of tourists had begun.

By 1864, the press of tourism and of private entrepreneurs was becoming a threat to the beauty of the valley; overdevelopment and overgrazing were already a severe problem.

In that year, a bill was passed in Congress and signed by President Abraham Lincoln requiring the state of California to preserve and protect Yosemite Valley and the Mariposa Grove of Giant Sequoias in a natural, undisturbed condition. This was the first practical application of an idea that resulted in today's national park system.

During the twenty years that followed, toll roads were built, a stage line was started, and hotels sprang up to cater to the increasing numbers of visitors. Largely through the efforts of John Muir, the Sierra Club's first president, Congress acted in 1890 to create Yosemite National Park. The bill was signed by President Theodore Roosevelt. The national park was composed of lands surrounding an original state park. In 1906, after a decade of lobbying by Sierra Club secretary William

Colby, California ceded its part to the federal government, and the two segments were combined.

The national park was administered by the cavalry until 1916, when the National Park Service was established in the Department of the Interior, and Yosemite was finally put under civilian management. Tourism grew steadily in the years that followed as Yosemite's fame spread: by the 1940s, Yosemite had over 500,000 visitors a year; by the mid-1970s, more than 2.5 million people from around the world visited the park annually.

G E O L O G Y

Yosemite National Park lies midway along the 400-mile-long range of "snowy mountains," the Sierra Nevada, poetically described by John Muir as "the range of light." To the west and paralleling the Sierra Nevada is California's Central Valley, and to the east is the vast desert of eastern California and the basin and range country of Nevada.

El Portal, near a west entrance to the park, is at an elevation of 2,100 feet; the land climbs steeply along the Merced Canyon to 4,000 feet, the level of the floor of Yosemite Valley. Most of the park—the high country—is the rugged granite terrain of forests, alpine meadows, and bare rock that surrounds the valley. Much of this area is 5,000 to 10,000 feet in elevation, with major peaks like Mount Lyell, Mount Dana, Mount Clark, and Mount Conness reaching into the thin air above 11,000 feet to more than 13,000 feet. Tioga Pass, the park's east entrance, is almost 10,000 feet high.

Two major rivers drain Yosemite. The Merced—mostly placid as it winds through Yosemite Valley, but wild and foaming both above and below this stretch—channels rain water and snowmelt from the park's southern half. The Tuolumne drains the northern half. Both rivers head near the park's eastern boundary—along the Sierra crest—flowing westward down the range's less-steep western slopes and out to the San Joaquin River in the Central Valley.

Most of the park has been chiseled out of granite by erosion. This bedrock, which appears buff to gray from a distance and salt-and-pepper close up, is partly clothed by variously colored lichen, evergreen forests, and flower-filled meadows. In winter, almost all the high country is covered by snow, but the valley walls are too steep for snow to collect, and the valley floor is low enough that its snow cover is intermittent.

But snow and vegetation only partly hide the granite; exposed slabs, boulders, ridges, ledges, cliffs, domes, and peaks abound, many of which are entirely treeless. From numberless vantage points, visitors can look out on vast "seas of granite." This is a park of grand vistas, huge in scale and evoking a sense of eternity.

Ancient Beginnings

Ageless as they seem, Yosemite's granites are not the Sierra's oldest rocks—not by some 200 million years. Some of the beds of slate exposed in the Merced Canyon along California 140 to the west of the park were deposited in an ancient ocean as layers of mud and sand roughly 450 million years ago. Later they were twisted and metamorphosed within mountain ranges ancestral to the present Sierra. Only the contorted layers and a few ancient marine fossils document this distant beginning.

The next chapter written in the rocks is related to the drifting apart of North America and Europe, which began about 200 million years ago. As one of the earth's crustal plates slowly carried North America westward, the Atlantic Ocean opened and the Pacific coast was crumpled by mountain building. Since oceanic crust is generally heavier than continental crust, the Pacific plate buckled beneath the North American plate, creating a deep oceanic trench. The adjacent continental crust was folded and fractured, and molten rock from below squeezed upward to form a volcanic mountain range similar to the present-day Andes in South America.

Much of the molten rock, or magma, that fed these ancient Sierran volcanoes cooled slowly, deep underground, forming the vast granite core that is exposed in the present Sierra Nevada. All this activity occurred on a time scale that was slow, even in geologic terms. The granites of Yosemite and the neighboring Sierra have been dated by geologists to be as old as 200 million years and as young as 60 million years, with many in between. As a result, Yosemite's many distinct granites are of a wide range of colors, textures, and mineral ingredients, evident in the cliff walls of the valley.

The gold veins in the foothills of the Sierra, like those in the Mother Lode Country to the west of the park, formed from the distilling action of hot waters associated with the volcanism of this same granite-forming period.

Uplift and Erosion

Granite is formed deep in the earth, perhaps 7 miles beneath the overlying volcanoes. The granites of Yosemite have been uplifted some 7 miles, and 4 to 5 miles of rock have been eroded from above them to expose the granite core. This is not to say that the Sierra was ever 7 miles high. The process of uplift, with its attendant earthquake activity, was slow and episodic; 7 miles up in 60 million years is an average of

The Tuolumne River is one of the largest rivers in the park.

only 7 inches every 1,000 years. Erosion by rain and streams kept pace with much of the uplift, and the Sierra is probably higher now than it was earlier in its history.

One of the interesting aspects of the last 3 million years of uplift of the Sierra is that it was not symmetrical. Instead, the major uplift was on the eastern scarp of the range. The western flank was tilted toward the Central Valley of California. This westward tilting accounts for the less-steep western slopes and for a Sierra crest that is nearer to the eastern side of the range.

Glaciation

Fire and ice have been Yosemite's major creators. The earth's internal fires melted the magma that cooled to form granite, and rivers of glacial ice carved the present peaks and valleys.

During the last few million years, the earth's climate has cooled enough that great ice sheets have formed and melted several times. Apparently the uplift of the Sierra has also accelerated, raising the peaks to higher, cooler elevations. The result has been several periods of major mountain glaciation. Ice caps as much as 1 mile thick accumulated in the high country, sending slow-moving rivers of ice down the preexisting valleys. The major glaciers that ground down the Merced and Tuolumne canyons were thick and heavy, and several generations of ice carved the deep U-shaped valleys seen today.

Overleaf: Snow-covered Sierra Nevada seen from Tuolumne Meadows, a favorite starting point for hiking, backpacking, and mountaineering trips.

The work of the glaciers was aided by great bedrock cracks—called joints by geologists—that formed as the granite cooled and was exposed by erosion. Sometimes these joints are flat or convex, and exfoliate (flake off) to form the great granite domes. In other places they are almost vertical and helped form the massive cliff of El Capitan in the valley and the steep-sided summits of Cathedral and Unicorn peaks in the Tuolumne Meadows area. A combination of exfoliation and vertical joints, and the patient carving of glacial ice, formed Half Dome.

With each ebb and flow of the erosive ice, Yosemite's face was sculpted closer to its present form. While freezing and thawing water dislodged granite blocks from exposed summits above, glacial ice plucked rocks from the flanks of the high peaks, resulting in the bowl-shaped cirques exposed today. Downslope, aprons and rivers of glacial ice carved and polished the granite. Millions of rocks of all sizes, trapped in the moving ice, engraved scratches on rock surfaces and later were left strewn across the landscape as "erratics" when the ice melted.

In part of Yosemite Valley, ice quarried 3,000 feet or more of bedrock from the valley floor. When the ice melted, only 10,000 years ago, a glacial lake filled the valley, into which hundreds of feet of mud and sand were deposited. These sediments produced the flat floor of the present-day valley.

Our own century enjoys a glacial minimum during which almost all of Yosemite's ice has retreated, leaving mere remnant glaciers on the high peaks. But in the perspective of geologic time, we can expect the ice to return, renewing its sculpture of Yosemite and the great Sierra Nevada.

Waterfalls

Yosemite's magnificent waterfalls and cascades are products of the same forces that shaped Yosemite Valley's distinctive cliffs and domes. While Yosemite Valley was being carved more and more deeply by glacial action, the tributary ice streams like Yosemite Creek cut much more slowly; their valleys were left hanging above the major glacial valleys as the ice melted, and their waters poured down the main canyon walls or leaped into space where the walls were steepest.

The classic example of this hanging valley type of fall is Yosemite Falls; the Upper Fall plummets 1,430 feet, and after a series of cascades for 675 feet, the Lower Fall plunges another 320 feet. Yosemite Falls, at 2,425 feet, is the highest waterfall in North America and the second-highest in the world after Angel Fall (3,212 feet) in Venezuela. Indeed, five of Yosemite's waterfalls are among the ten highest on earth; even Vernal Fall, at 317 feet, is almost twice as high as Niagara.

A Jeffrey pine on the sheer granite of 3,073-foot-high Sentinel Dome.

Bridalveil Fall is another fine example of the hanging valley type of waterfall. Falling 620 feet, its misty waters seem to float in the valley breezes.

A different type of waterfall resulted from the action of glaciers plucking huge blocks out of streambeds where the granite was jointed, thus producing "glacial stairways." Vernal and Nevada are falls of this type; in Merced Canyon, the Merced River drops 2,000 feet in 1.5 miles in a section called the Giant's Stairway, with 317-foot Vernal Fall and 594-foot Nevada Fall pouring over two of the steps.

In many places in Yosemite, falls cascade over irregularly fractured granite or over more gently sloping, smooth cliffs instead of leaping freely. The Cascades in Cascade Creek and the 1,250-foot Royal Arch Cascade are good examples.

Spring is the season to see Yosemite's many splendid falls. The rapid melting of the heavy winter snowpack gives the falls a booming vitality. By autumn, some of the falls are dry, or nearly so. This is in part related to the watershed area that each waterfall drains. For example, Ribbon Fall near El Capitan drains only 4 square miles, whereas Nevada Fall drains 118. In consequence, Ribbon Fall often disappears before summer is over, while Nevada Fall thunders all year round. Even in winter, the waterfalls have a stark beauty. Yosemite Falls grows a huge curtain of frost and a great ice cone at the base of the Upper Fall, icy reminders of the glacial origin of its hanging valley.

Climate and Precipitation

Yosemite's mild climate makes travel a pleasure in almost any season. In summer, days are warm and dry; temperatures sometimes reach as high as 100° F in the valley and 75° F in the high country, but nights are always cool. Summer skies are usually blue and cloudless, with an occasional thundershower in the afternoon.

Winter temperatures can fall as low as 5° F to 10° F, although the usual range is from 20° F to 40° F and sometimes as high as 65° F or so. The first snowfall usually comes to the valley before Christmas; snows in the high country come earlier and are so heavy that the cross-Sierra Tioga Road is closed to cars for six to nine months of the year, even though the floor of Yosemite Valley may be largely snowless much of the winter. Even in winter, the skies are brilliantly clear between storms; the icy beauty of Yosemite's snow-crowned cliffs and trees shining under the deep-blue sky is an unforgettable sight.

Trees, Plants, and Flowers

At first glance, Yosemite's shining granite domes and leaping waterfalls seem to be its most spectacular attractions. At a closer focus, though, the diversity of Yosemite's plant life is just as intriguing. With altitudes ranging from 2,000 feet on the western boundary to 13,000 feet at the eastern summit, there are innumerable local environments hospitable to plants with differing needs. Thirty-seven kinds of native trees grow in the park (both broad-leaved and cone-bearing evergreens) and more than 1,400 flowering plants, as well as innumerable shrubs, grasses, sedges, ferns, and fungi. They are distributed in broad vegetation zones or belts, overlapping in places, that are determined largely by altitude.

While most of Yosemite is at a high elevation, the park boundary at El Portal and parts of the Wawona and Big Oak Flat roads are in the foothill woodland zone of 2,000 to 3,000 feet. At this elevation, the most conspicuous trees are the digger pine, a spreading rangy tree with grayish needles, and the handsome, tall ponderosa, or yellow, pine. There are live oaks here, too, and California buckeye, which in early summer is covered with long clusters of white blossoms. In spring this zone is blanketed with blue and purple lupine, orange-gold California poppies, and dozens of other wildflowers, and dotted with western redbuds, small shrubs that are completely swathed in brilliant magenta blossoms. Hillsides are covered with dense brush or chaparral, mostly the hardy California lilac and purple-barked, gnarled manzanita.

Opposite: A winter frost in Yosemite Valley.

Beginning at about 3,000 feet is the mixed-conifer forest, a broad zone of diverse tree species extending to about 7,000 feet in elevation. In this zone, depending on rainfall and suitable soil, are mixtures of ponderosa pine; Jeffrey pine; sugar pine, with its foot-long cones; incense cedar, a large tree that is often mistaken for a giant sequoia, and is in fact not a cedar but a member of the cypress family; and Douglas fir, which is not really a fir and, just to complicate matters, looks like a spruce. Also in this zone, which includes Yosemite Valley, are fine stands of black oak and, scattered through the forest and along the Merced River, lovely California dogwood, which in May and June blooms lavishly with large, creamy white flowers.

The magnificent giant sequoias—the largest living things known—grow best at this elevation. There are three groves within the park: the Mariposa, Tuolumne, and Merced Groves of Giant Sequoias. These trees—some of which are almost 3,000 years old—average 250 feet in height and 15 to 20 feet in diameter. A "big tree" is so massive that it is almost impossible to comprehend that it is a living, growing plant.

These huge trees have cinnamon-colored bark that is sometimes 2 feet thick, and bear tiny cones about the size of a hen's egg.

The lavish wildflowers of this zone vary as the seasons progress, from the brilliant red snow plant that pushes through the forest floor just as the snow is retreating, to the autumn-blooming meadow goldenrod. The lovely western azalea blooms in the valley meadows in June, as do the tall, showy cow parsnip, milkweed (which harbors the monarch butterfly), and such small flowers as violets, pussy paws, and brodiaea.

The most extensive of Yosemite's forests grow between 6,500 and 9,000 feet; this is sometimes called the lodgepole pine—red fir belt. In areas of suitable moisture and soil, the stately red fir grows in almost pure stands; where soils are too soggy or too thin for red fir, the smaller lodgepole pine dominates.

Counterclockwise from opposite top: Pygmy owl on cow parsnip; Anderson thistle; shooting stars; monarch on a milkweed; raccoon.

Along the trails and in mountain meadows in this zone are an abundance of wildflowers, including the shooting star, monkey flower (yellow, pink, and red varieties), larkspur, and paintbrush. Occasionally it is possible to find the rare Washington lily, a large white blossom on a 6-foot stalk.

Above 9,000 feet, the forest thins out to small groves and scattered trees: western white pine, mountain hemlock, and, at the highest elevations, whitebark pine. Among the few struggling whitebark pines that grow above timberline there is still a fine community of wildflowers, among them mats of spreading phlox, bell-shaped white heather, alpine pentstemon, and Dana's lupine.

Wildlife

The most conspicuous animal in Yosemite National Park is the mule deer, which is often seen browsing in meadows singly or in small bands. They are the only hoofed animals in the park, although the Sierra bighorn once lived in the high country. Gentle and inquisitive, mule deer are nonetheless wild animals and should not be touched or fed.

The same caution applies to the Sierra black bear, which in spite of its name can vary in color from light yellow through brown to black. This is the only species of bear still found in the park.

It is sometimes possible to catch sight of a coyote, raccoon, gray fox, or porcupine and rarely, a bobcat or mountain lion. Squirrels are very common; the gray squirrel with its long, bushy tail is active almost all year. There are five species of chipmunk in the park, as well as the Sierra chickaree, or red squirrel, which lives at the higher altitudes.

Other high-mountain animals include the Sierra marmot, the largest local representative of the squirrel family; the grayish yellow California badger; and the cony or pika, a small, elusive creature that resembles a rabbit and is more often known by its high nasal chirp, than by sight.

Birds are abundant in Yosemite, with a population of more than 220 species. The most immediately obvious in the valley are the crested Steller's jay, a brash "camp robber"; several kinds of woodpeckers and flickers; and the western meadowlark, with its beautiful song.

The birdlife also varies with elevation; at higher altitudes are found (among many others) the mountain bluebird, Clark's nutcracker, and mountain chickadee. A most unusual bird that sometimes can be seen along fast-moving mountain streams is the water ouzel, or dipper; it bobs up and down on a streamside rock for a few moments and then makes a dash into the stream, going completely underwater to hunt for larvae on the bottom.

Tuolumne Meadows is the largest high-mountain meadow in the Sierra Nevada.

S I T E S ,   T R A I L S ,   A N D   T R I P S

Yosemite National Park is so large and so scenically varied that the problem for the visitor is not finding something to see or do, but choosing among the riches. Much of the spectacular scenery can be seen from the park's roads, but to experience more fully this extraordinary mountain environment, try to sample at least a few of the more than 750 miles of trails available to hikers and horseback parties.

Yosemite Valley

Yosemite Valley is a logical starting point for a tour of the park; for many, this "Incomparable Valley" is a destination in itself. Because of the very heavy summer visitation to the valley, it is a good idea to make camping reservations early.

The roads in Yosemite Valley are arranged in a one-way system, with those in the eastern part of the valley closed to cars. However, a free shuttle bus operates on the valley loop road, including the restricted Mirror Lake Drive, making frequent stops at scenic spots; it is an excellent way to see the valley.

The Yosemite Valley Visitor Center is located in Yosemite Village; it has exhibits on the park's natural features and human history. Here also is information on trails and campgrounds, and many publications about Yosemite National Park and the Sierra. The collections of the *Indian Cultural Museum* and the model Ahwahneechee village show how Yosemite's early inhabitants lived.

The one-way road leads west from the Visitor Center, and in about .5 mile reaches the Yosemite Falls parking area. A short trail (.2 mile) goes to the bridge at the base of 2,425-foot *Yosemite Falls*. In the spring, the bridge shakes with the thundering drop of water, and sightseers are sprayed with the fine mist. In late summer, the falls wane and in some years are dry by autumn. In winter, a beautiful ice cone (really frozen spray from the falls) builds up at the base of the Upper Fall.

The *Yosemite Falls Trail* starts from a point .5 mile farther along the loop road. This is a steep (2,700-foot ascent in 3.5 miles) but spectacular trail, offering unrivaled views of Yosemite Falls and Yosemite Valley.

The loop road follows along the Merced River with fine views of Yosemite's cliffs, spires, and domes, The prominent peaks rising one above the other on the right are the *Three Brothers*. These are named for the three sons of Tenaya, who was chief of the Yosemite Indians at the time Yosemite Valley was first entered by white explorers.

The low ridge that the road crosses in this area is the terminal moraine of the last glacier in Yosemite Valley; it is a line of rock rubble, left when the glacier melted.

Just before the Pohono Bridge is *Valley View*, or The Gates of the Valley, with a panoramic vista of Yosemite's granite peaks and domes, Bridalveil Fall, and, in the foreground, tranquil Bridalveil Meadow and the Merced River.

Turn left at the next intersection; the road crosses Pohono Bridge and then the meadow where the Mariposa Battalion camped during its foray into Yosemite Valley in 1851.

At the next intersection, jog a few hundred yards to the right on the Wawona Road to the Bridalveil Fall parking area, for a view of this ethereal waterfall. *Bridalveil Fall* was called Pohono, or "puffing wind," by the Indians. A short (.2 mile) trail leads to the base of the fall.

Backtrack to the valley loop road, for another fine view across the river to *El Capitan*, a sheer, granite promontory that rises almost 4,000 feet above the valley floor. On the right loom *Cathedral Rocks* (sometimes called the Three Graces) and then *Cathedral Spires*, two towering shafts of granite 2,300 and 3,000 feet above Yosemite Valley.

Past Cathedral Spires, the next huge granite tower is 3,073-foot *Sentinel Rock*. To the right of the rock, *Sentinel Fall* cascades down the cliffs in springtime. Near the base of Sentinel Rock is the start of the *Four-Mile Trail* to Glacier Point, a steep but easy scenic trail that, in spite of its name, is almost 5 miles long.

Past Sentinel Rock, the road breaks out of the forest into an open meadow, with another view of stately Yosemite Falls. Continue right at the next intersection to visit the Sierra Club's *LeConte Lodge,* a memo-

Lost Arrow, a spiral cliff near Yosemite Point, is a challenge for mountain climbers.

rial to geologist Joseph LeConte, with exhibits and a library (open only in the summer). About 1 mile farther is Curry Village. A large parking area is located here; the roads to Happy Isles and Mirror Lake are open only to the shuttle buses that leave from Curry Village and to bicyclists and foot travelers.

At *Happy Isles*, 1 mile past Curry Village, the Merced River reaches the valley floor in a tumble of white water, branching into several channels. A pleasant trail crosses bridges among the small islands in the river, and a nature center nearby features exhibits about Yosemite's ecology.

Happy Isles is the trail head for many of Yosemite's finest trails, the most notable being the *John Muir Trail*, which starts here and leads to Tuolumne Meadows, then south through the Sierra to Mount Whitney, 212 miles away. Many shorter hiking trips begin here too, starting along the same trail. Just .9 mile up the John Muir Trail is Vernal Fall Bridge, from which there is a magnificent view of this 317-foot water-fall and the tumultuous waters at its base. The steep, 1-mile *Mist Trail* leads to the top of *Vernal Fall*, and another 2.4 miles to the top of 594-foot *Nevada Fall*.

As the trail continues 1.2 miles through Little Yosemite Valley, a 2.1-mile trail to the top of Half Dome branches off to the left. The last part of the *Half Dome Trail* is via a cable-stairway up the rounded northeast side of the dome—a strenuous but exciting climb, rewarded by dramatic views of Yosemite Valley and the High Sierra. *Half Dome*, a huge granite rock formation, towers almost 1 mile above the valley floor. A rounded dome, its west side (facing Yosemite Valley) is a sheer, 2,000-foot cliff. John Muir called Half Dome "the most beautiful and most sublime of all the wonderful Yosemite rocks." (Winter condi-tions require closure of portions of these trails; closed areas are posted. Inquire at the Yosemite Valley Visitor Center before starting the trip.)

From the valley loop road once again, 1.6 miles from Happy Isles is *Mirror Lake*. Silting in now, so it continues to get smaller, Mirror Lake still reflects the mountains and domes that surround it. The *Mirror Lake Trail*, a 3-mile loop, circles the lake.

From the west edge of Mirror Lake are striking views of the cliffs and domes, the most imposing of which is Half Dome. Across Mirror Lake to the north is Mount Watkins. On windless mornings when the lake is still, a perfect reflection of Mount Watkins can be seen on its surface. As the road turns back to the west, it passes pillarlike *Washington Column* and above it the finely modeled *North Dome*. On the granite

Opposite: The west side of Half Dome is a sheer 2,000-foot cliff.

walls of the valley are the sweeping curves of the *Royal Arches*, a product of glaciation and exfoliation.

The road crosses the Ahwahnee Meadow near the historic Ahwahnee Hotel, and from here is one of the best views of *Glacier Point*, a stark cliff of granite soaring 3,242 feet above the valley. From the Ahwahnee Meadow, it is .6 mile back to the Visitor Center.

Glacier Point, Wawona, and the Big Trees

The Wawona Road (California 41) leaves Yosemite Valley from the road junction near Bridalveil Fall. It first climbs 1.5 miles to the eastern end of the Wawona Tunnel, where a point called *Discovery View* provides one of the most memorable panoramic views of Yosemite Valley: cliffs, domes, and forested floor, with Bridalveil Fall in the foreground. An interpretive sign identifies by outline the features of Yosemite's profile.

From the Wawona Tunnel, the road winds through lovely forests of ponderosa pine, incense cedar, and black oak for 7.7 miles to the Chinquapin intersection, named for the glossy, green shrub common in this area. Here the Glacier Point Road (16 miles) turns off to the left. This road is usually closed above Badger Pass Ski Area by snow in late autumn, and remains closed all winter.

Five miles past Chinquapin, a short side road turns right to Badger Pass Ski Area, Yosemite's winter sports center, where there are both downhill skiing and the trail heads for some excellent cross-country trips. In the spring, the Badger Pass Meadow is a favorite haunt of wildflower-lovers.

After 3.2 miles, the road crosses Bridalveil Creek, the headwater of Bridalveil Fall. Farther along the road are grand views into the backcountry, with the whole length of the Clark Range in view.

The parking area for the short (1 mile) *Sentinel Dome Trail* is about 5 miles past Bridalveil Creek. After an easy walk, the last part of which is a scramble up the curved side of the dome, the view is a grand 360° panorama of the park. At the top of Sentinel Dome is the famous gnarled Jeffrey pine, a prime subject of countless photographs. Now dead, it was a victim of drought in the late 1970s.

The 1.1-mile *Taft Point Trail* leads from the same parking area to the rim overlooking Yosemite Valley, with superb views of Yosemite Falls and El Capitan. The last several hundred feet of this trail skirt the valley's sheer 3,000-foot rim.

At the end of a series of steep downhill switchbacks is Glacier Point; probably no other easily accessible viewpoint offers the scenic splendor found here.

Trails of Yosemite National Park

Four-Mile Trail: Starts 1.25 miles from Yosemite Village on Southside Drive at Post V18 (Four-Mile Trail parking area) or at Glacier Point; 4.8 miles; 3 to 4 hours one way from Yosemite Valley floor; 3,200-foot ascent; built in 1871 as the route to Glacier Point before roads were available; strenuous, with steep switchbacks; carry water.

Mirror Lake Loop Trail: Starts and ends at Mirror Lake; 3 miles round trip; 1 to 2 hours; 60-foot ascent; loop skirts Mirror Lake with magnificent view of Half Dome and continues up Tenaya Canyon; passes glacial polish (.2 mile from start), the Snow Creek Trail (to Tenaya Lake), and at its maximum distance from Mirror Lake (1.3 miles) crosses Tenaya Creek, then passes down opposite side of canyon; level, with a few up-and-down areas.

Yosemite Falls Trail: Starts at Sunnyside Campground; 7.2 miles round trip; 2,700-foot ascent; strenuous climb to the top of Yosemite Falls, 2,425 feet above the valley floor; a panoramic view of Yosemite Valley from the world's second highest free-leaping waterfall; steep, with many switchbacks; guardrails at scenic points, but extreme caution should be exercised at all times; summer months are hot and dry; carry water.

Panorama Trail: Starts at Glacier Point or Happy Isles; ends at Yosemite Valley floor; 3,200-foot descent; 8.5 miles; descends 1.5 miles (1,300 feet in elevation) to pass across top of Illilouette Fall, after which it climbs up and around shoulder above Panorama Cliffs, then descends to valley floor by either horse or foot trail; a popular, though very strenuous, all-day hike is to go up to the Glacier Point Four-Mile Trail and return to the valley via the Panorama Trail; closed in winter.

Yosemite Falls, which sometimes dries up by fall, is best viewed in late spring and early summer.

Pohono Trail: Starts at Glacier Point; ends at Wawona Tunnel; 13 miles; 6 to 8 hours; 1,800-foot descent; follows close (within about 1 mile) to the south rim of Yosemite Valley; at Taft, Crocker, and Dewey points, trail comes right to the rim to offer outstanding views of the valley; may be taken in either direction, although it is less difficult from Glacier Point; known for its abundant and varied spring and early summer wildflowers; closed in winter.

Half Dome Trail: Starts at Happy Isles (concrete bridge); 16.8 miles round trip; 10 to 12 hours (many prefer to make hike in 2 days and camp in Little Yosemite Valley); 4,800-foot ascent; follows the Vernal and Nevada Falls Trail to the top of Nevada Fall and on to Little Yosemite Valley, then branches off to follow Clouds Rest Trail around the back side of Half Dome to the base; beyond Nevada Fall, the trail is for both pack animals (which have the right of way) and people; the last 600 feet going up the side of Half Dome is very steep and protected with cables (cables down and trail closed in winter); wilderness permit, obtained at Visitor Center, required for overnight stay.

Inspiration Point Trail: Starts and ends at east end of Wawona Tunnel; 2.5 miles round trip; 2 to 3 hours; 1,200-foot ascent; strenuous climb to historic Old Inspiration Point on the old Wawona Road, built in 1875 and used until the new road and tunnel were completed in 1933; steep uphill, with many switchbacks; carry water.

Vernal and Nevada Falls Trail: Starts and ends at Happy Isles (concrete bridge); 1.5 miles to Vernal Fall; 3.4 miles (6 to 8 hours) round trip to Nevada Fall; climb of 1,900 feet requiring only moderate exertion on paved trail for first .8 mile from Happy Isles to Vernal Fall Bridge; .7 mile beyond bridge to top of Vernal Fall via the Mist Trail; strenuous and steep rest of trail; Nevada Fall is start of the 212-mile John Muir Trail to Mount Whitney in Sequoia and Kings Canyon national parks; very wet from spray in early spring and summer; guardrails along steep sections and at top of each fall; caution should be used at all times.

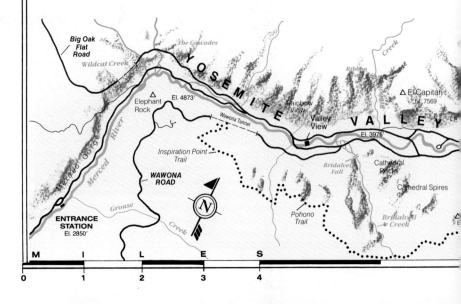

Lower Yosemite Falls Trail: Starts at Yosemite Falls shuttle bus stop/parking area at Post V3 near Yosemite Lodge; ends at bottom of falls; .5 hour.

Bridalveil Fall Trail: Starts at Bridalveil Fall parking area at Post W1; ends at bottom of falls; .5 hour.

Curry Village to Mirror Lake: Starts at Valley Stable or Mirror Lake Junction shuttle bus stops; ends at Mirror Lake; 2 miles round trip; 1 to 2 hours; paved route.

Taft Point Trail: Starts at Glacier Point Road; ends at Taft Point; 1.2 miles; 2 hours; easy climb; excellent views of El Capitan and Yosemite Falls; no guard-rails along 2,000-foot cliffs.

Sentinel Dome Trail: Starts on Glacier Point Road; ends at nearly treeless summit of Sentinel Dome, at 8,100 feet; 2.5 miles round trip; 2 hours; 420-foot ascent; excellent view of Yosemite Valley.

May Lake Trail: Starts and ends along Tioga Road at Post T21 (hike begins at end of 1.8-mile road); 2.5 miles round trip; 2 hours; 450-foot ascent; hike among stands of fir and pine; at 9,300-foot elevation.

Lembert Dome Trail: Starts and ends at Dog Lake trail head just off Tioga Road near Tuolumne River Bridge, at Post T31; 2.4 miles round trip; 2 hours; 850-foot ascent; glacial polish; outstanding views, at 9,450-foot elevation.

High Sierra Camps Loop Trail: Starts and ends at Tuolumne Meadows; traverses about 50 miles of outstanding scenery (passing 8 summer camps, located an average of 6 miles apart, which provide meals and tent accommodations by reservation); elevation range is 7,900 to 10,200 feet.

See map on pages 200–201.

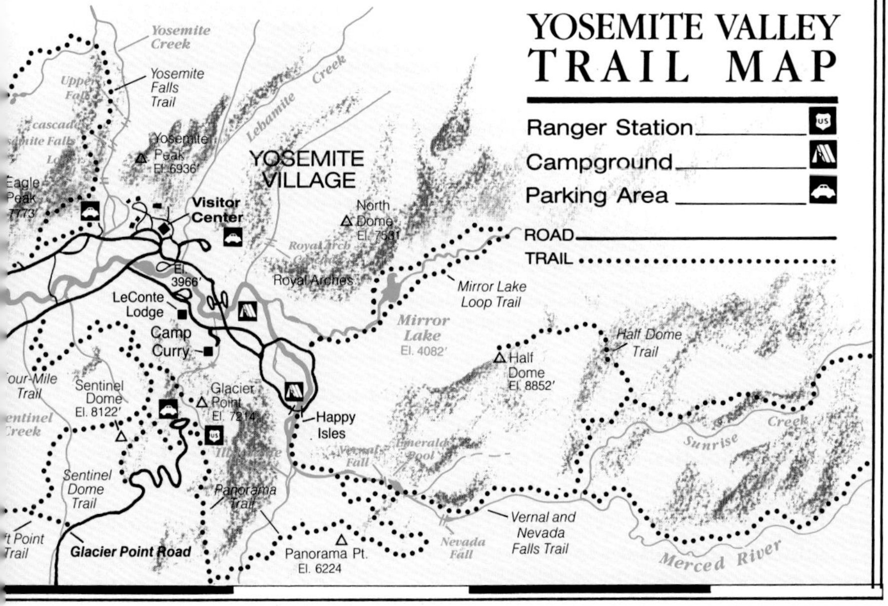

YOSEMITE VALLEY
TRAIL MAP

Ranger Station
Campground
Parking Area
ROAD
TRAIL

From the parking area, walk 300 yards to Glacier Point for a bird's-eye view of the valley below and the vast expanse of the High Sierra with its polished domes and snow-covered peaks, Vernal Fall and Nevada Fall to the east, and the full drop of Yosemite Falls across the valley.

From Glacier Point, retrace the route to Chinquapin, and turn left on the Wawona Road. The road winds gently downhill through lovely forests of ponderosa pine, incense cedar, and black oak to Wawona, originally a trail-side camp built by Galen Clark, the first Guardian of the Yosemite Grant. Located here is the *Pioneer Yosemite History Center*, where a covered bridge near the camp's original site and several historic buildings relocated to the center from their former settings recreate Yosemite's past. During the summer, a living-history program, including stagecoach rides, helps visitors relive part of that past. Nearby is the beautiful and historic Wawona Hotel, still in operation.

From Wawona, continue south on the Wawona Road, past the turn-off to the south entrance of the park, to the *Mariposa Grove of Giant Sequoias*, 6.6 miles from Wawona.

This magnificent grove contains at least 500 mature giant sequoias, the huge reddish brown trees that are among the oldest and largest living things on earth. The largest tree in the grove is the Grizzly Giant, with a base diameter of 30 feet, girth of 94.2 feet, and height of 200 feet. It is thought to be about 2,700 years old.

Most of the grove can be visited only by walking or by riding the free tram system (early May to mid-October). Ride the tram round-trip, or get off at one of the stops and walk back along the trails. Near the parking area is the *Pillars of Heaven Nature Trail*, a .5-mile self-guiding loop through part of the grove.

The Tioga Road and the High Country

To many people, the high country—roughly from 7,000 to above 13,000 feet in elevation—is the most exhilarating part of Yosemite National Park. This vast region of sparkling lakes and streams, flowery meadows, and bare granite peaks rising above timberline is accessible by car only during summer and early autumn. In these high altitudes, the air seems clearer and the light more dazzling; the invitation to walk the high trails is almost irresistible.

Leave Yosemite Valley via the Big Oak Flat Road to Crane Flat, where the Tioga Road begins. (Other roads from Crane Flat lead to the *Tuolumne* and *Merced Groves of Giant Sequoias*, and to Hetch Hetchy, a valley that was similar to Yosemite Valley until it was dammed in 1914 to provide a water supply for San Francisco.) The Tioga Road (California 120) climbs from 6,200 feet through red fir and lodgepole pine forests to Tioga Pass, the park's east entrance, at an elevation of

Yosemite's Cathedral Peak, 10,940 feet, is in the Tuolumne Meadows area.

9,941 feet. It is the highest road pass in California. There are grand views of the high country from many points along the road, and campgrounds in several places provide a more "primitive" camping experience than do those in Yosemite Valley.

At 18.7 miles past Crane Flat, the road crosses Yosemite Creek, the headwater of Yosemite Falls; and 5.1 miles farther is the start of the 3.7-mile *North Dome Trail*.

Two miles beyond is the May Lake Junction. Turn here onto a section of the Old Tioga Road; it winds past Snow Flat, a meadow where some of Yosemite's deepest snows accumulate each winter, and ends at the *May Lake Trail*. This 1.2-mile trail leads to May Lake High Sierra Camp.

On the Tioga Road again, *Olmstead Point*, 2.2 miles beyond the May Lake Junction, provides some of the most breath-taking vistas anywhere in Yosemite. The view to the west is down Tenaya Canyon with its vast expanses of polished and sculpted granite, 9,926-foot Clouds Rest, and the unfamiliar, rounded back view of Half Dome. To the east is *Tenaya Lake*, a beautiful blue lake fringed with dark trees and sur-

Overleaf: Yosemite Valley and Bridalveil Fall.

Pacific dogwood grows along the Merced River.

rounded by glacially smoothed domes and cliffs. The Indian name for Tenaya Lake was Pywiack, or "lake of the shining rocks"; here can be seen some of the best examples of glacial polish.

The road skirts the shore of Tenaya Lake at the base of 9,786-foot *Polly Dome* and passes *Fairview Dome* to reach *Tuolumne Meadows*, the largest high-mountain meadow in the Sierra.

One of the most prominent landmarks of Tuolumne Meadows is *Lembert Dome*, an asymmetric dome of polished granite with a distinctive profile—a good example of the sculpturing effect of ice. It is possible to scramble to the top from a path that branches from the *Dog Lake Trail*, and enjoy a 360° view of Tuolumne Meadows, Unicorn Peak, Cathedral Peak, Mount Conness, Mount Dana, Mount Gibbs, and many high peaks in the distance.

From Tuolumne Meadows, the Tioga Road climbs through lodgepole pine forests and follows along the sparkling Dana Fork of the Tuolumne River to Dana Meadows, ultimately reaching Tioga Pass.

Besides being a place of great natural beauty, Tuolumne Meadows is a favorite starting point for hiking, backpacking, and mountaineering. Many trails into the backcountry originate here, and other, longer trails pass through; the *Pacific Crest Trail* and the *John Muir Trail* meet here and follow the same route to Mount Whitney.

Even a short hike from Tuolumne Meadows can provide a sample of the magic of Yosemite's high country. A loop trail circles the meadows; this is a nice hike to take while adjusting to the higher, thinner air.

A 3-mile trail leads to *Elizabeth Lake,* a lovely subalpine lake nestled at the foot of craggy Unicorn Peak; and a slightly longer trail (part of the John Muir Trail) goes to equally beautiful *Cathedral Lakes.* The first mile or two of one of the longer trails can make a pleasant afternoon's hike. A 2-hour walk eastward along the Lyell Fork of the Tuolumne River on the John Muir Trail affords a fine combination of river, meadow, and mountain; a similar walk westward on the Pacific Crest Trail is an almost irresistible appetizer for a longer hike.

The High Sierra Loop

The High Sierra camps make accessible to the unseasoned hiker some of the most beautiful backcountry in the park. There are six camps arranged roughly in a circle, at distances averaging 8 miles apart. The camps provide beds, restrooms, hot showers, and meals (in a central dining tent). The camps usually are open from early July through early September, and reservations are necessary. The National Park Service also maintains a public campground at each camp.

A High Sierra loop trip starts at Tuolumne Meadows Lodge, the only camp accessible by car. It is a good idea to plan a night or two at Tuolumne Meadows to adjust to the altitude (8,600 feet). In the meadows area you can participate in ranger programs and naturalist-guided hikes, or take guided horseback rides that leave from the Tuolumne Stables.

The trail to Glen Aulin High Sierra Camp from Tuolumne Meadows (7.6 miles) passes through open meadows with views of the Cathedral Range. It follows the Tuolumne River over sparkling expanses of granite and past cascades and waterfalls that signal the beginning of the river's plunge to the Grand Canyon of the Tuolumne River. Glen Aulin Camp is located at the foot of *White Cascade* beside a large pool that invites swimming. Follow the trail farther downriver through the Glen Aulin itself—through stands of fir, pine, and aspen—to *Waterwheel Falls,* where during the early summer, water is tossed backward in "wheels" (arcs) 30 to 40 feet high.

Leaving Glen Aulin, the *McGee Lake Trail* climbs 8.6 miles to May Lake High Sierra Camp, at 9,270 feet. The trail passes McGee Lake, and offers views of Mount Conness to the east, Mount Hoffmann to the west, and Mount Clark to the south. It goes through rock gardens in which grow many Sierra wildflowers like pentstemon, paintbrush, and mountain daisy. The camp sits on the eastern shore of *May Lake* amid mountain hemlocks, with Mount Hoffman (10,850 feet) towering behind. A ridge behind camp offers a spectacular panoramic view, from Tenaya Canyon with Half Dome to Tenaya Lake and the many distant peaks beyond.

The next day's hike (8 miles) descends about 1,100 feet and crosses the Tioga Road above Tenaya Lake. The trail then climbs up a series of switchbacks on an exposed slope of granite boulders to Forsyth Pass, eventually reaching three *Sunrise Lakes*, two of which lie directly beside the trail and offer good swimming and fishing. The trail then crosses a pass and drops 1 mile to Long Meadow and Sunrise High Sierra Camp, at 9,400 feet. The camp is located on a grassy bench 30 to 40 feet above the meadow, with tents arranged picturesquely among the boulders. The large screen windows in the dining tent frame a view of Mount Clark, which glows with alpen glow at sunset, as does Mount Florence to the east. You can stroll by the meandering stream in Long Meadow and watch the deer feed at dusk.

From Sunrise Camp, the trail to Merced Lake follows the Echo Creek drainage down through glens filled with wildflowers to meet the Merced River about 2 miles below camp. The Merced Lake High Sierra Camp sits at the east end of *Merced Lake* in a tall forest of Jeffrey pine, lodgepole pine, and white fir. At the 7,275-foot elevation, nights are comparatively warm. Fishing is good at Merced Lake and at Washburn Lake, 3 miles up the Merced River.

Between Merced Lake and Vogelsang High Sierra Camp there is a choice of trails. One goes up Lewis Creek and over 10,700-foot Vogelsang Pass in 9 miles. This is the steeper trail and affords a stunning view of many of the peaks along the Sierra crest. The other trail follows Fletcher Creek in a more gradual, 7.6-mile ascent, passing through open meadows and near granite domes.

Vogelsang, at 10,160 feet, is the highest camp on the loop. For a fine view, climb Vogelsang Peak (11,516 feet) above the camp. There are numerous lakes in the area around camp, with several kinds of trout, making this camp a favorite of fishermen. Glaciation is much in evidence, with glacial cirques and polished slopes, and the step-formation of the nearby canyons.

The trail back to Tuolumne Meadows (7.2 miles) crosses Tuolumne Pass and follows Rafferty Creek down to the Lyell Fork of the Tuolumne River. Here it joins the John Muir Trail. An alternate route is the longer, more scenic *Ireland Creek Trail* (12.3 miles).

Opposite: Horsetail Falls at sunset.

ANIMALS & PLANTS

OF THE PACIFIC SOUTHWEST
AND HAWAII

This appendix provides a sample of animals and plants commonly found in the national parks of the Pacific Southwest and Hawaii. The codes have been used to indicate the parks in which these animals and plants are most often seen.

CI	Channel Islands	KC	Kings Canyon	SQ	Sequoia
HL	Haleakala	LV	Lassen Volcanic	YO	Yosemite
HV	Hawaii Volcanoes	RW	Redwood		

MAMMALS

AMERICAN RIVER OTTER LV, RW, YO

The river otter is one of the largest members of the weasel family, measuring 3–4.25 ft. and weighing up to 30 lbs. Seeing it is really a chance occurrence, but when seen it is a major attraction, distinguished by clownlike actions—floating on its back in the water, sliding in the snow, and generally frolicking about. The river otter has a dark-brown coat, lighter belly, silver-gray throat, and whitish whiskers. Its long tail is thick at the base and tapers to a point, and its feet are webbed. It feeds mainly on fish, but also eats mice and terrestrial invertebrates.

BADGER KC, LV, SQ, YO

The nocturnal badger is seldom seen in heavily visited areas. Generally a little over 2 ft. long, including a 5-in. tail, it has a flattish body, with short, bowed legs. Its burrow has an 8–12-in. elliptical opening, and is marked by a large mound of earth and debris; the badger can bury itself faster than a person can dig with a shovel. It feeds on rodents.

BIGHORN SHEEP KC, SQ

Also known as the "mountain sheep" or the "Rocky Mountain bighorn sheep," it is one of the most spectacular animals in the parks. Rams are 3–3.5 ft. in height, 127–316 lbs., and with a horn spread of 33 in. (the horns curve up and back over ears); ewes are 4.25–5.25 ft. in height and weigh 74–200 lbs. Color varies from dark brown to pale tan; generally the belly, rump patch, back of legs, muzzle, and eye patch are white. The bighorn's diet is mostly grasses, sedges, and woody plants, and its habitat is alpine meadows and foothills near rocky cliffs.

BLACK BEAR KC, LV, RW, SQ, YO

The black bear may be a brownish or cinnamon color, but it can easily be distinguished from the grizzly and brown bears by its straight-profiled face, rather than the dished face of the others, and by its comparatively smaller size (3 ft. at the shoulder, 4.5–6.25 ft. long, 203–595 lbs.) and humpless shoulders. The black bear feeds on grasses, buds, leaves, berries, nuts, bark, insects, rodents, the fawns of deer and elk, and fish, particularly salmon; a scrounger by nature, it will forage near campsites. This is a powerful and potentially dangerous animal despite its clownlike antics; although primarily nocturnal, it is sometimes seen during the day, sometimes "galloping" as fast as 30 miles an hour.

BOBCAT KC, LV, RW, SQ, YO

The bobcat is North America's most common wild cat; because it is nocturnal and secretive, it is seldom seen. It is tawny in color, with indistinct black spots, a pale or white belly, and a short, stubby tail with 2 or 3 black bars. It weighs 14–68 lbs. and measures 2.3–4 ft. long; the males are larger than the females. In the late winter, the male may be heard yowling at night, much like a domesticated cat. Kits are born in a den, usually in thickets or under rocks and logs. The bobcat feeds on rodents and especially ground-nesting birds.

BRUSH RABBIT
CI, KC, RW, SQ, YO

A small reddish-brown animal mottled with black, the brush rabbit measures 11.5–14.75 in., has short 2.5-in. ears, and a .75–1.75-in. tail. Primarily nocturnal, it nests in thick brushy areas. The brush rabbit's favorite food is clover, but it eats grass and various berries as well as woody vegetation in the winter.

CALIFORNIA SEA LION CI, RW

The "trained seal" of the circus might be found cavorting much the same way as the sea lion in the waters

along Redwood's coast and particularly around the Channel Islands, tossing objects in the air and catching them on its nose, and generally clowning and showing off. The male sea lion weighs up to 660 lbs. and measures 6.5–8.5 ft.; the female is 5–6.5 ft. in length and weighs 100–220 lbs. Although sea lions appear off the shores of all Pacific coast national parks, only Channel Islands has a resident population. An extremely intelligent animal, the sea lion enlisted for a year's training for the circus could have a 12-year show biz career. It feeds on squid, octopus, abalone, and other types of fish, which it usually hunts at night.

COYOTE
KC, LV, RW, SQ, YO

The coyote is the smallest species of wild dog; although resembling a domestic dog, it is often mistaken for a wolf. The coyote is seen fairly regularly in the western parks: its evening "howl" has made it legendary. It weights about 75 lbs., stands about 2 ft. at the shoulder, and is 3.5–4 ft. long, including a tail of 12–15 in. Its fur is brownish- to reddish-gray—at the lower altitudes more tan and red, at the higher altitudes more gray and black. The coyote has a varied diet

of deer, elk, rabbit, rodents, snakes, birds, and insects. A typical den is a wide-mouthed earthen tunnel, 5–30 ft. long, which may be the former residence of a fox or badger.

DEER MOUSE
CI, KC, LV, SQ, YO

There are about 100 species of rats or mice in North America, and probably the most common in the Southwest is the deer mouse. A grayish to reddish-brown mouse about 5–8.75 in. long, including a 2–5-in. tail, it feeds on seeds, nuts, small fruits, berries, and insects. It usually burrows in the ground, though some may nest in raised areas or have refuge burrows.

FISHER
KC, LV, SQ, YO

The fisher closely resembles but is larger than both the marten and the mink. Its long, thin body is dark brown with a broad grayish head and a bushy tail. The male may measure up to 40 in. and weigh 18 lbs.; the female is smaller. It preys mostly on snowshoe hares, porcupines, squirrels, and mice. Fishers tolerate one another only during the mating season; for the most part they are loners and thus are rarely seen. Their fur is considered valuable, and for this reason the population has dropped in recent years.

GRAY FOX
KC, LV, RW, SQ, YO

Of the six species of foxes in North America, the gray fox is the most commonly found in national parks; yet, being nocturnal, it is seldom seen. It is gray, with a black stripe running down the top of its tail, stands 14–15 in. at the shoulder, and is 3–4 ft. long, including a 9–17-in. tail. The gray fox feeds on rabbits and rodents that happen by its lair and, in summer, on fruit and berries.

GRAY WHALE
CI, RW

Seeing whales along California's coast is mostly a chance occurrence, but the gray whale is almost certain to be spotted at Channel Islands and along Redwood's shores if one is patient. This is a spectacular sight, even if it is only for seconds at a time. One cannot fail to be excited at seeing only 2–3 ft. of what is actually a 60–70-ft.-long animal. The gray whale, the one most commonly spotted, journeys south to Mexican waters in the autumn and north to the open Pacific in the spring. In addition to the gray, the goose-beaked whale has been spotted from Redwood; there also have been sightings of the sperm whale and, on very rare occasions, the great blue whale.

LONG-TAILED WEASEL
KC, LV, RW, SQ, YO

Wholly carnivorous, the long-tailed weasel feeds on rats, rabbits, birds, and even other weasels when killing instincts are triggered by the smell of blood. The animal's name is derived from a 6.5-in. brown tail with a black tip. The body is brown with a white chest.

MOUNTAIN LION
KC, LV, RW, SQ, YO

Often called cougar or puma, the mountain lion is a most secretive mammal, living mostly in mountainous areas and seldom seen; it is a rather docile cat, rarely attacking humans, but its scream can be terrifying. Yellowish to tawny, with a long, black-tipped tail, it weighs up to 275 lbs. and measures 5–9 ft., including a 2–3-ft. tail. The mountain lion feeds on deer, coyote, beaver, mice, hares, raccoons, birds, and grasshoppers.

MULE DEER
KC, LV, SQ, YO

The mule deer is a fairly common species of the deer family seen in the western parks, particularly in the early morning and late evening. It is characterized by its large, mulelike ears, from which it gets its name, and white rump, although it should not be confused with the white-tailed deer—also seen in some western parks. It weighs up to 400 lbs.

and stands 3–3.5 ft. at the shoulder. The male loses its antlers in the late winter and is generally solitary in its roamings. The mule deer eats acorns, berries, cactus fruits, twigs, buds, grasses, herbs, tree bark, and mushrooms.

NORTHERN ELEPHANT SEAL CI

Not the prettiest of the seal family, this giant mammal is the largest aquatic carnivore, weighing up to 7,700 lbs. and measuring up to 21.5 ft. Both male and female are a brown or gray color above and lighter shade of either color below. In 1892, as few as 20 elephant seals had survived the massive whaling industry's search for blubber oil. Now more than 65,000 populate the shores of California from Baja to San Francisco. They feed on ratfish, hagfish, squid, small sharks, and other deep-water life, which they can hunt while submerged for 40 minutes at a depth of 200 ft.

NORTHERN FLYING SQUIRREL KC, LV, SQ, YO

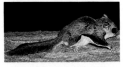

Nocturnal and seldom seen, the northern flying squirrel glides from tree to tree by spreading a loose fold of skin between its forelegs

and hind legs. It measures 10.5–14.5 in. and is brown above and white below. Like most squirrels, it eats nuts, acorns, seeds, berries, some insects, and, on occasion, vertebrate flesh.

PIKA LV, YO

Sometimes called the "whistling hare," this small furry mammal, which closely resembles the guinea pig, has a pudgy brownish body, is 6.5–8.5 in. long, has short, rounded ears, and lacks a discernible tail. It feeds mostly on green plants and burrows among rocks.

PORCUPINE KC, LV, RW, SQ, YO

Contrary to legend, porcupines *cannot* throw or "shoot" their quills, although the quills are rather loosely attached and may shake off if the porcupine threshes its tail about in self-defense. Classified as a rodent, it is the only quilled mammal. About 3 ft. long, 1 ft. high, and 35 lbs., it lives mostly in coniferous forests, but may also inhabit brushy areas of the Southwest. It survives mostly on a diet of the wood directly beneath tree bark, although it also eats buds and twigs from a variety of trees and bushes.

RACCOON KC, LV, RW, SQ, YO

The notorious black-masked raccoon raids garbage cans in national parks just as it does in the suburbs; nocturnal, the raccoon can be seen around park campgrounds. It is reddish-brown with black above and gray below, and measures 2–3 ft., including a 7.5–16-in. bushy tail with alternating black and brown rings. Its diet includes grapes, nuts, insects, rodents, turtles, frogs, and birds' eggs; dens are usually in hollow trees, caves, rock clefts, or culverts.

ROOSEVELT ELK RW

The great Roosevelt elk, taking its name from famed hunter and conservationist President Theodore Roosevelt, is found in only two of our national parks, Redwood and Olympic. It is larger than the familiar Rocky Mountain elk—much broader and more massive. A typical specimen may be 8 ft. long, with a 3.2-ft. antler spread. Primarily grazers, this species, like other elk, feeds on grasses and woody vegetation.

BIRDS

AMERICAN KESTREL
CI, KC, RW, SQ, YO

Until recently, this small falcon was known as the "sparrow hawk." The kestrel measures 9–12 in. from bill to tail and has a wingspread of 22–23 in. It has blue-gray wings and head with a buff breast and nape. The kestrel does not build a nest of its own, but lays its eggs without nesting or borrows another bird's nest in tree holes or building niches. It can be seen perched on trees and telephone poles, from which it swoops rapidly upon its grasshopper and rodent prey.

AMERICAN ROBIN
KC, LV, RW, SQ, YO

Best known of all North American birds, once called "robin," the American robin is gray-brown, with puffed-out, red or orange breast, white throat, and blackish head and tail. It measures

9–11 in. The robin feeds primarily on worms pulled from the ground. In cold weather, the nest is built of twigs and mud and lined with fine material in low, densely leafed or needled trees and bushes; in hot weather, the nest is high in maple or sycamore trees.

BARN OWL
CI, HV, RW

The barn owl is a medium-size owl measuring 14–20 in. The animal has a white heart-shaped face edged with tan; its back is light tan with pearl-gray streaks, and its front is white. The barn owl is often mistaken for the all-white snowy owl when seen in the glare of automobile headlights. It feeds on mice and rats and can be seen perched in trees.

BREWER'S BLACKBIRD
KC, LV, RW, SQ, YO

The male Brewer's blackbird has an iridescent purple-black head, glossy green-violet body, and yellow eyes; the female is a light gray-brown with brown eyes. It is 8–10 in. long and is a very social bird, mixing with other blackbirds, such as the red-winged. Its range is wide, from British Columbia to northern Baja California and east to the Great Lakes, and it feeds primarily on seeds and insects.

BROWN PELICAN
CI, RW

Though it was at one time near extinction after a history of 30 million years, the brown pelican is making a comeback now that DDT has been banned. Chemical pollutants, absorbed from a fish diet, affected the pelican's calcium metabolism, resulting in thin-shelled eggs that failed to survive incubation. This large, heavy bird with an immense dark bill is easily recognizable as it glides low over the water and then dives to catch fish. It measures 4–4.5 ft. and breeds among the Channel Islands; it can be seen along the coast at Redwood.

CALIFORNIA QUAIL
HV, KC, RW, SQ, YO

Following breeding seasons, this small, plump quail becomes quite social and can be found in large groups in public parks and gardens. Measuring 9–11 in., it has a black forward-curving plume atop a chestnut-brown head; the forehead is creamy and the throat is black, and both are edged in white; the breast is grayish-blue, the back is brown, and the belly is creamy, with brown markings.

CLARK'S NUTCRACKER
KC, LV, SQ, YO

The 12–13-in. Clark's nutcracker is light gray with dark eyes and has a long, sharply pointed bill. Its wings are black, with a patch of white at the trailing edge. It can be found near camp and picnic sites, where it begs or steals food scraps.

CORMORANT
CI, RW

Three varieties of cormorant are found along the California coast: pelagic (smallest, 25–30 in.), Brandt's, and double-crested (largest, 30–36 in.). All three are nearly iridescent black with long necks, and all fly over water; the double-crested cormorant, however, will fly over land to take shortcuts. The bird nests on coastal or offshore rocks and feeds by diving into water for its prey.

DIPPER
KC, LV, RW, SQ, YO

Almost comical as it appears to water-ski over the surface, the dipper really walks in shallow water; in deeper spots, it walks on the bottom with half-open wings while feeding on insects. Uniformly slate-gray, the dipper resembles a wren with a stubby tail and yellowish feet.

GREAT HORNED OWL
KC, RW, SQ, YO

The great horned owl is common to all of North America, from Mexico to the tree line in Canada. It is 1.5–2 ft. from tail to top of head, gray-brown above, with a fine dark-gray horizontal barring below, large yellow eyes, and ear tufts set far apart. It nests in trees, crevices, or cliffs, often in a nest once occupied by a hawk. The owl hunts rabbits, rodents, ducks, crows, and other owls, and it has been seen capturing a skunk.

HAIRY WOODPECKER
KC, LV, SQ, YO

A medium-size woodpecker, but larger than the downy, the hairy woodpecker has a white head with black crown, eyemask, and "whiskers." Male has red patch at base of crown, and black tail with white outer feathers; female has no red patch. Both are 8.5–10.5 in. from bill to tail. It feeds by pecking a hole in tree bark and, with long, flexible tongue, extracting grubs; it nests in tree cavities.

HEERMANN'S GULL
CI, RW

The Heermann's gull is a medium-size gull, mostly dark, with a red bill and a snow-white head that blends into a gray neck and back; the wings and tail are slate black and trimmed with white. Heermann's gulls follow fishing boats and steal fish from other birds, particularly the brown pelican. They measure 18–21 in. in length and do not nest in either Redwood or Channel Islands.

HERMIT THRUSH
KC, LV, SQ, YO

Some consider the hermit thrush's softly uttered *chup* to be the most beautiful bird song in North America. This little bird measures 6.5–8 in. in length, and is olive-brown with a white, spotted breast and streaked throat. It flicks its tail and

wings in a constant nervous fashion. The thrush nests on or just above the ground in a neat cup of grass, moss, and leaves, and it generally forages on the ground on seeds and insects.

HERRING GULL
RW

This large white bird with gray wings and back measures 22.5–26 in. and populates both the Atlantic and Pacific coasts. Its wing tips are black with white spots, and its bill and eyes are both yellow. A loud *ke-yah* squeals through the air as the herring gull scoops up surface fish and scavenges almost anywhere, from beaches to city dumps.

MOUNTAIN CHICKADEE KC, LV, SQ, YO

The mountain chickadee is a small, constantly active insect seeker. It is 5–5.75 in. long, gray, with a black cap, white eye stripe, and pale gray sides. The chickadee nests in a hair- or fur-lined natural cavity or woodpecker tree hole.

NENE (HAWAIIAN GOOSE) HL, HV

The nene, or Hawaiian goose, is Hawaii's state bird. At one time endangered and nearly extinct (as recently as 32 years ago, only 30 or so were known to exist), it is slowly making a comeback on the island of Hawaii, where it nests between 4,000 and 8,000 ft. on Mauna Loa, adapting to life on lava flows far removed from water. The nene (pronounced "ney-ney") is approximately 20 in. tall, is brown and gray with black markings, and resembles its ancestor, the Canada goose, with one major difference: its feet have lost their webbing. The nene is a dry-land nester, feeding on berries; because it nests on the ground, it is the prey of the mongoose, and thus its population is constantly in danger.

OREGON JUNCO
KC, LV, RW, SQ, YO

The Oregon junco is the western junco, and its coloring is distinctly different from that of its eastern and northern cousins; this bird has a black hood and a chestnut mantle, with a white chest and buff sides. It measures 5–6.25 in. and feeds on seeds and small fruits.

PEREGRINE FALCON
CI, HV

At one time in grave danger of extinction, experimental breeding is now saving this much prized falcon. It measures 15–21 in. long and has a slate-gray back with a white throat and a finely barred breast. The bird's wingspan can be as much as 40–45 in., as the peregrine dramatically swoops and dives in now familiar flights. It nests in a hollow or on inaccessible cliff ledges; in cities it will nest on the ledges of buildings, where it then feeds mainly on pigeons.

PINE SISKIN
KC, LV, RW, SQ, YO

The pine siskin is a small grayish-brown bird that, like the chickadee, will hang upside down to feed on seed pods and catkins. It measures only 4.5–5.25 in., and has a buff breast with yellow on its wings, and a notched tail.

RED-TAILED HAWK
CI, KC, LV, RW, SQ, YO

The red-tailed hawk is one of the larger birds of this genus, measuring 19–25 in. tall, with a wingspan of 48–54 in. It has a dark-brown back, a light-brown chest with a dark belly band, and a finely streaked grayish tail. Frequently seen perched atop fence posts or telephone poles, the bird will sit inordinately still for a long time, then suddenly swoop down on a squirrel, or a rabbit, or some other prey.

RUFOUS HUMMINGBIRD
KC, LV, SQ, YO

The male rufous hummingbird is identified by distinctive black throat and white

collar below; the female is greenish above, whitish below. Both are 3.5–3.75 in. from bill to tail. It nests in a feltlike cup in shrub or tree, and feeds on insects, spiders, and flower nectar.

SPOTTED SANDPIPER
KC, LV, RW, SQ, YO

The spotted sandpiper is among the smallest of the sandpipers, measuring 7.5–8 in; it can nearly always be distinguished from other sandpipers by its jerky, uneven flight patterns. In the fall it has an olive-brown back with a white breast, light eye-stripe, and white eye-ring; in the spring, its breast is marked with dark spots.

STELLER'S JAY
KC, LV, RW, SQ, YO

The Steller's jay is common to campsites and picnic areas in parks. The only western jay with a crest, it measures 12–13.5 in. and is blackish on the upper half of the body, including the head, and bluish-gray on the lower part. The eyebrow is oddly and lightly streaked, and the tail has black crossbars. It nests in a neat, twiggy bowl well-hidden in conifers and feeds on seeds, fruits, nuts, the eggs of other birds, mice, and frogs.

TUFTED PUFFIN
RW

The tufted puffin is most commonly seen sitting upright on sea cliffs along the Siberian, Alaskan, and British Columbian coastlines; fortunately, a few nests are found along the California coasts. Occasionally seen off Redwood's shores, it measures 14.5–15.5 in. and is distinguished by its stubby black body, white face, yellowish tufts beside the eyes, and a large orange-red bill. In the winter the bird undergoes some dramatic changes: the colored bill plates are molted and the bill is actually smaller and duller, the face turns dusky, and the tufts disappear. The tufted puffin nests singly or in colonies along vertical sea cliffs and feeds at sea.

AMPHIBIANS, ECHINODERMS, AND REPTILES

BLOOD STAR CI

A walk around the tide pools of Frenchy's Cove will reveal many creatures of the sea. The blood star is only one of numerous starfish; 5 stiff, slender, smooth arms lacking spines. It generally measures 20–25 cm. in diameter, is usually bright red to orange, and ranges from the intertidal zone to 2,200 ft. out. A tide pool is a collection of tidal water in rocky areas along the shore and is generally filled with life, but well-meaning collectors are rapidly diminishing these precious life zones. Collecting is forbidden at Channel Islands.

CALIFORNIA NEWT
KC, SQ, YO

The newt belongs to the salamander family and is secretive, voiceless, and lizardlike in appearance. The California newt, found in the Sierra, is about 5–7.75 in. long, rough-skinned, tan to reddish-brown above, and yellow below. During rainy seasons, it is very visible; during hot, dry times, it is mostly in the shadows and damp areas. It preys on insects, mice, snakes, and other small animals.

PACIFIC TREE FROG
KC, LV, RW, SQ, YO

Hollywood filmmakers use the high-pitched voice of the mighty 2-in.-long Pacific tree frog for outdoor night sounds, thus making it famous all over the world. Generally found close to water, its colors range from green to light tan to black, but it has the familiar black stripe through the eyes and usually a dark triangle between the eyes. It feeds primarily on insects.

SEA BAT STARFISH CI

This starfish can be found at Frenchy's Cove on Channel islands. It has 5 (sometimes 4–9) arms that are not distinctly separated, giving it an octagonal appearance. The body is fat, with a scaly surface, and its color varies from red to yellow-orange to brown. The sea bat starfish is generally found on mud bottoms and in the sand, although some are found clinging to rocks; the animal ranges from the intertidal zones to 90 ft. out. They are scavengers and congregate in large numbers.

WESTERN FENCE LIZARD
CI, KC, RW, SQ, YO

One of the most common in the West, this spiny lizard can be olive, brownish, or black, with blotches or wavy crossbars down the back. The undersurface of the legs is generally yellowish-orange, and there are blue patches on the belly. It measures 6–9.25 in. long and is seen year round.

WESTERN POND TURTLE
KC, LV, SQ

The western pond turtle, with the unlikely Latin name

of *Clemmys marmorata*, is most commonly seen basking alone in the sun. It measures 3.5–7 in. in length, and its smooth, broad, low shell is olive to dark brown, sometimes with dark flecks and lines running from the center of scutes or scales. Its home is mostly in still and slow-moving water, sometimes in brackish water, and it feeds on mollusks and other small animals as well as on aquatic plants.

WESTERN RATTLESNAKE
KC, SQ, YO

The western rattlesnake varies in color from cream to black with blotches. It has a stout body and a tapering tail, with a series of interlocking pieces of dry skin at the end commonly called a "rattle." It has vertically elliptical pupils in the eyes when in bright light. A light stripe behind the eye extends to behind the corner of the mouth. Its scales are distinctly keeled. The total length of this snake can run to 5.5 ft. in length. It is primarily found in the foothills, but has been seen at heights of 11,000 ft. The den of this snake is located on rocky outcrops and stream courses, and in northern areas it is found in rock crevices in large numbers. The western rattler eats lizards, birds, frogs, and small mammals.

WESTERN TERRESTRIAL GARTER SNAKE
KC, SQ, YO

There are four subspecies of this garter snake, so the colors and marks vary somewhat. The wandering garter has a narrow, dull yellow or brown back stripe that fades toward the tail; the light areas are marked with small dark spots that are sometimes enlarged, sometimes absent altogether, and at other times fused and mottled. It measures 1.5–3.5 ft. in length. This snake can occasionally be seen basking in the sun during the morning hours. It feeds on tadpoles, frogs, fish, mice, and small birds.

WESTERN TOAD
KC, LV, RW, SQ, YO

The western toad is a large toad, measuring up to 5 in., that is gray to green with a light-colored stripe down the middle of its back. Its warts are tinged with red and surrounded by black blotches. The western toad is quite active at night; at higher altitudes, it is active during the day as well. It feeds mostly on plants and insects but also eats fruits and vegetables. Those found around populated areas have been known to eat dog food set out for pets.

FLOWERS, SHRUBS, AND TREES

ARROW-LEAF BALSAM ROOT
KC, LV, SQ

The arrow-leaf balsam root is a nearly leafless stalk with 1 large brilliant yellow flower head growing from a cluster of silver-gray leaves. The flower is 4–5 in. in diameter. The plant grows 8–32 in. in the open. The Indians prepared medicine from these roots.

CAMAS LILY
KC, LV, SQ, YO

Sometimes the common camas lily is so prevalent that it can blanket an entire meadow in blue-violet. This star-shaped flower is generally 1.5–2.5 in. wide, the grasslike leaves 2 in. long; the plant grows to 20 in.

COLUMBIA LILY
RW, YO

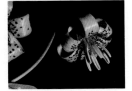

Other names for this large, mostly orange, and immensely popular western wildflower are Oregon and tiger lily. The flower itself measures 2–3 in. wide in 6 petallike segments that curve back toward the stem. The leaves are 2–4 in. in diameter; the plant grows to a height of 4 ft.

COAST REDWOOD
RW

The coast redwood is the world's tallest tree, ranging in height from an average of 200 ft. to the tallest in the park at 367.8 ft. The age of the coast redwood at maturity is 400–500 years, although the oldest recorded through annual rings is 2,200 years. It has a reddish-brown trunk and is quite large at the base, tapering only slightly; the diameter is 10–15 ft. The leaves are needlelike and uneven; cones are .5– 1.25 in. long. The genus name commemorates the Indian chief Sequoyah, or Sequoia, inventor of the Cherokee alphabet. This tree has been the source of constant controversy between conservationists and the logging industry throughout the years.

DOGWOOD
KC, RW, SQ, YO

The flower of the Pacific dogwood is larger than that of the eastern or flowering dogwood; the flower is 4–6 in. wide with 4 yellow-greenish petals split in the middle, giving an impression of 8 petals, and has petal-like leaves, all of which make up the "flower." The tree grows to a height of 50 ft. with a dense, rounded crown and horizontal branches.

FOXGLOVE
RW, YO

Spires of hanging flowers all turned to one side and all resembling little bells top tall, leafy stalks that cover the wooded and bushy slopes of the Pacific region. The Latin name is *Digitalis purpurea*; digitalis, the heart stimulant, which is quite toxic when not used properly, is derived from this plant, which is in itself poisonous to livestock. The white-pinkish flower is 1–1.5 in. in diameter, and the plant grows to a height of 7 ft.

GIANT COREOPSIS
CI, LV

This yellow-flowered member of the sunflower family resembles a small tree, with its long leafless stalks that branch at the top. It may grow to a height of 10 ft. in the southern California coastal area, especially on dunes and bluffs.

GIANT SEQUOIA
KC, SQ, YO

This rare species is among the world's oldest trees; among those felled some have been ring-measured at 3,200 years. Almost all of the giant sequoias are protected within 3 national parks —Yosemite, Kings Canyon, and Sequoia—in 4 national forests, and in several California state forests and parks. The sequoia grows to 250 ft. and has a trunk diameter of 20 ft. Its leaves are evergreen (blue-

green) needles with cones that are 1.75–3.75 in. long. Many of the virgin trees were lost in the early days of California logging.

INCENSE CEDAR
KC, LV, RW, SQ, YO

The incense cedar is a large, resinous, aromatic tree that grows to 150 ft. with a tapering, irregular, 3–5-ft. trunk, and a narrow, columnar and open, irregular crown. Its branches are flat, with wedge-shaped joints and scalelike leaves; its cones are .75–1 in. in length and are oblong, hanging from a slender, leafy stalk.

LUPINE
CI, KC, LV, RW, SQ, YO

There are several varieties of the lupine in national parks; pictured is the yellow bush lupine, a large, round, bushy plant with tall, 2–9-ft. stands of palmately compound leaves and sweet-smelling, yellow "pea flowers." The lupine was once believed to be "wolflike" in that it devoured the nutri-

ents of the soil; in fact, its name is derived from the Latin *lupus*, or wolf. Actually, the lupine prefers poor soil, from which it draws no further nutrient. The tree lupine grows rapidly, has deep roots, and is excellent for the stabilization of poor or sandy soils, especially along coastlines. Sections of the city of San Francisco, considered sandy and unstable, were once reclaimed by the tree lupine.

MONKEY FLOWER
CI, KC, LV, RW, SQ, YO

The monkey flower is a leafy plant ranging from spindly and tiny to large and bushy; it can grow to 3 ft. Its yellow, bilaterally symmetrical flowers measure .5–1.5 in. on slender stalks, and bloom from March to September.

MOUNTAIN HEMLOCK
KC, LV, RW, YO

The mountain hemlock is a 30–100-ft.-high tree with a tapering, 1–3-ft. trunk and a conical crown of slender, horizontal branches. Its needles are evergreen and are usually crowded at the end of short side twigs curved upward. The cones are 1–3

in. long and cylindrical; they go from purplish to brown in color. This hemlock provides nesting sites and seeds for birds as well as forage for sheep and goats.

OHIA LEHUA-METROSIDEROS
HL, HV

The most common tree in Hawaii, the ohia lehua-metrosideros consists of a swarm of hybrids; beautiful flowers, mostly red and yellow, appear throughout the year. It grows from near sea level to about 8,200 ft. On dry lava it will grow 10 ft. tall, but in wetter areas it can grow 20–30 ft. tall. The wood is hard and dark red and was used by ancient Hawaiians for spears, mallets, and idols. Today it is used for the flooring and keel blocks of ships.

OXALIS
LV, RW

The oxalis, or redwood sorrel, is a low plant that grows in patches with 3 heart-shaped leaflets and a funnel-shaped, white or rose-pink

flower at the end of each stalk. The flowers are .5–.75 in. wide with 5 petals, sometimes with blue veins. The plant grows to 7 in. and frequently forms a solid carpet beneath the redwoods.

PONDEROSA PINE
KC, LV, SQ, YO

The most widely distributed and common pine in North America, the ponderosa pine is a large evergreen with a broad, open, conical crown of spreading branches. It is 60–130 ft. high and 2.5–4 ft. in diameter, with stiff dark-green needles and 2–6-in. cones. It is the most commercially valuable western pine.

PUKIAWE-STYPHELIA
HL, HV

Pukiawe-styphelia is an abundant shrub with white, pink, red, or mahogany brown berries that occurs throughout both parks. In Hawaii Volcanoes National Park they are found mostly in the open

shrubland along the Mauna Loa Road; at Haleakala, in the crater and along the upper slopes.

QUAKING ASPEN
KC, LV, SQ, YO

The most widely distributed tree in North America, the quaking aspen grows to a height of 80–100 ft. Its leaves are 1.25–3 in. long and nearly round, shiny green above, dull green beneath, and turn golden-yellow in autumn before dropping; the "quaking" comes from leaves that tremble in the slightest breeze. The bark is the favorite of beaver and rabbits; deer, elk, moose, sheep, and goats feed on twigs and foliage.

REDBUD TREE
KC, SQ, YO

The redbud tree is a large shrub or small tree that has a rounded crown of many spreading branches and purplish-pink flowers. It grows to 16 ft. and has a trunk diameter of only 4 in. The Indians once made bows from its wood.

SILVERSWORD
HL, HV

One of the national parks' most unusual plants, the silversword is found only in the two volcanic parks of Hawaii. A lustrous silvery down covering thick, daggerlike leaves gives the plant its name. Surprisingly, though it resembles the yucca of the lily family, it belongs to the Compositae family, along with sunflowers, asters, and chrysanthemums. After a growth of 7–20 years, the plant flowers once and then dies.

SNOW PLANT
KC, LV, SQ, YO

A stout, fleshy plant with bright red, corolla bell-shaped flowers, the snow plant grows to a height of 24 in. and flowers from April to July, poking its head through the forest floor just as the snows begin to recede.

SUGAR PINE
KC, LV, SQ, YO

Often called the "king of the pines," the sugar pine is one of the most beautiful of the tall, majestic trees of California. It is a large, tall, 100–160-ft. tree with a straight 3–6-ft.-diameter trunk and horizontal branches that form a high conical crown. The cones measure 11–18 in. in length and have been recorded at 21 in.; they are a shiny, light brown in color. The sugar pine is a major lumber species and played an important role in the building of early California.

WESTERN AZALEA
KC, RW, SQ, YO

This shrub grows from southern California to southwestern Oregon and is generally found in open areas near the coast. The flowers—

April to August—are quite fragrant and range in color from white to deep pink. It will grow to a height of 17 in.; the flowers are about 2.5 in. in diameter; and the leaves are 1.25–3.5 in. in length.

PHOTO CREDITS

Page 10: © Roy Murphy
13: © Hara
16, 18–19: © Bob Evans/
Peter Arnold, Inc.
20: © Robert Gildart
21, both: © Bob Evans/Peter
Arnold, Inc.
**22, 23, clockwise from
bottom left:** © Howard
Hall/Tom Stack & As-
soc.; © Howard Hall/
Tom Stack & Assoc.;
© Bob Evans/Peter Ar-
nold, Inc.; © F. Gohier/
Photo Researchers, Inc.
26–27: © Frans Lanting
28: © David Muench
31, 35: Bishop Museum
37: © David Muench
38: © Ed Cooper
40–41: © David Muench
43, 46–47: © Ed Cooper
49: © Werner Stoy/Camera
Hawaii, Inc.
50: © Laura Bremner
50–51, 55: © Ed Cooper
56: © David Muench
63, 64: © Tai Sing Loo/
Bishop Museum
65: © Ed Cooper
67: © David Muench
69: © Ed Cooper
70-71: © Laura Bremner
74: © Keith H. Murakami/
Tom Stack & Assoc.
77: © Ed Cooper
82–83: © Camera Hawaii, Inc.
86: © Werner Stoy/Camera

Hawaii, Inc.
89: © Camera Hawaii, Inc.
90: © Jeff Gnass
93: © Ed Cooper
97: Sequoia and Kings Canyon National Parks
101: © D.C. Lowe
102–103: © David Muench
107: © Jeff Gnass
111: © Galen Rowell
112, both: © D.C. Lowe
115: © Manuel Rodriguez
116: © David Muench
122, 123: Lassen Volcanic
National Park
125: © Pat O'Hara
127: © Holiday Films
130: © Warren Garst/Tom
Stack & Assoc.
133: © Bill Perry
134–135: © Jeff Gnass
137: © David Muench
138: © Jeff Gnass
140, 143: © David Muench
147, 149: Redwood National
Park
150: © Rick McIntyre
153: © Stephen Trimble
154–155, left to right:
© Gary Milburn/Tom
Stack & Assoc.; © David
Muench; © John
Richardson
158–159: © David Muench
163: © Ed Cooper
164: © David Muench
168–169: © Manuel
Rodriguez

171, 174–175: Sequoia and
Kings Canyon N. P.
177: © David Muench
178: © Roy Murphy
**181, clockwise from top
left:** © Manuel
Rodriguez; © Galen
Rowell; © Rod Planck/
Tom Stack & Assoc.;
© John Gerlach/Tom
Stack & Assoc.
184–185: © Jeff Gnass
187, 191: © David Muench
193: © Jeff Gnass
195: © David Muench
196: © Galen Rowell
199: © J. Mark Blackburn/
International Stock Photo
203: Yosemite National Park
207: © David Sumner
208–209, 211, 212: © Ed
Cooper
**214, 215, counterclock-
wise from top left:**
© Ed Cooper; © John
Gerlach/Tom Stack &
Assoc.; © David
Muench; © Holiday
Films; © Tom J. Ulrich/
Click/Chicago
217: © Manuel Rodriguez
219: © Galen Rowell
221: © Manuel Rodriguez
223: © D.C. Lowe
227: © Donna Dannen
228–229: © D.C. Lowe
230: © Ed Cooper
233: © Galen Rowell

Appendix of Animals and Plants Photo Credits

236, col. 1, top: © E.P.I.
Nancy Adams/Tom Stack &
Assoc., **bottom:** © Roy
Murphy; **col. 2, top:** © G.C.
Kelley/Tom Stack & Assoc.,
bottom: © Roy Murphy; **col.
3:** © Roy Murphy.
237, col. 1, top: © Robert

McKenzie/Tom Stack &
Assoc., **bottom:** © Brian
Parker/Tom Stack & Assoc.;
col. 2: © Roy Murphy; **col. 3,
top:** © Joe McDonald/Tom
Stack & Assoc., **bottom:**
© Gary Milburn/Tom Stack
& Assoc.

238, col. 1, top: © Bob
McKeever/Tom Stack &
Assoc., **bottom:** © Steve
Martin/Tom Stack & Assoc.;
col. 2: © Larry R. Ditto/Tom
Stack & Assoc.; **col. 3, top:**
© Roy Murphy, **bottom:**
© Rod Planck/Tom Stack

239, col. 1, top: © Phil & Loretta Hermann/Tom Stack & Assoc., bottom: © Larry Dech/Tom Stack & Assoc.; col. 2, top: © C. Summers/Tom Stack & Assoc., bottom: © William R. Eastman III/Tom Stack & Assoc.; col. 3, top: © Roy Murphy, bottom: © Phil & Loretta Hermann/Tom Stack & Assoc.
240, col. 1, top: © Christopher Crowley/Tom Stack & Assoc., bottom: © Stephen Trimble; col. 2, top: © Don & Pat Valenti/Tom Stack & Assoc., bottom: © Anthony Mercieca/Tom Stack & Assoc.; col. 3: © John Gerlach/Tom Stack & Assoc.
241, col. 1, top: © Len Rue, Jr./Tom Stack & Assoc., bottom: © G.C. Kelley/Tom Stack & Assoc.; col. 2, top: © Roy Murphy, bottom: © C. Summers/Tom Stack & Assoc.; col. 3, top: © Stephen Trimble, bottom: © Rod Planck/Tom Stack
242, col. 1, top: © John Gerlach/Tom Stack & Assoc., bottom: © Larry Ditto/Tom

Stack & Assoc.; col. 2, top: © Alan D. Briere/Tom Stack & Assoc., bottom: © Anthony Mercieca/Tom Stack & Assoc.; col. 3, top: © Gary Randall/Tom Stack & Assoc., bottom: © Anthony Mercieca/Tom Stack & Assoc.
243, col. 1, top: © Brian Parker/Tom Stack & Assoc., bottom: © John Shaw/Tom Stack & Assoc.; col. 2, top: © C. Summers/Tom Stack & Assoc.; bottom: © Alan G. Nelson/Tom Stack & Assoc.; col. 3, top: © Prof. R.C. Simpson/Tom Stack & Assoc., bottom: © Anthony Mercieca/Tom Stack & Assoc.
244: © Kevin Schafer/Tom Stack & Assoc.
245, col. 1, top: © Tom Stack/Tom Stack & Assoc., bottom: © Roy Murphy; col. 2, top: © Jim Yuskavitch/Tom Stack & Assoc., bottom: © David McCray/Tom Stack & Assoc.; col. 3, top: © John Gerlach/Tom Stack & Assoc., bottom: © Lysbeth Corsi/Tom Stack & Assoc.
246, col. 1: © Rick McIntyre/

Tom Stack & Assoc.; col. 2, top: © Jim Yuskavitch/Tom Stack & Assoc., bottom: © John Gerlach/Tom Stack & Assoc.
247, col. 1, top: © Jeff Gnass, center: © John Gerlach/Tom Stack & Assoc., bottom: © Jeff Gnass; col. 2: © Roy Murphy; col. 3, top: © David Lavender, bottom: © Jeff Gnass.
248, col. 1, top: © Russ Finley, bottom: © David Lavender; col. 2, top: © Roy Murphy, bottom: © Ed Cooper; col. 3, top: © John Gerlach/Tom Stack & Assoc., bottom: © Jeff Gnass.
249, col. 1, top: © Camera Hawaii, Inc., bottom: © Manuel Rodriguez; col. 2, top: © Stephen Trimble, bottom: © Ed Cooper; col. 3, top: © Tom Stack/Tom Stack & Assoc., bottom: © Ed Cooper.
250, col. 1, top: © Ed Cooper, bottom: © Roy Murphy; col. 2, top: © Roy Murphy, bottom: © Ed Cooper.

INDEX   *Numbers in italics indicate illustrations.*

acid rain, 194
acorns, Indians and, 170,
    202
adaptation, plant, 73
Agate Beach (Redwood),
    163
Age of Dinosaurs, 152, 180
ahinahina. See silversword
ahupuaa (land districts), 34
Ahwahnee, 202, 204
Ahwahneechee Indians, 202,
    204
Ahwahneechee village
    (model), 217
Ahwahnee Hotel (Yosemite),
    222
Ahwahnee Meadow (Yose-
    mite), 222
akala, 44
Alanui Kahiko Overlook
    (Hawaii), 78
alder, 157
algae, 130, 183
Almanor, Lake (Lassen), 123
Alta Plateau (Sequoia), 188
Alta Trail (Sequoia), 188
altitude, effects of, 179, 193,
    213, 216
amakihi, 48, 75
Amblu Kai. *See* Lassen Peak
American Association for
    the Advancement of
    Science, 175-76
Anacapa Island (Channel
    Islands), 17, 24
anemone, sea, 21
    strawberry, *22*
Angel Wings (Sequoia), 193
animals, exotic, 85
    vs. native animals, 36, 48,
        62, 75
    vs. native plants, 35, 36,
        44, 48
apapane, *45*, 48, 75, 85
Arch Point Loop Trail
    (Channel Islands), 25
Arch Rock (Channel Islands),
    13
Arguello, Don Luis, 124
art, Hawaiian, 62, 78, 80
artifacts, Indian, 96

ash, mountain, 132
aspen, quaking, *249*
Atsugewi Indians, 122-23,
    124
azalea, 110, 154
    western, 215
Azalea Campground (Kings
    Canyon), 113
Azalea Trail (Kings Canyon),
    108, 110

badger, *236*
    California, 216
Badger Flat (Lassen), 133,
    136
Badger Pass Ski Area (Yose-
    mite), 222
Bald Hills Road (Redwood),
    160, 162
balsam root, arrow-leaf,
    138, 247
bamboo, *46-47*
Bathtub Lake (Lassen), 139
beach trips, 163
Bear Lakes (Lassen), 132
bear, black, *130,* 130, 143,
    216, 236
beaver, 143
Big Arroyo (Sequoia), 193
Big Basin Redwoods State
    Park, 148
bighorn sheep, 216, *236*
Big Oak Flat Road (Yose-
    mite), 213, 226
Bird Park Trail (Hawaii), 80,
    85
birdwatching, 155, 157, 162,
    163
blackberries, 155
blackbird, Brewer's. *240*
Black Kaweah (Sequoia),
    193
Black Rock Desert (Nevada),
    135
bleeding hearts, 154
blood star, *245*
bluebird, mountain, 216
Boat Creek Trail (Redwood),
    163
bobcat, *155,* 216, *236,* 236-
    37

Boiling Springs Lake (Las-
    sen), 128, 139
Boiling Springs Lake Trail
    (Lassen), 133, 139
Bottomless Pit (Haleakala),
    53
Boy Scout Tree (Redwood),
    156
Boy Scout Tree Trail (Red-
    wood), 156
Brewer, Mount (Kings Can-
    yon), 98
Brewer, William H., 98, 99
Bridalveil Creek (Yosemite),
    222
Bridalveil Fall (Yosemite),
    211, 218, 222, 225,
    228-29
Bridalveil Fall Trail (Yose-
    mite), 225
Bridalveil Meadow (Yose-
    mite), 218
brodiaea, 215
Broken Mountain. *See* Lassen
    Peak
Brokeoff Mountain (Lassen),
    126, 131, 139
Bubbs Creek (Kings Can-
    yon), 96, 98, 99, 108,
    110, 113, 114
Bubbs Creek Canyon (Kings
    Canyon), 110
buckeye, California, 180,
    213
Bullfrog Lake (Kings Can-
    yon), *112*
Bumpass Hell (Lassen), *127,*
    128
Bumpass Hell Trail (Lassen),
    131, 132, 138
Butte Lake (Lassen), 133,
    138
Butte Lake Campground, 136
butterfly, monarch, *215*
Byron Ledge Trail (Hawaii),
    80

Cabrilho, Joao Rodrigues
    16-17, 146
calderas, 68, 72, 126
caliche, 24-25

253

California Current, 152
California State Geological Survey, 98, 173
Cameron Meadows (Lassen), 133
camping:
  dangers, 24
  environment and, 113, 114, 194
Canyon View Nature Trail (Channel Islands), 25
carbon dioxide, 68, *69*
cardinal, 85
Carter, Jimmy, 149
Cascade Creek (Yosemite), 211
cataracts, 104-105
Cathedral Lake (Yosemite), 231
Cathedral Peak (Yosemite), 210, *227,* 230
Cathedral Range (Yosemite), 231
Cathedral Rocks (Yosemite), 218
Cathedral Spires (Yosemite), 218
cedar, incense, 48, 180, 214, 222, 226, *248*
Cedar Grove (Kings Canyon), 96, 99, 100, 105-106, 108
Central Valley (Kings Canyon), 98
Chain of Craters Road (Hawaii), 76, 78, 79, 80, 88
Channel Islands National Park, 10-27
  general information, 12-13
  geology, 17
  history, 16-17
  map, *14-15*
  natural history, 20-21
  sites, trails, and trips, 24-25
Chaos Crags (Lassen), 126, 129, 135, 136
Chaos Jumbles (Lassen), 124, 135, 136
chaparral, 167, 213
checkermallow, *21*
chickadee, mountain, 216, *242*
chickaree, 130, 155, 182, 216

Chihuahua Mine (Sequoia), 188
Chilula Indians, 146
Chimney Log (Sequoia), 188
chinquapin, 192, 222
Chinquapin intersection (Yosemite), 222, 226
chipmunk, 130, 217
chuck-ah, 202
chuckar, 45
Chumash Indians, 16
Cinder Cone (Lassen), 124, 128, 129, *133,* 136, 138-39
cinder cones, 39, *40-41,* 48, *65,* 87
Cinder Cone Trail (Lassen), 133, 138
Circle Meadow (Sequoia), 187, 188
cirques, 104, 193, 210, 232
Clark, Galen, 199, 202, 226
Clark, Mount, 205
Clark Range (Yosemite), 222
Clouds Rest (Yosemite), 227
Clouds Rest Trail (Yosemite), 224
Club, Mount, 231, 232
Cluster Lakes (Lassen), 132
Clynne, Michael, 125
Coastal Trail (Redwood), 160, 163
Coast Range, 108, 112
Coast Range orogeny, 151
coconut, 88
Conrad, Mount, 126
Congress Trail (Sequoia), 187, 188
Congress, Mount, 205, 230, 231
conservationists vs. colonists (Sequoia), 175-76
Cook, Captain James, 35, 62
Copper Creek (Kings Canyon), 105
Copper Creek Trail (Kings Canyon), 108, 110
Coprosma, 44
coreopsis, giant yellow, 13, 21, *26-27, 248*
cormorant, 21, *241*
Cotter, Dick, 98-99
coyote, 217, *237*
Crandell, Dwight, 136
Crane Flat (Yosemite), 226, 227

Crater Butte (Lassen), 128
Crater Rim Road (Hawaii), 79, 82, 84, 85
Crater Rim Trail (Hawaii), 80, 87
Crescent Beach (Redwood), 163
Crescent Beach Overlook (Redwood), 160
Crescent City, California, 147, 157, 163
Crescent Creek (Sequoia), 187, 188
Crescent Meadow (Sequoia), 172, *187,* 188, 192
Crespi, Fray Juan, 146
Crocker Point (Yosemite), 224
cryptomeria, 48
Crystal Lake (Lassen), 139
Crystal Lake Trail (Sequoia), 188, 190-91
culture, Indian, 170-71, 202, 204
Curry Village (Yosemite), 220, 225
cypress, 183

Damnation Creek (Redwood), 160
Damnation Creek Trail (Redwood), 157
Dana, Mount, 205, 230
Dead Giant (Kings Canyon), 112
Dead Giant Loop Trail, 108-109, 112
deer, 143, 232
  black-tailed, 130
  mule, 130, 216, *238*
Deer Cove Creek (Kings Canyon), 105
Del Norte Coast Redwoods State Park, 157, *158-59,* 160, 162
deodar, 48
Dersch Meadows (Lassen), 134
Devastation Trail (Hawaii), 80, 84
Devil's Kitchen (Lassen), 128, 133, 138
Dewey Point (Yosemite), 224
Diller, Mount, 126
dipper, 216, *241*
Discovery View Trail (Yosemite), 222

Dittmar Volcano (Lassen), 125
Dog Lake Trail (Yosemite), 225, 230
dogwood, 214, *230, 247*
domes, 105
Don Cecil Trail (Kings Canyon), 106, 108
Douglas Memorial Bridge (Redwood), 160
Dragon Peak (Kings Canyon), 114
Drakesbad (Lassen), 136, 139
duck, wood, 130

Eagle Lake Trail (Sequoia), 188, 191, 192
earthquakes, 83, 88
East Anacapa Island (Channel Islands), *13,* 25
Echo Lake (Lassen), 132
ecology, 42, 183, 194
El Capitan (Yosemite), *196,* 210, 211, 218, 222, 225
elepaio, 75, 85
Elephant Seal Cove Trail (Channel Islands), 25
Elizabeth Lake (Yosemite), 231
elk, Roosevelt, *143,* 155, 162, 163, *239*
Ella Falls (Kings Canyon), 109, 112-13
Ellis, William, 62, 64, 68
Ellsworth Trail (Redwood), 156
El Portal (Yosemite), 205, 213
Emerald Lake (Lassen), 131
endangered species, 17, 21, 24, 31, 36, 42, 54, 75, *143. See also names*
Enderts Beach Trail (Redwood), 160, 163
environmental issues, 35, 36, 54, 62, 100, 113, 114, 124, 128, 149, 174, 194, 204
erosion, *38,* 104-105, 125, 126, 129, 151, 193-94, 205, 206-207, 210, 211
  volcanoes and, 38, 39
  water and, 76, 78, 104-105, 151, 207, 210, 211

"erratics," 210
eucalyptus, 48
European explorers, 16-17
evergreens, 179
evolution, 42, 45, 72
Evolution Valley (Kings Canyon), 100
exfoliation, 210, 222
exploitation, 17, 148
extinction, 62, 75

Fairfield Peak (Lassen), 128
Fairview Dome (Yosemite), 230
falcon, peregrine, *243*
False Klamath Cove (Redwood), 157, 160, 163
Farewell Gap (Sequoia), 191
farming, 24, 54
faulting, 17
Fern Canyon Trail (Redwood), 162
Fern Falls (Redwood), 156
ferns, 52, *55,* 73, 85, 88, 162
Fin Dome (Kings Canyon), 114
fir, 130, 132, 134, 154, 155, 162, 180, 183, 193, 214, 232
fire, 183, 186, 287
Fire Mountain (Lassen), 124
fisher, *237*
fishing, 130, 155, 192, 232
fissure vents, 87
flicker, 216
Flint Rock Head Overlook (Redwood), 160
Florence, Mount, 232
folding, 17
Footprints Trail (Hawaii), 62, 87-88
Forest Lake (Lassen), 132
forest, mixed-conifer, 214
Forsyth Pass (Yosemite), 232
fossils, 24-25
Four Mile Trail (Yosemite), 218, 223
fox, *20,* 21, 217, *238*
foxglove, *247*
fractures, *69,* 77
Franciscan Formation (Redwood), 150
Franklin Lake Trail (Sequoia), 191
freeze-thaw action, 210

Frémont, John Charles, 98
Freshwater Lagoon (Redwood), 151
frog, Pacific tree, *245*
Frypan Meadow (Kings Canyon), 106, 108
fuchsia, 74
Fuji, Mount, 125

garter snake, *246*
gases, 77
General Grant Grove, 98, 100, 105, *107,* 108-109, 110, 112, 113
General Grant National Park, 100, 176
geranium, 44, 86
Giant Forest (Sequoia), 99, *164,* 168-69, 172, 180, 183, *184-85,* 186, *187,* 188, 190, 193
  Administration Building, *174-75*
Gibbs, Mount, 230
ginger, 74
glacial action, 151, 192, 207, 210, 211, 222, 232
  and erosion, 104-105
Glacier Point (Yosemite), 218, 222, 223, 225, 226
goat, wild, 35, 44, 55
Goddard, Mount, 99
gold, 148, 156, 172, 204, 206
Gold Bluffs Beach, *143,* 148, 163
goldenrod, 215
goose:
  Canada, 45, 130
  Hawaiian (nene), 31, 45, 53, *74,* 75, *242*
granite, 104, 105, 205-207, 210, 211
Granite Pass (Kings Canyon), 99
grazing, 24, 31, 35, 36, 44, 100, 173-74
Great Western Divide, 98, 167, 180
Gregg, Dr. Josiah, 148
gull, 21, *242*
gypsum, 82

Halape Trail (Hawaii), 79, 88
Haleakala Crater (Haleakala), *35, 37,* 38-39, *43,* 48, 52, 64

Haleakala National Park,
28-55
general information,
30-31
geology, 36-39
history, 34-36
map, *32-33*
natural history, 42, 44-45
sites, trails, and trips, 48-54
Halemaumau Crater (Hawaii), 56, *82-83*, 84, 87
Halemaumau Trail (Hawaii),
80, 87
Halemauu Trail (Haleakala),
48, 50, 52, 53
Half Dome (Yosemite), 210,
220, *221*, 223, 224, 227,
232
Halona Kahakai (Hawaii),
78
Hana Road (Haleakala), *50-51*, 54
Happy Isles (Yosemite), 220,
223, 224
Harrison, Benjamin, 176
Hat Lake (Lassen), 134
Hawaiian Planting Area (Haleakala), 51, 54
Hawaiian Volcano Observatory (Hawaii), 64, 72,
83
Hawaii Volcanoes National
Park, 56-89
general information, 58-59
geology, 65-72
history, 59, 62-64
map, *60-61*
natural history, 72-75
sites, trails, and trips, 76,
78-88
trail map, *81*
hawk, red-tailed, *243*
Hazelwood Nature Trail (Sequoia), 186, 188
Heceta, Bruno de, 146
heiaus, 62. 76
Helen, Lake (Lassen), 131
hemlock, 130, 134, 139, 154,
216, 232, *248*
Hetch Hetchy, 226
Hidden Beach (Redwood),
160
High Sierra Camps Loop Trail
(Yosemite), 225, 231,
232

High Sierra Trail (Sequoia),
188, 192
Hiiaka Crater (Hawaii), 79
hiking, 52, 54, 80, 81, 86,
87, 88, 105-106, 108,
131, 135-36, 160, 162,
190, 192, 194, 220, 223,
224, 225, 231
Hilina Pali (Hawaii), 79, 88
Hilo (Hawaii), 76
Hiouchi Trail (Redwood),156
Hobbs Wall Trail (Redwood),
157, 162
Hockett, John Benjamin, 173
Hoffman, Mount, 231, 232
Holei Pali Overlook (Hawaii),
78
Holei Sea Arch (Hawaii), 76
holei tree, 85
honeycreepers, 45
horns, 104
horse, 194
Horseshoe Lake, 132, 133,
136
Horsetail Falls (Yosemite),
233
Hosmer Grove (Haleakala),
48, 50
Hotel Creek Trail (Kings Canyon), 105, 106, 108
Hot Rock (Lassen), 122, 135
hot-spot theory, 66
House of the Sun Visitor Center (Haleakala), 48, 49
Howland Hill Road (Redwood), *147*, 156, 157
huckleberry, 154, 156, 162
Huckleberry Meadow (Sequoia), 186, 188
Humboldt coast, 146, 148
Humboldt Trail (Lassen),
135
Hume Lake (Sequoia), 108,
112
hummingbird, *243*
hydrogen sulfide, 82

ice ages, 36. *See also* glacial
action
ice plant, 21
iiwi, 45, 48, 75, 85
Illilouette Fall (Yosemite),
223
Indian Cultural Museum
(Yosemite), 217

Indians. *See* Native Americans
industry, 100
intrusions, 66, 68
iris, *155*
iron, 151
ironwood tree, 21
Ishi (Yana Indian), 122

Jagger, Thomas, 64
jay, 216, *243*
Jedediah Smith Redwoods
State Park, 146, 156-57
John Muir Trail, 108, 110,
111, 114, 192, 220, 224,
230, 231, 232
Johnson, Lyndon B., 149
joints, 210
junco, *242*
juniper, 48, 193
Juniper Lake (Lassen),133,
136

ka-cha-vee, 202
Kaena Point (Hawaii), 67
Kaimu Black Sands Beach
(Hawaii), 76
Kalahaku Overlook (Haleakala), 48-49
Kalapana (Hawaii), 64, 76
Kamehameha, Chief, 62, 88
Kamoamoa (Hawaii), 76
Kau Desert (Hawaii), 62,
79, 85, 88
Kaupo Trail (Haleakala), 51,
52, 54
Kaweah River and Canyon
(Sequoia), 167, 170,
180, 190, *191*, 194
Keaau (Hawaii), 76
Ke Ala Kahiko Trail (Hawaii),
80
Ke ala Komo (Hawaii), 78, 88
Keanoe Valley (Haleakala),
48
Keanae Peninsula (Haleakala), *50-51*
Keanakakoi Crater (Hawaii),
84
Kearsarge Pass (Kings Canyon), 96, 98
kelp fish, *22*
Kent, William, 148
Keoua, Chief, 62, 88
Kern-Kaweah Divide (Sequoia), 193

Kerr Ranch Schist, 151
kestrel, *240*
Kilauea Iki (Hawaii), 80, 84, 87, *99*
Kilauea Volcano, 36, 53, *57,* 59, 62, 64, 66, 68, 69, 72, 74, 76, 77, 78, 79, 80, 82, 83, 84, 85, 87, 88
King, Clarence, 98-99, 173-74
Kings Canyon, *90,* 97
Kings Canyon National Park, 90-115
  general information, 92-93, 96
  geology, 101, 104-105
  map, *94-95*
  history, 96-100
  sites, trails, and trips, 105-106, 108-10, 112-14
  trail map, *109*
Kings Creek (Lassen), *137*
Kings Creek Falls Trail (Lassen), 132
Kings Creek Meadow (Lassen), *137*
Kings River (Kings Canyon), *90,* 93, 96, 97, 98, 99, 100, 104, 105, 106, 110, 113, 114
Kipahulu (Haleakala), 44, *45, 46-47,* 51, 54
kipuka, 78
Kipuka Ki (Hawaii), 85
Kipuka Nene (Hawaii), 79, 88
Klamath Cove (Redwood), 160
Klamath River, 147, 151
koa, acacia, 73, 82, 83, 85
koali, 85
Kokoolau Crater (Hawaii), 79
kukui, 78, 85
kupaoa, 44

Lady Bird Johnson Grove (Redwood), 160, 162
Lae Apuki (Hawaii), 76
Langley, Mount, 173, 195
La Perouse, Jean François Galoup de, 39
larkspur, 216
Lassen Peak, 64, 116, 119, *123,* 124, *125,* 126, 128, 131, *134-35,* 139, 179

Lassen Peak Trail (Lassen), 131, 132, 139
Lassen, Peter, 124
Lassen Volcanic National Park, 116-39
  general information, 118-19
  geology, 125-29
  history, 119, 122-24
  map, *120-21*
  natural history, 129-30
  sites, trails, and trips, 131-36, 138-39
Last Chance Trail (Redwood), 157
Laughing Waters Cascades (Kings Canyon), 113
lava, *38,* 53, 66, *67,* 68-72, *70-71,* 74, 76, 84, 85, 87, 88, *89,* 125, 126
  aa, 53, 68, 72, 78, 86, 87
  caves, 72
  domes, 126
  flows, 78
  formations, *31, 116*
  molten, as energy, 84
  pahoehoe, 53, 69, 78, 79, 86, 87
  tubes, 72, 87
LeConte, Joseph, 220
Leleiwi Overlook (Haleakala), 48
Lembert Dome, 225, 230
Lewis Creek Trail (Kings Canyon), 106, 108
lichens, 105
Lieffer Trail (Redwood), 156
lilies, 129, 132, 192, 216, *247*
Lincoln, Abraham, 204
Little Bald Hills Trail (Redwood), 156-57
Little Crystal Lake (Sequoia), 191
Little Willow Lake (Lassen), 133
Little Yosemite Valley (Yosemite), 220, 224
lizard, western fence, *246*
lobelia, woody, 45
logging, 99, 124, 148, *149,* 157
Log Meadow Loop Trail (Sequoia), 186-87, 188
Loihi Volcano, 65

Lone Pine Creek (Sequoia), *178*
Long Meadow (Yosemite), 232
Lookout Peak (Kings Canyon), 106, 108
Loomis, B. E., 119, 126
Lost Arrow (Yosemite), *219*
Lost Man Creek Trail, 160
Lua Manu Crater (Hawaii), 79
lupine, 129, 155, 192, 213, 217, *248*
Lyell, Mount, 205

Maalaea Bay (Haleakala), *43*
McGee Lake Trail (Yosemite), 231
McKenzie, Bert, 126
madrone, 154, 162
magma, 66, 68, 69, 79, 84, 104, 206, 207
Maidu Indians, 123
Maidu Volcano (Lassen), 125
Makahiku Falls (Halaekala), 54
mamane, 44, 48, 74, 75
manzanita, 110, 162, *184-85,* 192, 213
Manzanita Lake (Lassen), *125,* 136, 139
Manzanita Trail (Kings Canyon), 108, 110
Mariposa Battalion, 204, 218
Mariposa Grove (Yosemite), *203,* 204, 214, 226
marmot, 114, 130, 216
Marquesas, 59
marten, 130
Mather, Stephen, 176
Maui, 36, 39
Maui Nui, 36
Mauna Kea (Haleakala), *40-41*
Mauna Loa Strip Road (Hawaii), 75, 80, 81, 85, 86
Mauna Loa Trail (Hawaii), 80, 81, 86
Mauna Loa Volcano, 36, *40-41,* 59, 64, 68, 72, 74, 79, *82-83,* 85, 86, 87
Mauna Ulu (Hawaii), 78, 84, 88
May Lake Trail (Yosemite), 225, 227, 232

meadowlark, 216
Merced Canyon (Yosemite),
205, 206, 211, 214, 226
Merced Lake (Yosemite), 232
Merced River (Yosemite),
205, 211, 218, 220, 230,
232
metamorphic rock, 104, 105
migrations, Indian, 170-71
milkweed, 215
Mill Creek Falls Trail (Lassen),
132
mining, 148, 172-73, 190,
191, 204
Mirror Lake (Yosemite), 220,
223, 225
missionaries, 35
Mist Falls (Kings Canyon),
108, 110, 114
Mist Trail (Yosemite), 220,
224
Miwok-speaking people, 202,
204
Mokuaweoweo Caldera (Hawaii), 81
molds, tree, *86*
Molokini (Haleakala), 39
Monaches, 96, 170, 171, 172
Monarch Divide (Kings Canyon), 93, 106, 108
Monarch Lakes Trail (Sequoia), 188, 190
mongoose, 36, 75
monkey flower, 129, 216,
248
monkshood, 129
Mono Indians, 171, 172
Moraga, Gabriel, 97
morning glory, 73, 74
Moro Rock (Sequoia), 167,
172, 180, 188, 191, 194
Mosquito Lake Trail (Sequoia), 192
mountain lion, *181,* 216, *238*
mouse, deer, *237*
mudflows, 126, 128
Muir, John, 97, 99, 100,
130, 152, 167, 173,
175, 186, 202, *203,* 204,
205, 220
Muir Hut (Kings Canyon),
111
Muir Woods (Redwood),148
mule-ear, mountain, 129
Muliwa a Pele (Hawaii), 78-79

Mullineaux, Donal, 136
mynah, 75
mythology, 34-35, 53, 59,
62, 66, 74, 83, 87, 122-24

Napau Trail (Hawaii), 79, 88
nasturtium, 85
National Geographic Society, 149
National Park Service, 17, 36,
44, 45, 75, 113, 114, 136,
149, 176, 204-205, 231
Native Americans, 96, 119,
122-24, 146, 170-71,
172-73, 204. *See also
names*
Nature Conservancy, 17, 36,
45
Na Ulu arches (Hawaii), 78
naupaka, 74
nene. *See* goose, Hawaiian
Nevada Fall (Yosemite), 211,
220, 224, 226
newt, California, *245*
noni, 78
nukupuu, 45
nutcracker, Clark's, 114, 216,
241

oaks, 183, 202, 213, 214,
222, 226
oats, wild, 167
Observatory Trail (Hawaii),
80
obsidian, 171
Oheo (Haleakala), 54
ohelo, 44, 74, 75, 83, 88
ohia lehua-metrosideros, 44,
45, 48, 73, 75, 82, 84,
85, 88, *249*
Oili Puu (Haleakala), 53
olapa, 44
Olmstead Point (Yosemite),
227
orchids, 74, 82, 192
otter:
river, *236*
sea, 17, 154, 155
Owens Valley (Kings Canyon), 96, 99
owl, *214, 240, 241*
oxalis, 154, *249*

Pacific Crest Trail (Lassen),
133

Pacific Crest Trail (Yosemite), 230, 231
Pacific high, 152
Pacific Plate, 65, 66, 101,
206
Pahoa (Hawaii), 76
paintbrush, 192, 216, 231
Painted Dunes (Lassen), 138
Paiute Indians, 96, 98, 172,
202
Panoramic Point (Kings Canyon), 108, 112
Paradise Meadow Trail
(Lassen), 133
Paradise Valley (Kings Canyon), 99, 110, 114
Paradise Valley Trail (Kings
Canyon), 108, 110
parrotbill, 45
parsnip, cow, *214*
Patrick's Point State Park,
163
Pauhi Crater (Hawaii), 79
Pele, 35, 53, 59, 62, 66, 74,
83, 84, 87
Pele's hair, 69
Pele's Paint Pot (Haleakala),
53
pelican, *21, 240*
pentstemon, 216, 231
Peterson Trail (Redwood),
157
petrel, 45, 53
petroglyphs, 62, 78
pheasant, 45, 75
phlox, 216
pika, 114, 216, *239*
pili, 53
Pillars of Heaven Nature
Trail (Yosemite), 226
pines, 21, 48, 130, 132, 133,
134, 139, *177,* 180,
183, 193, 194, *211,*
213, 214, 216, 217,
222, 226, 232, *243,*
249, 250
pinnipeds, 20
plants, exotic, 21, 24, 48,
53, 62, 75, 85
plover, golden, 45
Pohono Trail (Yosemite),
218, 224
Point Bennett (Channel
Islands), *18-19,* 25
Polly Dome (Yosemite), 23

Polynesians, 34, 59
poppies, California, 213
porcupine, 143, 216, *239*
porpoise, 20, 143, 155
Potwisha Indian, 170, 172
Prairie Creek (Redwood),
  143
Prairie Creek Redwoods
  State Park, 162, 163
precipitation, 179
Prospect Peak (Lassen), 131
puffin, tufted, *244*
Pukalani (Haleakala), 48
pukiawe-styphelia, 52, 88,
  249
Puhimau Crater (Hawaii), 79
pumice, 69, 75, 84
Puu Huluhulu Trail
  (Hawaii), 79
Puu Nole (Haleakala), 53
Puu o Pele (Haleakala), 53
Pu'u Puai Overlook
  (Hawaii), 80, 84
Puu Ulaula Overlook (Hale-
  akala), *49*

quail, 75, *241*
quartz, 101

rabbit, brush, *237*
raccoon, *215,* 216, 239
Rae Lakes (Kings Canyon),
  112, 113, 114
Rainbow Mountain (Se-
  quoia), 188
"rain shadow," 179
ranching, 122
rat, 36, 75
rattlesnake, western, *245*
Reading Peak (Lassen), 131
recreational development
  (Sequoia), 190
redbuds, 213, *249*
Red Hill (Haleakala), 49, 53
Red Hill (Hawaii), 86-87
redwood, coast *(Sequoia
  sempervirens),* *140,* 143,
  146-47, 148-49, 152-54,
  153, 157, *158-59,* 162,
  163, 182, *247*
Redwood Canyon (Kings
  Canyon), 100
Redwood Creek Trail (Red-
  wood), 151, 160,
  162-63

Redwood National Park,
  140-63
  general information,
    142-43
  geology, 150-51
  history, 146-49
  map, north area, *144-45*
  natural history, 152-55
  sites, trails, and trips,
    156-57, 160-63
  trail map, south area, *161*
repopulation, animal and
  plant, 24, 44, 54, 75, 88
Requa Hill (Redwood), 160
Revelation Trail (Redwood),
  162
rhododendron, *140,* 154,
  156, 157
Ribbon Fall (Yosemite), 211
Ridge Lakes Trail (Lassen),
  132
Rixford, Mount, 114
Roaring River (Kings Can-
  yon), 98, 106
robin, *240*
roof pendants, 114
Roosevelt, Franklin D., 17
Royal Arch (Yosemite), 211,
  222
ruins, 35, 62

Saddler Skyline Trail (Red-
  wood), 162
St. Helens, Mount, 119, 136
salal, *140,* 154
salmon, 146, 155
salmonberry, 154
sandalwood, 74
sandpiper, 21, *243*
San Joaquin Valley (Kings
  Canyon), 108, 112,
  168-69
San Miguel Island, *16,* 17,
  18-19, 24-25
San Miguel Trail (Channel
  Islands), 25
Santa Barbara Island, 17, 24
Santa Cruz Island, 17, 25
Santa Rosa Island, 17, 25
Save-the-Redwoods League,
  148
Sawtooth Pass (Sequoia),
  188, 190
Scientific Research Reserve,
  45

scree, 194
sealers and whalers, 17
sea lion, California, *10,* 24,
  143, 155, 163, *237*
seal, 17, 24, 42, 73, 143,
  155, *239*
"sea stacks," *150,* 151
sedimentary deposition,
  101, 128, 134, 150,
  151, 206, 210
seismographs, 83
Sentinel Campground (Kings
  Canyon), 108
Sentinel Dome (Yosemite),
  211, 222, 225
Sentinel Falls (Yosemite),
  218
sequoia, giant *(Sequoiadendron giganteum),* 164,
  167, 180, 182-83, 186,
  194, 214-15, 226, *248*
Sequoia Lake Overlook
  (Kings Canyon), 108,
  112
Sequoia National Forest,
  108, 112
Sequoia National Park, 100,
  164-95
  general information,
    166-67
  geology, 178
  history, 170-76
  map, *94-95*
  natural history, 179-86
  sites, trails, and trips,
    186-94
  trail map, *189*
Sequoia Natural History
  Association, 186
Shasta, Mount, 116, 124, 139
Shasta City, California, 135
sheep, 100, 173-74
shooting star, 129, 192,
  214-15, 216
shrew, 155
Sierra Club, 149, 218, 220
Sierra Nevada, *93,* 111, 167,
  167, 172, 177, 205,
  208, 208, 209
Signal Peak (Channel
  Islands), 24
silver, 172-73
silversword, *28,* 31, 36, 42,
  44, 48-49, 53-54, 86,
  250

Silversword Trail (Haleakala), 53-54
Simpson Trail (Redwood),157
single habitat life forms, 21
Sixty Lake Basin (Kings Canyon), *102-103*
skiing, 222
skunk cabbage, 157
slate, 206
Sliding Sands Trail (Haleakala), 50-51, 52, 53
Smith, Jedediah, 98, 124, 147
smog, 194
Snag Lake (Lassen), 133, 138
Snow Creek Trail (Yosemite), 223, 227
snow plant, 129, *181,* 192, 215, *250*
snowshoeing, *134-35*
soapberry, 85
Soldiers Trail (Sequoia), 188
Southern Pacific Railway, 106, 110
Spanish explorers, 96-97, 124, 146-47, 171, 177
spatter cones, 87
"Specter of Brocken" phenomenon, 48
springs, thermal, 128-29, 138
spruce, 48, 154, 157, 163, 214
squirrel, 130, 155, *181,* 216, 239
stalactites, 72
starfish, *22, 245*
steam, 68, *69,* 82, 87, 126, 128
Steaming Bluff (Hawaii), 82
Stewart, George, 175
strawberry, wild, 85
sulphur, 79, 82, 84
sulphur dioxide, 68, *69, 84*
Sulphur Works (Lassen), 125, 128, 131, 139
Summit Lake (Lassen), 132, 134
Summit Trail (Hawaii), 80, 81
Sunset Rock (Sequoia), 168-69
Sunset Trail (Kings Canyon), 109, 112-13
superstitions, 53, 62, 66, 83
Swanson, George, 167
Swanson, John, 167

swimming, 231, 232

Taft, William Howard, *203*
Taft Point Trail (Yosemite), 222, 225
Tall Trees Grove (Redwood), 151, 160, 162
tanoak, 154
tarn, 192
taro, *50-51*
Tehama, Mount, 125, 126, 131, 132
Tehipete Valley (Kings Canyon), 99, 100, 105
Tenaya, California, 218
Tenaya Canyon and Lake (Yosemite), 223, 227, 230, 232
Terminal Geyser (Lassen), 128
Tharp, Hale D., 167, 170, 172
thistle, 155, *214*
Three Brothers (Sequoia), 180
thrush, 85, *242*
Thurston, Asa, 62
Thurston, Lorrin, 64
Thurston Lava Tube (Hawaii), 63, 80, 85, 87
ti, 74, 85
tidepools, *18-19*
Timber Gap Trail (Sequoia), 188, 190
Tioga Pass (Yosemite), 205, 226-27, 230
Tioga Road (Yosemite), 213, 225, 226, 227, 230, 232
toad, western, *246*
Tolowa Indians, 146
tourism, 36, 44, 192, 204, 205
Tree Fern Forest Trail (Hawaii), *63*
trillium, 156
tritonia, 74
trout, 130, 155, 232
tsunami, 76
Tubatulabal Indians, 170
Tunnel View (Yosemite), 222
Tuolumne Meadows (Yosemite), 208-209, 210, 214, *217,* 220, 225, 226, 230, 231, 232

Tuolumne River, 205, *207,* 225, 230, 231, 232
turtle, western pond, *246*
Twin Lakes (Lassen), 132
Tyndall, Mount, 99

umacha, 202
Unicorn Peak (Yosemite), 210, 230
U.S. Army, 173
U.S. Cavalry, 188
U.S. Congress, 64, 100, 149, 204
U.S. Department of Interior, 205
United States Exploring Expedition (1841), 35
U.S. Geological Survey, 72, 83, 136, 173
uplift, 101, 104, 151, 206-207

Vancouver, Capt. George, 35, 39
Vernal Fall (Yosemite), *199,* 210, 211, 220, 224, 226
Viola Falls (Kings Canyon), 109, 112
violets, 215
Visalia, California, 172
Visalia Delta (newspaper), 174, 175
visually handicapped, trails for, 162
volcanic eruption, 36, 38-39, 59, 62, *64,* 66, 68, 72, 79, 82, 84, 87, 88, *89,* 119, *123,* 125-29, 135-36, 138, 139, 206
volcanoes, 36-41, 65-72, 125
formation of, 38, 66, 68
Volcano House (Hawaii), 76, 79, 87

Wahaula Visitor Center (Hawaii), 76, 80
Waimoku Falls Trail (Haleakala), 51, 54
Walker, Joseph, 204
Walker Pass (Sequoia), 171, 172
Warner Valley, 133
Washburn Lake (Yosemite), 232
water:
and erosion, 76, 78, 104-

105, 151, 207, 210,
211
as life determinant, 21,
44, 74
potability of, 160
and volcanoes, 38-39
Water Mountain (Lassen),
124
Waterwheel Falls (Yose-
mite), 231
Watkins, Mount, 220
Wawona Hotel (Yosemite),
226
Wawona Road (Yosemite),
213, 218, 222, 224, 226
weasel, long-tailed, *238*
whale, California gray, 20,
22-23, 143, 155, 163,
238
White Cascade (Yosemite),
231
White Chief Trail (Sequoia),
191, 192
White Hill Trail (Haleakala),
50

Whitney, Josiah, 173
Whitney, Mount, 99, 100,
170, 173, 176, *178,*
179, 192, *195,* 220,
224, 231
Widow Lake (Lassen), 139
wiliwili, 74
Wilkes, Lt. Charles, 35, 124
Williamson, Mount, 99
Wilson, Woodrow, 36
Wobonuch Indians, 170
Woksaki Indians, 170
woodpecker, 181, 216, *241*
World Heritage Site (Red-
wood), 160
wren, 156

Yana Indians, 119, 122
Yellowstone National Park,
176
Yokut Indians, 170, 171
Yosemite Falls (Yosemite),
210, 211, 218, 222,
223, 225, 226, 227
Yosemite Indians, 218

Yosemite National Park,
100, 176, 196-233
general information,
198-99, 202
geology, 205-207, 210-11
history, 202-205
map, *200-201*
natural history, 213-17
sites, trails, and trips, 217-
20, 222-27, 230-32
trail map, *224-25*
Yosemite Point (Yosemite), 219
Yosemite Valley (Yosemite),
196, 199, 202, 204,
217-22, 223, 224, 225,
226, 227, *228-29*
Yosemite Village (Yose-
mite), 217, 223
yucca, 180
Yurok Indians, 146

Zumwalt, D.K., 106, 110
Zumwalt Meadow Trail
(Kings Canyon), 106,
108, 110

The text was set in Garamond Book by
U.S. Lithograph Inc., New York.
The book was printed and bound by
Dai Nippon Printing Co., Ltd., Tokyo.